ADVANCE PRAISE FOR A WEEKEND OR THE WORLD

"I can't help but feel if I'd read this book before I started traveling, I would have saved a sh*tload of cash and time. Stress and sleep too! Especially if you're new to travel, just read the book. It's filled with a whole heap of helpful information and resources. It will just make all your future travel so much easier and better."

–JULIAN LUCA, Founder and CEO of TRAVA Travel

"An absolute must-read for not only new adventurers but for us avid travelers as well. A fabulous insight to the not-so-often-asked questions or thoughts."

–TIFFANY WIDDOWSON, Team Leader at
Flight Centre Australia and avid traveler/adventurer

"Andre's book reads like one long, entertaining conversation with a good friend. Even seasoned travelers have something to learn from this book."

–LAUREN FARMER, Polar Expedition Guide and travel photographer

"The ultimate travel guide. Watson has provided an exhaustive list on how best to travel. There is something for everyone here."

—**EMILY D. McCARTHY,** Head of Community at GORUCK

"Travel is all about choices. Andre will teach you, with ease, everything you need to consider to ensure each of your future trips will be a trip of a lifetime."

—**ANNETTE BOMBOSCH,** PhD, Biologist and Polar Expedition Guide

"Do you want to travel, but don't know how? Andre's book gives an excellent introduction to the basics of travelling where he covers all the essential things as well as most day-to-day situations. Whether you've never travelled before or you're a seasoned traveler, there is something for you here."

—**JAKOB KIERKEGAARD,** kierkegaardsrejser.blogspot.com

"Andre Watson offers a very personal account of his travel experiences. This book will provoke those new to travel and those with extensive experience into planning the best possible trip"

—**GERARD BAKER,** Author and Antarctic Expedition Guide

A WEEKEND

OR

THE WORLD

A WEEKEND
OR
THE WORLD

A COMPLETE HOW-TO TRAVEL GUIDE

ANDRE WATSON

HOUNDSTOOTH
PRESS

A WEEKEND OR THE WORLD
A Complete How-To Travel Guide

ISBN   978-1-5445-2811-3 *Hardcover*

        978-1-5445-2809-0 *Paperback*

        978-1-5445-2810-6 *Ebook*

        978-1-5445-2812-0 *Audiobook*

CONTENTS

Dedicated to all of the brave men of Special Operations who have volunteered to be in harm's way and whose knowledge and life lessons have taught me so much and taken me so far.

WHO IS THIS BOOK FOR?

Almost everyone I know wants to travel around and see the world. But surprisingly, few people I know actually have. Why is this?

After finally traveling all over the world myself, many of my friends and coworkers started to ask me things like:

- How did you save up so much money?

- Was it safe?

- How did you decide where to go?

- How did you eat if you didn't know the language?

- How did you find a place to sleep?

- How were you able to find directions?

- Are "squat toilets" real? How do you use one?

After hearing many similar questions over and over again, I started to realize that while many people I knew wanted to travel, they just weren't sure *how* to travel. The desire was there. They had destinations in mind. They just weren't sure where to start.

Many of them were also talking themselves out of travel adventures because of all the scary what-ifs. What if I get robbed? What if traveling costs a lot of money? What if I screw this up and end up stranded in another country?

If any of the questions mentioned so far sound like the questions you've had about traveling, I have good news. This book is for you.

In this book, we'll talk about how to plan your trip, how to manage your daily concerns while traveling, and we'll talk about what it's like coming home. This book contains all the knowledge you need to make your trip actually happen. Anyone can do it. The way this book is structured, we'll go through each general travel topic and discuss the key details you need to know. Then we'll fit these things together into the bigger picture for your travels. By the end, you'll know so much about traveling that nothing you come across should deter you from getting out there and seeing the world.

Even if you're an experienced traveler already, I guarantee you'll find something in here you either haven't come across or haven't considered before. This book contains a lot of my accumulated travel knowledge. If you're looking to step up your travel game or have ever wondered if you could be doing things better, this book is for you, too.

Oddly, there are very few other resources out there that explain *how* to travel. There are a wealth of guidebooks for different locations, but these don't actually guide you through how to plan or take your trip.

Of the few resources that do teach general travel, most focus on why you should want to travel at all. They talk about how traveling causes you to discover yourself and how you learn to understand people with different cultures and viewpoints. They also talk about how you end up learning that you don't need many possessions, and how this frees up your life to focus on the things you really care about.

Don't get me wrong, these things are all correct and are all amazing benefits of traveling. But I have only met a couple of people, out of thousands of travelers, who have specifically cited these things as their *reason* for traveling. These things are all self-growth things, and trying to make self-growth happen is not really something you can plan in advance.

On the contrary, most of the travelers I know have certain destinations in mind that they want to visit, and these are usually historical sites, major cultural centers, or natural wonders. The weird conflict that seems to come up between what I see as destination-driven travel and the commonly talked about growth-driven travel in the other how-to-travel resources is that there's an implication that if you aren't traveling for a certain self-growth purpose, then you're not traveling correctly. I've actually heard conversations during my own travels in which a group of travelers were talking about another traveler and I'd hear someone say, "Oh, well they're not a *real traveler.*"

I say that attitude is completely and utterly false, not to mention inappropriately judgmental.

If you want to travel to beaches and relax in all-inclusive resorts, you're a traveler. If you want to live in yurts with locals in Mongolia, you're a traveler. If you want to live in a big city in Australia and work there for a year, you're a traveler.

Because of this, what you won't find in this book is an end-goal-driven approach or a "right" way to travel. I believe people should go where they want to go and how they want to go there, for their personal reasons. I do my best to try and accommodate everyone's travel styles for planning purposes in here. For the non-planning portion, I look at things from the perspective of a budget traveler because their case requires the most attention and hands-on execution. If you understand how to take a trip where every detail is up to you, you can understand how to take a trip in a more "packaged" way, too.

Also, what you aren't going to find in this book is an explanation of what I consider to be everyday things. I assume you know what Facebook is and how to install apps on your phone. I also assume you understand how to use websites and are comfortable purchasing things online. I further assume you understand how to connect to Wi-Fi with your devices and are using debit and credit cards for the majority of your purchases these days. Nothing too crazy there, right? I feel the vast majority of us have a solid grasp of these topics, so I'm not going to cover them in this book even though those are all relevant to traveling.

This is more like a manual that teaches you good travel practices. My recommendation is to read this book through once before you buy anything for your trip. Then, as your trip starts to become more of a reality, come back to particular sections as they become relevant for you. If you do this, you should be good to go when your departure date finally arrives.

Before we begin, an interesting observation I've noticed is that many people who start traveling for the first time tend to start with a "safer," more "packaged" trip. This could be taking a bus tour through Europe, an all-inclusive trip to Cancún, or a cruise ship around the Caribbean. But as they start traveling more, they tend to shift from the more luxurious and less-planned style of travel to the less luxurious and more independent style of travel. Once they start to feel more comfortable with travel, they see less of a need to take more resort-style trips and start slowly looking more like budget travelers. At this point, they really start getting immersed in cultures and making their own adventures. With the people who go through this progression, I think the initial trips were understandably planned at their level of comfort with the unknown, but that's really what this book is all about—trying to make the unknown known. That is also part of the reason why the non-planning sections were written from a more budget-oriented perspective. I think most people as they gain travel experience tend to slide more toward that style of travel. Maybe just from reading this book, you may slide a little in that direction before setting off on your trip. It's something to think about as you go through this book and start traveling. Your travel habits will likely change over time and that's okay.

There's no wrong way to travel. I'll help you make it happen like an expert the first time, and you'll be a pro after that.

So are you ready? Turn the page.

INTRODUCTION

When I was twenty-four, one of my roommates walked into the living room and saw the other three of us roommates in the house sitting there watching TV. He sat down and said, "Hey, guys, just wanted to let you all know that I'm moving out in a couple of months. I'm going to go travel in South America, and I'm figuring I'll be gone about a year or so. You guys might want to, ya know, find another roommate or something."

All of us started laughing and making fun of him like this was ridiculous. I even said something to the effect of, "You're crazy. You're going to get kidnapped. It was nice knowing you."

But he wasn't fazed by our comments. We asked him some more questions, and it turned out he'd been researching this trip for a while and was pretty much ready to go. The backpack that had shown up in his room was actually what he was planning on using to go traveling. We hadn't asked him about it and just assumed he was getting into camping.

As his news started to sink in more, I was actually a little miffed at myself. I had wanted to travel the world and see what it had to offer, too, but I'd never really seriously considered it because I thought it was out of my reach.

Suddenly seeing someone in my inner circle doing something that I had been idly dreaming about shattered the illusion that I couldn't go travel around the world. If my roommate could do it, I could do it, too.

This whole internal dialogue was actually even more ironic because I'm a dual citizen of both the United States and Germany. I'm no stranger to traveling.

My mother was native German, and she started dating my father in California just as he joined the United States Air Force. My father could have been stationed at any air base in the world but just happened to be assigned to Rhein-Main Air Force Base in Wiesbaden, Germany, which is where I was born a few years later.

Because of the close proximity of this base to my mother's village outside of Nuremberg, we frequently traveled back and forth to my grandparents' place. I spent the first five years of my life speaking English and German in equal amounts.

A few years later, my father transitioned out of active-duty military service and became a commercial airline pilot for American Airlines for the rest of his career. Because he was an employee of the airlines and got discounted flights and we had close family in Germany, we took trips every year to spend time with our relatives.

This means I had literally spent my entire life, from birth to graduating high school, traveling between the United States and Germany.

So when my roommate said that he was going to travel around the world, and I had considered that to be out of my reach, I immediately realized it was almost absurd that I felt this way. If anyone was already accustomed to traveling around the world, it was me.

Why had I not just gone out and traveled to other places before this? Honestly, I don't know. It just seemed there were so many details, and it would be so difficult and scary, that I hadn't considered I could really go out there and travel around the world.

Roughly a year before my roommate announced his soon-to-be travel, I found myself in a very unusual situation. Even now, it's strange how this worked out, but I was at a dinner among many longtime friends who were part of a club. Just recently, I had joined this club and I was definitely the new guy. We all got seated randomly at various tables, and although I was twenty-three, it just happened by chance that everyone else at my ten-person table was a World War II veteran and over the age of eighty. All of them were wearing their unit pins and service medals from World War II. I was the youngest person at the table by a huge margin and had no medals or honors to my name. In fact, I'd only been out of university for about a year.

While I was eating dinner and talking with these veterans, it suddenly occurred to me that there were literally centuries of wisdom within the people sitting at the table around me. Not only that, but they were heroes and men who had seen hardship and struggle in their lives. They had conquered their fears in order to help out the world.

I finally worked up the nerve to ask everyone at the table, "Hey, I have a question for you guys. You guys are obviously much older than me and have seen a whole bunch of things in your lifetime. I'm essentially just getting started in my life and only entered the 'adult real world' within the last year. If you had any key piece of advice for someone like me who is just starting out, what would it be?"

What shocked me was that there was no hesitation at all from any of them at the table, and they were almost stumbling over each other, all of them saying the same thing, which was some form of, "Don't hesitate to do the things you're interested in doing. When you're our age, you won't be starting a business, making a family, writing books, or going on adventures. When you decide that you want to do something, don't sit there and wait around. ***Do it.***"

This has been the best advice that I have ever received.

Hearing this advice, and then later hearing my roommate's announcement, really gave me pause to reevaluate my life. Here I had gotten this amazing expert advice on not waiting around to make my dreams come true, and then there I was, looking directly at a huge desire in my life that I was making no progress on. I decided to stop making excuses. I knew I wanted to travel and I was going to start making that happen.

Because these events finally got my brain moving, I started to think about where I wanted to travel and started doing enough research and planning to actually get moving on a travel plan. It took me months of research, reading, and rereading things to figure out what I needed to do for my trip. It was a very difficult and laborious process, and I was still confused about a lot of things, despite having already traveled to Germany many times. Further, I was nervous about eventually starting my trip. Did I miss something? Was I ready? Was my plan going to work?

My hesitation to travel was also slightly ridiculous considering that for a large part of my life, I was hell-bent on joining Special Operations in the US military. Due to the ironies of life, I ended up never joining the military, but the thought of jumping out of airplanes, shooting guns, and staying up for days without sleep sounded awesome to me for a long time. Somehow, despite my attraction to dangerous situations, I was still nervous about taking my first big trip. So I can definitely understand why many people are hesitant to take the first leap and get going on their dream trips.

Although I had a full travel itinerary planned out, I didn't start actually traveling until three years later. This was mostly because I needed to save up the money to take a big trip, but when I did travel the first time, I spent seven months traveling around the world and it was amazing. To be honest, though, I was still anxiety-ridden when I started actually traveling because I still wasn't sure what to expect, even after all of my research. After a couple of weeks, I settled into life on the road, and the worry started to disappear. Within a month, I couldn't believe how confused and worried I had been in the beginning. Then travel was no big deal anymore.

Since that first trip, I have lived in Australia, I have lived in the United Kingdom, and I have traveled a lot more. At this point, I have been to roughly sixty countries covering all seven continents during a time span of more than two years of travel. My travels have also drastically changed my worldview, led me into all sorts of adventures, and have taught me that people are just people regardless of where they're from.

I wouldn't take back my traveling for anything.

Frankly, it's made me a better person and given me the drive to help make the world a better place.

Since doing all of this traveling and blogging about it for my friends, a number of my friends, coworkers, and even acquaintances have approached me and told me that they want to go traveling as well, but it doesn't seem like something they can do or they just don't know where to start.

Luckily for them, I've been trained to share my knowledge.

Ever since a very young age, I knew I wanted to be a physicist. Most people aren't entirely sure what physics is, even if they've taken a class, so how did a young kid decide this was the field he wanted to go into? Honestly, I don't know.

I think I found out somewhere that physics described how things worked, and as a kid, I was insatiable with taking alarm clocks apart, building Lego projects, learning painting, practicing martial arts, and all sorts of other things. I just wanted knowledge and soaked it up like a sponge. Hearing that physics explained how things worked sounded incredibly appealing. As it turned out, when I did get into physics, physics is indeed the knowledge of how the universe operates.

When I went to university and studied physics, I was very lucky to have a very caring and awesome advisor who commented in class one time, "If you can't explain the concepts that we go over in this class to someone who doesn't understand physics at all, that means you don't understand the concepts yourself." This is paraphrasing a quote from Albert Einstein I later found out, and it's another great piece of advice that has stuck with me my entire life.

Because of my curiosity and the great life advice I have received, I have gotten involved with a number of different hobbies over the years. Most physicists I know are interested in a lot of different things. After all, we studied how the universe works, so we get interested in lots of stuff within the universe. Most of the things I have gotten into, though, I have unfortunately stumbled into without any sort of mentor. The number of insane mistakes that I've made has been almost stupidly comical. Because of this, I really want to help other people skip my own "learned that the hard way" sessions.

By combining all of these experiences, I have really tried to break things down for the people who have asked for my travel advice to make sure they are able to get going with their travels and that they're not worried about what they're about to face. However, it was not straightforward to figure out how to give this mentorship. Initially, I would tell someone to just buy me a couple of beers and we'll talk through everything. As you can imagine, this was a *terrible* way to teach someone a big topic area. There was too much to cover in a few hours, the conversation tended to veer off as more beers were consumed, and the next day, the person who came to me probably only remembered half of what we talked about. Instead, I started periodically providing support sessions as people were planning their trips. But it was difficult to coordinate sessions at the right points in their process, and sometimes information was still missed.

As a result, it started to dawn on me that I needed to write down my travel advice into some sort of coherent guide.

As I started to ponder this, I also realized I wanted to go further than just helping the people I know. I want everyone to get out there and experience traveling. I want everyone to have amazing adventures and growth. I'm sure there are tons of people out there who want to travel and just aren't sure where or how to start. That's who this book is for. This book is my breakdown of all the things you need to think about and do in order to start traveling.

That said, this book could easily have been 5,000 pages long. Traveling is essentially living but under different circumstances. If someone wrote a book about every single decision you make during the day and why you're making those decisions, you'd end up with a monumentally long book.

Rather than trying to explain every detail of everything travel related, I have taken an 80/20 approach. The 80/20 rule is the "Pareto principle," which stated originally that "80 percent of the land in Italy was owned by 20 percent of the population." This principle has been further expanded to everything in the sense that roughly "80 percent of something comes from 20 percent of something else." The way the 80/20 rule is applied most often, though, is that "80 percent of the benefit comes from 20 percent of the effort." Basically, you can expend little energy and get most of the benefit, but the last part of the benefit requires a ton of work.

This book is meant to be the 80/20 on traveling. I am going to talk about all sorts of things, but I simply can't cover everything that could possibly apply to traveling. This book is the 20 percent effort that's going to get you 80 percent of the way to traveling. By the time you're done with this, you should be able to figure out the last 20 percent of traveling on your own.

Some of that 80/20 is going to be a few of the previously mentioned hobbies that I got into which ended up helping my travels quite a bit. These include emergency medicine, off-grid medicine, survival, navigation, scuba diving, photography, martial arts, and security. I didn't *need* any of those to travel, however, so if any of those sound complicated or scary, I promise nothing presented in this book on those subjects will be that advanced. I will only pull on my knowledge of these things for the parts you need to know to make your travels easier.

Because of my desired military career that never happened, my research into and interactions with Special Operations groups have taught me a number of valuable lessons, and I am going to share some of these things that came from them to help you with your trip. I won't always call out the Special Operations groups as the source for some of my advice, but they have some very helpful insight on staying safe and, interestingly, on how to pack.

That said, this book is also going to teach you the essence of the Special Forces "Three Rules."

If you haven't heard of the Special Forces, these are the US Army's "Green Berets." Their official name is the Special Forces or SF. Unlike many other Special Operations military groups, the classic SF mission is to go into enemy territory, meet up with a group of people trying to overthrow the government in that country, and then train this group to effectively fight the government.

Please note, I don't mean to make any political statement here, and I also don't mean to promote or denigrate the military and its actions, but the guys in SF are effectively trained to be expert travelers in the most extreme sense. They go out for long periods of time with minimal supplies and under dangerous conditions. They are the hardest of the hardcore travelers. So their wisdom is very applicable for us regular travelers.

Out of the teachings of SF come the "Three Rules":

1. Always look cool.

2. Never get lost.

3. If you get lost, look cool.

This sounds like the most ridiculous advice ever until you think about it a little more.

What they're really saying is: Be confident. Know yourself and your capabilities. Know your plan, know where you're going, and know the contingencies. If for some reason your plan goes to hell, be calm, think through the problem, adjust, reevaluate, and figure things out. Be confident in your ability to fight through adversity.

These rules are also some of the best advice you'll ever hear.

What I intend to do with this book is get you to the point where you can apply the Three Rules to your traveling. You may not know everything that's going to happen, but you'll be confident, know what you're doing, and can handle issues and work through them as they occur.

Additionally, a quote that I like is, "No one rises to the occasion. Everyone falls to the level of their experience." With this book, I want to give you the travel knowledge that will easily gain you travel experience, and those combined will get you through any situation while traveling.

This book is meant to be for any traveler. Whether you are taking a short, relaxing weekend trip or traveling around the world for years out of a backpack, I've got you covered. It's all the same skill set.

This book is laid out in a progression. I'll help you figure out your traveling desires, then plan a trip, then get prepared for that trip, then actually take your trip, and then return home. By the time you've finished this, you'll already feel like you know what you're doing. After that, you just need to make it happen.

Let's get you started.

A NOTE ON COVID-19

The novel coronavirus that was discovered in December 2019 has completely upended the world. Besides the obvious and tragic human toll, borders have shut, trade has been interrupted, and supply and demand for goods has been all over the place. Trying to work on and publish this book during this time period has been one of the hardest things I've ever done. I wrote a book on travel, and as things started to shut down, I had to wonder a lot of things like: Are we ever going to travel normally again? Are hostels even going to exist in the future? Are immunization records going to be required everywhere now? What are cruises going to look like moving forward and is that industry even going to survive the shutdown?

Thankfully, there appears to be a light at the end of the tunnel, and a sense of normalcy is on the horizon. With vaccines being rolled out across the world, it does indeed appear that travel will eventually return to its pre-pandemic state of operation. It may take a couple of years for travel to fully get back to normal, but I have every confidence that it will.

That said, I don't really address COVID-19 in this book. The situation is changing so rapidly that anything I comment on would be irrelevant days or weeks later. So read this book, know that everything is still relevant, and check my blog at andrewatson.com/blog for any major updates that might affect the content of this book.

IMPORTANT TERMS

I'm going to default to certain units of measurement and use some specific terms frequently in this book, so it's important we're all on the same page right from the beginning. I really hope that this book makes its way all around the world, but likely, that means starting in countries that speak English as a first language simply because this book is already in English. That said, a huge percentage of the people in those countries do not speak American English, and I have really tried to make this book immediately readable to any English speaker even though this book is written in American English.

When I use terms that are specific to American English, I try to include Commonwealth English terms right afterward in parentheses. For example, if I reference a hoodie, it will show up as "hoodie (jumper)." If you haven't heard the term "Commonwealth" before, for the purposes of this book, I am referring to any former British territory that speaks English as a first language, except for the United States. There are of course many other Commonwealth countries that do not speak English as a first language, but the point for this book's sake is that all the English-as-a-first-language countries, except for the United States, speak roughly similar English due to their ties to the British Empire. One reason the United States is the outlier in how we speak is that the United States broke away from the British Empire somewhat earlier than other territories. For an explanation on what the Commonwealth is currently, check out the YouTube video, *The Difference between the United Kingdom, Great Britain, and England Explained.*

Similarly, because the United States is my "main" home as it were, I will generally be using imperial units, but I have tried to make every attempt to include metric units in parentheses after any imperial measurement. You'll see this conversion in the same manner like "3 ft (1 m)" throughout the book.

Because the United States and the United Kingdom are referenced a number of times in this guide, as of this sentence they will be referred to as the "US" and the "UK" respectively.

If I reference cost for things, those items will appear in US dollars, which I will mention as "dollars" or "USD," which is the international currency code for the US dollar currency.

As for other terms I frequently use throughout the book:

- **High-Income Country (HIC), Medium-Income Country (MIC), and Low-Income Country (LIC):** During the Cold War, from the end of World War II to the fall of the Soviet Union in 1991, "First World," "Second World," and "Third World" were common terms. The First World referred to the Allied World War II countries that opposed the Soviet Union. The Second World referred to the Communist countries allied with the Soviet Union. And the Third World referred to every other country. These terms are still in use today, but the connotations with those terms are largely incorrect and irrelevant nowadays, especially considering the Soviet Union hasn't existed for three decades. The replacement terms "developed" and "developing" are confusing and paint a misleading picture of the world because there is no agreed-upon standard to these terms. Before South

Korea dropped its "developing" status in 2019, they beat out France on a number of quality-of-life scales, but France was considered "developed" and South Korea was considered "developing." These terms also do not describe the world well because some developed countries have significant social and political issues. In 2016, the World Bank stopped using these terms and instead adopted the idea of HICs, MICs (including Upper Middle and Lower Middle), and LICs in order to clarify that their country classifications are referring to a country's economic status alone. As you can probably imagine, there is some correlation between economic status and infrastructure, which is why I include these terms in this book. HICs are generally going to have consistent transportation and clean drinking water even in remote areas. MICs generally have fairly good transportation but have running water that may be ill-advised to drink as a tourist. They will usually have pretty good access to clean bottled water, however. LICs may have urban areas that resemble MIC qualities, but more rural areas may have poor transportation and little access to clean water and medical help. I'm going to use these terms a bit in this book, but please note that I do not mean to judge any country or region with the use of these terms. They are included only to describe the relative difficulty that a tourist may experience in getting between locations and finding supplies while traveling in those locations.

- **University:** This breaks what I said about using American English first, and people in the US will likely find my wording with this term kind of weird. Anytime I reference the educational institution associated with earning a bachelor's degree, I will say "at university" or "in university" or something similar. Almost everyone in the US would normally say something like "at college" or "in college," but in most parts of the world outside the US, for example, the Commonwealth countries, college is actually the education usually received between the ages of sixteen and eighteen. In most of the world, university is what comes after college. In the US, for some reason, college and university are considered the same thing. In order to make this book friendlier to all English speakers and not just American English speakers, instead of using the US' "college" terminology, which gets really confusing for everyone else, I have instead just opted to use the more common "university" terminology. This will look slightly unusual to Americans but is hopefully not unreadable.

- **Metro versus Subway versus Rapid Transit System.** I try to say metro throughout this book because that's the more common generic term around the world.

PART 1

PREPLANNING FOR A BETTER TRIP

Most people who want to travel haven't really spent much time thinking about their motivations for traveling, but this is a key stage in planning a trip that everyone should dedicate some time toward.

Before you even start thinking about planning a trip somewhere, there are a few critical questions you should really spend some time thinking about. Answering these questions will not only make your trip easier to plan, but as you refine your answers, you could potentially change just about every characteristic of your original travel dream, including the destinations themselves. Our main goal in this preplanning section is to eventually figure out your traveler archetype. However, along the way, we're going to figure out your vision, your goals, your style, and even your limits. Once you know how all these things fit together and relate to your archetype, you'll be able to customize a perfect trip just for you.

WHAT DOES YOUR IDEAL TRIP LOOK LIKE?

The most important question you need to ask yourself is, "What do I want out of traveling?"

This may sound like a silly question, but really think about this. It's not as obvious as it seems. Close your eyes and imagine being on a trip to a destination that you've been considering. Take a few minutes to do this and try to make the vision in your head as realistic as you can. Imagine doing the activities you want to do and walking around and eating food. Pause for a few minutes here before you continue reading and really try to create this vision of yourself traveling.

Let's call this vision your *travel vision*. In your *travel vision*, were you sitting on the beach? Were you in a city? Were you hanging out with locals? Were other people speaking the same language as you? Were you on a ship? Were you climbing a mountain? Were you with traveling companions or were you solo? Were you at a resort or a regular hotel? Already, just by creating this visualization, your mind has made some major assumptions about your travel format and comfort level.

Taking this a step further, if your *travel vision* had you on a cruise ship, this is an environment where other people were cooking for you and you were in a single room that didn't change during your trip. Also, you were probably lounging quite a bit while having a pretty easy, relaxing vacation.

On the other hand, if your *travel vision* had you constantly partying and meeting new people while you hiked through picturesque scenery during the day, you were probably staying in hostels, changing rooms and cities often, and your meals were coming from street markets that don't exactly resemble restaurants.

No matter what your vision was, your imagined trip is really the visual answer to the question of "What do you want out of traveling?"

To give you my own *travel vision*, I saw myself going all over the world while meeting a bunch of people. I was doing outdoor activities, seeing major sights, and soaking up all the museums. In the evenings, I was partying together with locals and other travelers, and I was going back to a decent hotel room. I saw myself traveling between destinations by cruise ship whenever I could and working on cargo ships to travel between destinations whenever I couldn't. I pictured myself traveling for two to three years. I saw myself in a tour group whenever possible so that I'd have sort of a traveling group of friends. I even had a haphazard map of the world in my head of the major sights that I had heard of that I wanted to see.

Your vision is likely going to have been much different than mine, and that's totally fine. We all want different things.

Now let us back out of this *travel vision* a little and let's try to more fundamentally break down the specifics of what you saw. What is your vision *doing* for you? Are you fulfilling a desire to:

- Get away from stress for a while?

- Meet other people?

- Party with other people?

- Learn about other cultures?

- Learn a new language?

- See nature in ways that you haven't before?

- Explore?

- Try new food?

- Get closer to a partner?

- Belong to some sort of group?

- See art from all over the world?

- See history?

Don't worry, you can say yes to as many of these questions as you like. You can also have reasons to travel well beyond these questions. The reason behind your *travel vision* is going to have a huge influence on the next set of questions I'm about to ask, so really think about this. This would be another good opportunity to pause for a few minutes before you continue. Try to think about why you visualized that trip and what was appealing to you about that vision.

Hopefully, you have some solid thoughts about your vision. The more precisely you're able to answer this new question of "What does my *travel vision* tell me about what I want out of travel?" the easier it's going to be as we continue. Also, you will likely open up other travel options you hadn't considered before. Let's call your answers to this new question your *travel goals*.

The last thing you want to have happen is that you really wanted to climb Mount Everest but ended up on a cruise with your buddies (mates) instead. Or maybe you really want to hike across New Zealand but ended up in art museums across Europe. Either way, you probably wouldn't be entirely happy, especially if you could afford only one trip in the foreseeable future.

To help you refine your own answer to this exercise, I'll share my personal *travel goals* and hopefully, it will help you narrow in on your answer. For me, I travel because I want to understand people and the evolution of thought. I find it fascinating to see how different cultures handle different social situations and how different parts of the world have come up with multiple solutions to the same life problems. So for me, I like to be around the locals and see history through both sites and museums. That said, I also enjoy a little nature and a little partying. This basically means I want to go all over the world as long as there is some history and culture to see, and I might make a detour for some scenery or a good party spot. The key point for me, however, is discovering the local culture and history. That's what I want to get out of traveling. Those are my *travel goals*.

There's a really good chance that what I'm looking to get out of traveling probably doesn't exactly match what you're looking to get out of traveling. Or in other words, our *travel goals* are different. This means you and I would have very different destinations, budgets, and activities in mind for our trips. That's okay. The whole point of asking these questions is to figure out what you really want and then we'll talk about how to make that happen.

So now, please stop reading for a bit. Go take a walk, grab a meal, go to bed, meditate, or whatever allows you to think. Just put this book down for a while and really think some more about why you want to travel and what you want to get out of it. Really try to refine your *travel goals*.

DETERMINE HOW YOU WANT TO TRAVEL

Hopefully by now, you've really spent some time thinking about your *travel goals* and have a solid answer to the question, "What do you want out of traveling?" Being able to answer that question actually allows you to answer the next set of questions much more easily.

This next set of questions determines your *travel style* by looking at some different elements of travel planning and for each of these elements, figuring out how you prefer to travel from within a spectrum of options. The main factors that alter your experiences during travel often come down to a few primary things: accommodation, transportation, time, tours, and money.

I'm going to delve into how these factors can limit your trip next, but for now, don't worry about any real-world limitations you might have on these different elements of your *travel style*. Choose the option that best fits your *travel vision*. Some limitations can be surprisingly flexible if you're willing to work at them. Don't worry about your *travel goals* at the moment either. Think back to your *travel vision* and look at how your mind naturally chose some of these options.

ACCOMMODATIONS

A great starting point is accommodation. Think back to your *travel vision*:

How did you imagine your sleeping situation every night?

On one end of the spectrum, you could have been staying in five-star all-inclusive hotels throughout your trip. On the other end, you could have been camping every night. There are also a lot of options in the middle.

Accommodation Spectrum:

- Five-star luxury hotels

- Nice hotels but not necessarily five star

- A decent hotel, but it doesn't have to be fancy

- Any hotel will do, but I want my own room

- Airbnb-style rentals, either private or shared

- Private rooms in hostels (usually, but not always, means shared bathroom)

- Hostels (aka bunk beds in a shared room)

- Couch surfing at a stranger's place

- Camping/yurts/eco-lodges

I need to digress for a minute here. A lot of people I've mentored on traveling have scoffed at hostels and the thought of sharing a room with other people. Yes, hostels are effectively dorm rooms. But hostels are not that bad, I promise. I've spent more than a year of my life staying in hostels and I've never once had anything stolen. I've never seen anyone acting weird, and I've never really had any issues besides people being drunk. But that's also easily avoided.

To find good hostels, you just need to read the reviews from other people who have stayed at the hostel you're considering. If the hostel has a giant bar on-premises, chances are, you're going to be dealing with drunk people being loud, turning on lights in the middle of the night, and generally engaging in drunken stupidity. If you don't want to party or deal with this, then don't stay at a hostel with a giant bar on the premises. Pretty much any hostel without a bar and with decent reviews will be fine and issue-free.

Also, nearly every hostel has lockers to store your valuables and this locker can usually store your whole bag. I've only been to a few hostels that didn't have some sort of locker for your stuff. But if you think about it, what are you so worried about losing anyway? We'll talk more about this in the packing and security sections, but you shouldn't be traveling with your rare gold-coin collection or diamond-studded jewelry anyway, so you shouldn't have to worry about anything being stolen.

The only real downside to hostels is some reports I've heard from women about guys being creepy. But keep in mind, you can't really blame this on the hostel; this happens everywhere. However, a lot of hostels also have women-only dorms specifically for this reason.

Do you lack a little privacy being in a shared room? Of course. But the upside is that it's cheap. Like, really cheap. Another, even better upside is that staying in hostels is a fantastic way to meet people from around the world if that's one of your *travel goals*.

An additional concern I've heard is that you're around a bunch of strangers while you're sleeping. This is actually much less true than it seems. It's not like the corner bum packs up at night and heads to the local hostel. Hostels tend to be occupied by twenty- to thirty-year-old travelers, but a lot of hostels will allow people of any age to stay there. Regardless of age, though, everyone is a traveler first. And who goes traveling? It tends to be university-educated, or about-to-be-university-educated, fairly well-off people. The odds of having the local homeless staying in your hostel are so low that it's hardly even a possibility. Plus, the front desk staff is going to refuse to let anyone stay who is giving off the impression that they're not in the traveler category. So really, you're surrounded by people who are just like you in a hostel. They may be strangers, but they're strangers who are peers.

I mention this now because if you weren't considering hostels previously, but after reading this, you think that doesn't sound so bad, then keep it in mind as we proceed. I'll talk about the practicalities of hostels in depth later in the "Hostel Basic Procedures and Etiquette" section and you'll see how all the parts of a hostel fit together.

For now, though, let's get back on track. Which one of these accommodation options fits your desired *travel vision*?

In my case, I would actually prefer a decent hotel. But wait a second, didn't I just say that I've spent a ton of time in hostels? Yes, I have, but that's not my first choice when I think about where I want to stay. There are other reasons that my actual travel method is different from my most desired method, but I'll go through why this is the case very soon. For now, just focus on what you were naturally drawn to from the accommodations list.

LOCAL TRANSPORTATION

Now let's do the same thing with transportation.

What kind of transportation would you like to use during your travels?

Local Transportation Spectrum:

* Private transports, basically a hired driver that's not a taxi/ Uber

* Private bus, usually for tour groups

* Taxis/Uber/Tuk-tuks (a little three-wheeled open-aired mini-taxi)

* Shared taxis/Uber-Pool

* Public transport: buses, metros, light rail, etc.

* Walking, cycling

I think most of these are pretty self-explanatory, and almost certainly you're going to have some mix of these in a trip no matter how hard you try to stick to any particular type of transportation. But what are you drawn toward?

The private transportation options are really a sign that you don't want to have to think about where you're going. Meaning, someone else is handling the directions and driving. Whereas with public transportation, you're going to have to pay very close attention to where you're going, because no one is going to directly guide you. Further, you're going to have to do this while under the stress of being in a crowd and possibly in a country that doesn't have what you consider to be an easily readable language.

Depending on your destination, some or all of the options listed may be available, and one particular mode of transportation may be the preferred method in that locale. For instance, in India, tuk-tuks are the easiest way to get around in Delhi even though there's a metro system. But you can take private cars around there as well.

Again, don't worry about the reality of this for a specific trip right now. Just think about what you're drawn toward.

TIME

Let's talk about trip duration and how long you want to spend traveling. Don't worry about your life situation right now. Answer here with what you *want* to do.

How long do you want this trip to last?

Depending on your *travel vision*, you may be thinking to yourself right now, "What does he mean, how much time do I want to spend on a trip? It's a trip." Keep in mind, everyone has a unique vision of what traveling means to them. For some people, this is going to be using PTO (Paid Time Off) from work. For others, this is going to be a yearlong gap adventure. "Gap year" is traditionally when students take a year off before or after university to go see the world before they continue on to their next phase of life. For some other people, this is going to be a permanent "I don't ever want to work in a cubicle again" kind of decision and their trip could be years, if not decades. So what do you desire?

Time Spectrum:

- A weekend

- A couple of weeks

- A month

- A few months

- A year

- As long as you can

TOURS AND CONTROL

This is a really important question and one that I would not take lightly.

Do you want to participate in tour groups or avoid them?

I don't mean tours in the sense of having a guided tour through a museum. I mean tours where your hotels, your transportation, and your events are being coordinated by someone else.

Related to this question:

Do you see yourself traveling in a group or traveling solo?

This consideration is really about your desired during-the-day pace and level of control during a trip. If your *travel vision* had you lying on the beach in a tropical paradise, you probably don't want to plan out every single moment of your day because that likely wouldn't really feel relaxing. You probably also don't want to be in a formal tour group where someone else is dictating your schedule because that doesn't give you the freedom to relax. If your *travel vision* had you on your own and taking local trains in India, you probably don't want to be anywhere near a tour group either.

I'm going to revisit tours and groups much more in depth later because there are a lot of complicated decisions to make regarding tours. But again, just think about what you were drawn toward for now.

Tour Spectrum:

- A fully organized tour where everything is planned for you

- A partially organized tour where your transportation and accommodations are planned for you, but you are free to do as you wish in the locations you visit

- An "all-inclusive" hotel or cruise in which your meals and accommodations are handled, but you otherwise have free time

- Being in a group where you plan your own stuff

- Doing your own plans and going solo, with plans in place prior to departure

- Doing your own plans and going solo, and planning along the way

MONEY

This section isn't about budgeting for a trip—we'll get to that later. This section is about how much you are willing to spend on a trip. You may not have included this in your *travel vision*, and that's okay, because this question is a little bit separate.

How much money are you willing to spend on a trip?

Maybe you're rich and have no concerns at all about the cost of a trip. Maybe you're just out of university and want to keep the trip under a five-thousand-dollar budget. That's really what this is about.

Money Spectrum:

- Whatever, you have infinite money

- You're willing to spend a lot but within a reasonable limit

- You have a hard limit on what you're willing or able to spend

- You don't want to spend much

- You have no money, but you're going to make some part of this happen somehow through extreme budgeting

- You'll spend whatever it takes to accomplish your trip as you want to take it

The last option is kind of off the spectrum since you're essentially saying, "I'm limited on budget, but I'll do whatever it takes to make the trip I desire happen, so the budget is flexible if necessary." There's nothing wrong with being this person. It just means you'll do anything to make your exact trip happen, even if it's not currently within reach.

THE TRADE-OFF TRIANGLE EXERCISE

Let me explain a concept to you that's going to help you in the next section. I call this "the Trade-Off Triangle Exercise" and it's a concept that highlights the trade-offs you've made by selecting your *travel style* variables. This is mostly a thought experiment, so nothing concrete is going to come out of this. But going through this exercise really makes it clear what trade-offs you're making regarding your trip, even though they may not be obvious.

There are similar concepts to this in macroeconomics, software engineering, and general product development. In these other fields, their trade-off triangles are visual ways of describing trade-off decisions that occur in reaching a single outcome. A very common example of this is the product development idea of "fast, cheap, reliable." Every business wants their products to be all three, but usually you can only get two of those, and then you lose control of the third one. So, for example, something made fast and cheap is usually unreliable and of low quality. For another example, something very reliable and fast to produce is usually going to require advanced technologies and equipment, so it becomes very expensive. As a last example, something that tries to balance all three variables typically ends up being very generic and doesn't do anything overly well.

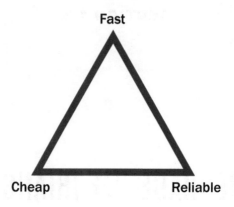

The product development trade-off triangle. You can choose where you want to be inside the triangle.

For our purposes, your trip is your outcome, but your trip depends on three tightly coupled variables. By figuring out the control you are gaining from making style decisions, you will also see where you are losing control with your decisions. Knowing this and seeing it visually can make you more aware of the consequences of the things you can't control as much.

For travel, there are three main concerns that can define the limits of your trip:

- Time

- Money

- Luxury Level

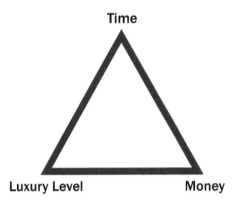

This is going to be our traveling trade-off triangle.

Think about each of these three variables. Remember all the things you discovered about yourself in the previous sections and ask things like:

- Are you using vacation time from work?

- Is budget a concern?

- Are you hard-set that only resorts will suffice for accommodation?

Try not to think about this in the sense that "I'm on a budget, so my luxury level is limited." Instead, think of it like you are "on a budget" and therefore money is limited. The conclusion that luxury has to be limited because of the money restriction will be the result of the rest of this exercise.

Let's take a closer look at your trade-off triangle now. The way this works is that you need to place a dot, representing your limits, in the part of the triangle that describes that limit. So if your only limit is money, then you'll be in the corner for money. If you are money and time limited, then you'll be on the middle of the edge that joins money and time.

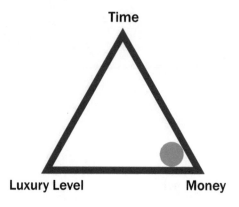

If you are money limited, place your dot in that corner. There are trade-offs here between time and luxury.

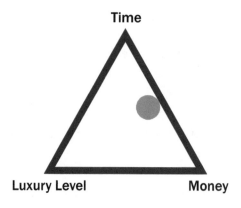

If you are money and time limited, your luxury level may be out of your control.

So now note in the triangle, if your dot is in one corner, then you have some choice between the two remaining variables and how they trade off. If your dot is on an edge, then you have very little control over the remaining variable. Essentially, if your dot is opposite from a corner, you have less control over that part of your trip.

In my case, money is my main limiter, so I have a trade-off to make between luxury and time for my travels. Because I want to go everywhere, that means I want to be traveling as long as possible, so time is the preference in the trade-off. As a result, luxury level is often out of my control and that lands me with low-luxury, budget-level travel options.

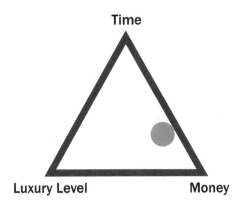

This is my travel trade-off triangle: I'm money limited, but I also have somewhat of a time limitation.

As another example, if you are only considering five-star hotels and you have two weeks off from work, then you are luxury and time limited, and therefore you lose control of the costs of that trip. This trip is likely going to be very expensive.

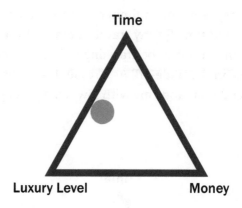

A fixed time, fixed luxury trip often loses control of cost.

Now that you know what you *can't* fully control in your trip based on your *travel vision, travel goals,* and *travel style,* are you okay with that loss of control? If your limiter was high luxury and time, then are you okay with spending potentially a lot of money for your trip? Similarly, if time and cost were limiters, are you okay with having a low luxury level? If the answer is no, you're going to need to make an adjustment somewhere in your planning.

Keep these things in mind for this next section.

ADJUST YOUR DESIRES TO MATCH YOUR GOALS

Now comes the really hard part. You've answered the questions about your *travel style* and you figured out your *travel goals*. If you're really, really lucky, then maybe your *vision, goals,* and *style* all line up perfectly. But if you're the other 999 out of 1,000 people, your *travel style* and your *travel goals* both support your *travel vision*, but your *travel style* and *travel goals* are out of sync. It's likely you're only just about to realize this. If you're thinking right now that your *vision, goals,* and *style* line up, I'm pretty much going to guarantee you they don't. Now you have to figure out *why* they don't line up.

Unfortunately, there are so many possible scenarios for this that there's no way I could cover them all without responding to emails from every single person reading this book, but let me go through this exercise with my personal answers so you can see what I mean.

So what do I want out of traveling?

My *travel goals* are that I want to see and experience culture all around the world, while doing some side activities, meeting people, and partying a little, too.

41

Due to my *travel vision*, however, my *travel style* landed me with a spectrum of choices that included decent hotels, taxis, and traveling for a year per trip. I'm also drawn toward large-scale tours because it's less hassle than having to plan out all of my own stuff. Finally, I know that no matter what my money situation is, I'm willing to spend whatever it takes to do these trips. However, realistically, it will take me time to save up the money.

But wait. There's a problem here and it's not obvious. If I compare my chosen spectrums for my *travel style* to my *travel goals*, they don't really line up. If I'm on a tour and staying in decent hotels, then how am I meeting other travelers and how am I interacting with the locals? Being on a tour is going to mean that I'm surrounded by a group. I'm on their timetable, and that means I won't be interacting with locals much to coordinate my own meals, points of interest, or even just getting around. I'll probably be on a bus, which means I can't stop easily to check things out if I see something interesting. Sure, I'll be staying in decent hotels, but I won't be meeting other people who aren't in my group because where can you hang out and meet people in a regular hotel? You can't, really. And partying? Unlikely. Out of a group of fifteen people, which would be a very large tour group, it's unlikely I'll be able to rally a handful of people who want to go out for a crazy night. Maybe a couple of people in the group will be interested, but then, because I'm on the group's tour schedule, I probably can't sleep off partying the next morning or I'll miss something critical on the tour.

What does this all mean? It means my *travel style* spectrums are not helping me to achieve my *travel goals*, even though both of them came from my *travel vision*. So I'm going to need to modify my spectrum of choices that make up my *travel style* into a reality that will help me accomplish my actual *travel goals*. Doesn't this mean my initial *travel vision* might have been a bit disconnected from my *travel goals*? Very likely!

Functionally for me, this means I need to make a few modifications to my spectrums to ensure I'm actually going to be traveling the way that serves me best:

- I want to meet other travelers, so I want to stay in hostels.

- I want to avoid tour groups so that I can stop whenever I want and move at my own pace.

- I also want to avoid tour groups so that I can see more specific sights and museums.

- I also want to avoid tour groups so I can party if I want to.

- I want to meet locals and interact with the culture, so I want to take public transportation and be on my own walking around.

The most difficult part of what I want out of traveling is that I want to travel to a lot of destinations because of my desire to understand different people and their cultures. Because of this, my desire to stay in hotels, paying for tour groups, using taxis, etc. are all going to dramatically increase my spending and limit how long my budget will allow me to travel. I can see this from my Tradeoff Triangle Exercise. If I want to travel for a full straight year, is that actually realistic if I'm blowing my hard-saved money on things that don't facilitate that goal? Not at all. I need to shift my spending toward accomplishing my goals and this is going to mean cutting luxuries for cost savings, which in the end means more interaction with others.

After saying this, what does my *travel style* have to look like now? I'm intentionally staying in hostels, using public transportation, and avoiding tour groups, which all mean that I'm essentially budget traveling. This will now allow me to achieve all of my *travel goals* because

I will get to interact with locals more, travel to more countries, experience more cultures, meet more people, do more activities, and even party more.

So does my *travel style* now match up with my *travel goals*? It does! And in fact, this *travel style* is how I've done somewhere around 90 percent of my traveling. The other 10 percent were countries where I'm not sure I could have gotten around without a guide initially due to language barriers and culture shock. I'll explain more about that later when we discuss tour groups in depth.

Note: Changing my *travel style* did mean that my *travel vision* also had to change a bit! Really, your *travel goals* are the driving factor in all of this.

Now it's your turn! You now need to do this process for yourself. If you travel the way that you selected in the *travel style* spectrums, is that actually going to allow you to meet your *travel goals*? Take some time after you finish reading this section and devote some serious thought to this. I would encourage you to do this while out for a jog, walking the dog, or doing a lap around the local mall by yourself. Don't try to think about this dilemma while watching TV, playing a video game, or driving home from work. You're distracted while doing those things and it's really easy to miss the point of this exercise and dismiss it with a "Nah, I'll be able to do my whole trip how I initially desired." If you dismiss this step, it's likely that you'll never go on your trip because you won't be able to get all the details to align correctly when you try to make your trip happen.

Something that you should really pay attention to while you think about this is that the less "packaged" your trip is—meaning, guides aren't doing things for you and the more you are planning and executing every aspect of your trip—the more immersed you are going to be in your environment while traveling. Less packaged means booking everything yourself, walking around everywhere, not taking large tours, etc. By no means am I saying that you have to travel this way, but if you book a full package trip where you'll be in buses with everyone else who booked the same package trip, then you can't really stop to interact with people or wander off and explore. The more you want to learn about a country and explore what it has to offer, the less packaged you will likely need to adjust your *travel style* to fit these desires.

As you're trying to make these adjustments to your *travel style* to match your *travel goals*, think back to your trade-off triangle and how changing anything affects the other aspects of your trip. If you've realized you're not happy with your control level due to your limits at any point, things start to get more difficult. If you aren't happy with your current limits and the resulting control level, that means your *travel vision* may not be possible in its current form. However, this does not mean you can't travel and soon—it just means you can't fulfill every aspect of the trip you want at the moment.

For example, if you want to take a yearlong trip and are on a limited budget, that means you've lost control of your luxury level. But maybe you find staying in a hostel to be absolutely unacceptable, meaning your limited budget may not be able to support your vision of nicer accommodation. In this situation, you may have to shift yourself into a different style of traveling in order to make your trip happen at all but within levels you're willing to tolerate. This could potentially mean a much shorter trip or maybe staying in lower-quality hotels. In a case like this, something has to give a little in order to bring your trip back into reality. All of this is a balancing act, and that's the whole point of these thought exercises and the Trade-off Triangle Exercise.

When I decided that I wanted to travel, I was twenty-four years old at the time. I didn't go through these exercises because I didn't know then what I know now about traveling. But I knew I wanted to travel to many places and that I had about four thousand dollars in savings, so I was very money limited. For me, going everywhere was by far the most important aspect of traveling, so time was my second limiter in that I wanted a long trip. As such, I lost control of my luxury level, and I was okay with that. But my savings weren't going to cover traveling for upwards of a year or two. I was stuck in a spot where my level of control for luxury was okay, but my finance limiter was preventing my time limiter from being realistic.

So I sat down and figured out that I needed to save a fair chunk of money, and this meant saving everything I could until I had the funds required to make that trip happen. Because the trip was really important to me, for the next three years I worked overtime, I stuck with my crappy car, I drank crappy beer, and I lived a pretty cheap lifestyle. After saving everything I could and then taking out a larger student loan than I needed for graduate school, I ended up with thirty-five thousand in the bank, and this was plenty to be able to hit the road for a long trip. But that thirty-five thousand wasn't going to take me everywhere I wanted to go in a single trip, so I hit the road and went as far as I could without getting into what I felt would be dangerous financial territory. Then I came home when my account neared my safety reserve (more on that when we talk about planning your trip). This ended up being a seven-month trip, though I probably could have stretched it to twelve months pretty easily if I had stuck to cheaper parts of the world, and I still maintained a good financial buffer for when I returned home.

You too can do the same thing. If cost is an issue, figure out how to save, and because this is a very common issue, we'll talk about it more in the "Avoid Excuses That Will Cancel Your Trip" section. If time is an issue, figure out how to get more time, even if it may mean leaving your job. If luxury is an issue, try going to a different area of the world that costs less, which will affect your overall trip cost and may allow for a much more luxurious trip within your current means.

Really think about what you need to do to match the *travel style* spectrums to the true *travel goals* defined from your *travel vision*, and try to get everything into somewhat of a realistic state. Talk yourself through why you need to change any of the choices in your spectrums, and when you're ready, continue on to the next section, where we'll determine your traveler archetype.

DETERMINE YOUR TRAVELER ARCHETYPE

Hopefully, you took some time to think about how your desired *travel vision* and *travel style* spectrums match up with your *travel goals*. Now let's see if we can figure out your traveler archetype. This will help you determine how you may want to travel and may also expose travel possibilities that you might not have considered. Once we've figured out your archetype, we'll talk about the various worldwide destinations that attract these archetypes and we'll talk about researching your trip.

Don't go into this exercise thinking it's a strict this-or-that activity and that these are the only options available. This exercise is meant to help you plan your trip and discover places you may want to go. That said, in my experience having met thousands of travelers along the road, most people have generally fit into one of these archetypes. However, that's not to say there aren't people out there who consistently fit into the description of two or three archetypes. If you're a multi-type and can change moods fairly easily, what that really means is that your desired travel destinations and options may be broader. If you are strictly more than one type all the time, your options may be more limited. No matter what, any of these situations are okay if they describe you.

Another thing to note is that while most people generally fit one archetype pretty well most of the time, there will be days or even whole trips when you'll be another archetype. It happens to me all the time. I may be doing the budget hosteling thing most of the time, but sometimes I've stopped for a day at a resort just to chill out on the beach and relax. I've also had days where all I do is search out nice food, which is also not the budgeting travel method. There are archetypes for all of these, but the important thing to consider is that most of the time, I am mainly one archetype. I just have some days or trips where I don't fit that mold. There may be things in every archetype that appeal to you or describe things that you like to do, but there is very likely going to be one main archetype that really speaks true to you and consider that when thinking about your plans and destinations.

Also, because of the adjustments from the last chapter, you may notice an archetype here that represents who you *want* to be, but you now realize that maybe there's another archetype that embodies who you're going to *need* to be to meet your *travel goals*. What I'd encourage you to do is look at the primary concerns of each archetype and see which archetype best fits your *travel goals*.

THE GAP YEAR

This archetype is typically an eighteen- to twenty-three-year-old traveler who is generally, but not always, traveling on money given to them from family specifically for the purpose of traveling. They usually travel directly before or after university. These folks tend to congregate around beaches and bars due to their age. They are usually not on tours or in museums. The main Gap Year goal is usually trying to see and experience the world, for as long as possible, as a sort of last hurrah before getting serious and entering the "adult" world. Because of the long trip desire, they're usually trying to keep trip costs very low.

Primary concerns:

- Cheap travel

- Partying

- Fun things to do

- Hostels

- Meeting lots of people

- Traveling for as long as possible

THE HIPPIE

These folks are typically twenty to thirtyish years old and are traveling on their own money. They tend to want to go somewhere and stay for a while, usually with like-minded people. They want to be free to explore and experience local culture but also have their own cultural pocket where they can hang out. They tend to like places that are known for being spiritual or places that are considered "hidden gems." They also tend to shun places that are "popular" regardless of the reason for that popularity. These folks also try to avoid Gap Year's hotspots if at all possible, because they see that style of tourism as feeding money into an industry that often cares little about the local people those industries claim to represent.

Primary concerns:

- Being around other Hippies

- Cost conscious, primarily chooses the lowest budget options for food and accommodations

- Being somewhere spiritual or around people who are "different" or underrepresented

- Avoiding popular tourist locations

THE ON-RETREAT

This is usually a twenty-five to forty-five-year-old working professional who is using their holiday time from work to get away and relax. They're on limited time and are very stressed out from trying to advance their professional career. Usually found at beach resorts or on cruise ships, they sometimes foray into other locales. They love picturesque areas that make them feel like they "got away from it all." Due to being so stressed out, these travelers rarely want to handle the minutiae of planning and executing a trip because this adds more stress into their already overworked lives.

Primary concerns:

- Calm and quiet

- Tranquil, picturesque environment

- Being pampered

- Very pointedly having the ability to avoid reality during their short stint away

- Typically enjoy guided day tours and activities

THE OUTDOORSMAN

This type is relatively rare. They're almost always twenty-five to forty years old and love camping and living in cabins in the woods. Much to my surprise, the few of these that I've come across have been very successful business owners and professionals. But the thing they really love is nature and its wonders. My surprise comes from the fact that these are typically people who are great at interacting with others but are choosing to be remote and out in nature away from people. The folks are usually traveling with a tent in their bag and aren't doing the "normal" urban touristy stuff.

Primary concerns:

- Going camping

- Going hiking

- Avoiding the main tourist areas

- Have money but are almost "living off the land" because they love nature

THE AVOIDER

This type isn't as rare as the Outdoorsman but they're fairly uncommon. In some cases, they could be described as extreme minimalists because of how little they choose to own. These types, in my opinion, seem to be running from something, possibly society itself. Typically, they do not want to be at "home" holding a traditional job. Rather, they'd prefer to be on the road forever. Avoiders have different life priorities than many of the rest of us and aren't going to let themselves get caught back in the "weekly grind." Most of the Avoiders I've come across have been in Central and South America.

Primary concerns:

- Not going home

- Working as they travel, usually with temporary odd jobs

- Living cheaply

- Owning nothing that can't fit into a single bag

THE DRIFTER

This is not someone who is homeless like the name may imply but more like a person who goes wherever the wind blows them. This is also a relatively uncommon type, but these are the people with the craziest stories. Stories like, "Oh, I was at a bar and heard some people talking about boats, which I knew nothing about, so I bought them a beer and it turned out they were professional fishermen. So after a few more drinks with them, I decided fishing sounded interesting and I signed on to the crew for three months during the next fishing season." These people are up for anything and will go with whatever interesting opportunities present themselves. These are your *Into the Wild* types and are living a lifestyle that makes them appear to be traveling when they're actually drifting. Slightly different than the Avoiders who are literally avoiding home, Drifter types are at home wherever they are currently.

Primary concerns:

- Adventure and experiences

- Finding out-of-the-norm things

- Learning about life

- Being free

THE EXPLORER

Somewhat uncommon, these folks are typically primarily trying to learn about the history and culture of the country they are visiting. They're serious about going to museums and interacting with locals. They will avoid other travelers if necessary to try and accomplish these goals. They are also interested in going to remote places that have unique options and cultures. They're seeking adventures but are also interested in learning and new experiences. These types will go to places that other types typically wouldn't consider as travel destinations. This is my type, so it was difficult to write this description objectively, but I've met others of this type and I think this description sums things up pretty well.

Primary concerns:

- Cheap traveling

- Traveling to many places

- Interacting with locals and learning about the culture

- Having varied experiences

- Going to museums and sights as well as local restaurants and bars

THE GET ME OUT OF MY COMFORT ZONE

Often with this type I hear, "I just want to experience culture shock." They often express feelings that their life at home has been handed to them and they know a lot of people around the world aren't so lucky. Often, these folks are newer to traveling and they tend to target countries with high poverty rates. Once these folks get their culture shock fill, they tend to want to get home as quickly as possible, and I've actually seen people cancel the rest of their travel plans right in the middle of a trip because they felt like they experienced the culture shock they were looking for and now had no further reason to continue their trip.

Primary concerns:

- Going to a place that is totally different than anything they know

- Having a short, intense trip and then quickly returning home

- Having a feeling of disorientation with their daily life while traveling

THE PENSIONER

These folks are usually fifty-five and older, and they want to use their career savings to finally take that dream trip they always planned. Because of retirement and large savings, this dream trip is usually composed of somewhat luxurious tours that follow the well-beaten tourist paths in a few select parts of the world. These trips can be quite long because the goal is to travel, relax, and enjoy the big trip. Because of the age involved, these folks are truly trying to make the most of their trips and usually take their time learning about and experiencing new cultures along their route.

Primary concerns:

- Comfortable travel

- Not having to fuss over little details in their trip

- Want to "see the sights"

- Have lots of time and money, so they want to take their time and really see the places they're visiting

THE CULTURIST

These are the folks who have an obsession with a particular country. In my experience, this is usually Japan or Latin America, but it could really be any country or region. This is someone who loves a country or culture so much that they've decided to start learning the language, they watch media in that language, and they have posters and books about that country or culture. And this is all before having even gone there. Usually going to this person's beloved country or culture is going to be a dream trip for them. These folks will tend to spend the majority of their time in modern cultural centers and not focus on other touristy stuff so much.

Primary concerns:

- Getting to their main country/region at all costs, no matter what

- Okay with extreme budgeting to make sure they see everything

- Want to interact with locals and culture

- Want to see the main sights

- For Japan, a lot of people travel in a group of friends because they know others who are just as excited to go there for the same reasons

THE *EAT PRAY LOVE*

Literally named after the book and movie, this is someone who is reevaluating their life and purpose after finding out that their supposed "success" in life wasn't as enjoyable as previously promised. These folks are usually over thirty and have done well in life by traditional standards but found something was lacking. They want to experience what else life has to offer and to find a direction in life that feels fulfilling to them as an individual. Because the movie focused on Italy, India, and Bali, most people of this type tend to want to go to those spots, but there are many more places available. For what it's worth, all of the things this type is looking to gain from traveling will come naturally from travel anyway, almost no matter where they go. The main thing these folks need to do is to get away from their day-to-day and reevaluate their definition of success.

Primary concerns:

- Exploring what life has to offer

- Finding a more meaningful sense of direction

- Experiencing spirituality

- Getting away from the beaten path that defines "traditional" success

THE FOODIE

This is someone who is really, really serious about their food. These folks want to experience great tasting food from tons of places and may even go so far as to plan their trip around where they're going to eat. They do an incredible amount of research before ever going to a destination by looking at recipes, shows, restaurant reviews, and menus. These folks would do well to look at the Michelin Guide and watch the Netflix show *Chef's Table*.

Primary concerns:

- Eating great food

- Eating lots of different types of food

- Trying the local specialties that they can't get elsewhere

THE NEWB

Typically, these are people who got up and went traveling because they saw that loads of people were obsessed with traveling, but they themselves had never really looked into traveling or planned anything for their trip. You will notice this type because they seem to be hanging around a lot in common areas but don't really seem like they have a plan. This isn't meant to insult these types of travelers at all, but it's in stark contrast to, for example, the Culturist, who probably has their trip planned out down to the most minute details months before they even leave, whereas the Newb might have thrown some clothes in a pack and headed to the airport with the ticket they bought the night before, and they might not even have the guidebook for their destination. Their lack of plan also means that other people are really important for them. Others are going to provide company as well as more on-the-fly planning information. This book would be really good for the Newb traveler type, but the irony of this type is that they probably won't seek it out before heading out on their trip!

Primary concerns:

- Leaving home and going on a trip

- Lack of plan almost certainly leads to budget concerns, so they're usually looking at cheaper options

- Being around people

- Open to just about any suggestion as to what to do once they're finally on the road

THE SEX TOURIST

I'm not going to give advice for this archetype and I think the name says it all. This traveler is primarily concerned with having sex with as many people as possible, from all different countries. These are usually men, but I have heard of a few women in this category. In all of those cases, it was from a female friend who was traveling with them who commented on how their travel companion is "going nuts for guys since they left home."

Primary concerns:

- Sex with many different people

- Privacy, so usually staying in private rooms

- Nothing else seems to be consistent to these people due to varying age, finances, etc.

* * *

Before you continue to the next chapter, which archetype did you see that best matches your *travel goals*, *travel vision*, and updated *travel style*? If you identified with a variant of an archetype that I didn't list, that's fine, too. Your archetype is going to come up a lot in the early part of this book, so check over your identified archetype once again just to make sure it's closest to your goals. If you aren't entirely sure at this point, that's okay.

If you felt you matched more than one archetype, try to think about which one primarily matches you or seems to describe you most of the time. In any case, as we continue on, you'll probably realize you lean more toward a certain archetype over the others, and then you can use that one to help guide you.

ROUGH BUDGET CALCULATIONS TO KEEP IN MIND

You don't need to specifically worry about your total trip cost yet, but it's worth keeping in mind, especially if you are budget limited and wondering what the rough costs are going to be while traveling in various parts of the world.

The reason I say this doesn't need to be finalized yet is that you can change all sorts of variables during your planning stages to adjust your budget. For example, you may have six months in Europe planned but realize this is way over your budget. However, that doesn't mean you can't spend *four* months in Europe instead with some careful adjustments. It's just worth knowing rough costs in advance so that if you are budget conscious, you can avoid considering a first trip that is far too expensive right from the start.

In general, a "see everything, do everything, get a taste of everything" trip, while moving at a solid clip, is going to cost about $1,500 a week in HICs, and $1,000 a week in MICs and LICs.

Now before you freak out, for any number of possible reasons while looking at those estimates, note that these are *my* costs as they have worked out for me in general, but note that I am the Explorer archetype. I am going to every museum and going to every sight that I possibly can. I'm taking tours in certain parts of the world, drinking a lot of beer, and heavily relying on planes for transportation, which is really the main cost contributor to both of those estimates. I am also moving really quickly in order to cut down on time, and therefore overall cost, but moving at what seems like a reasonable pace for me. I am also staying primarily in hostels in four- to six-bed dorms which are cheap but more expensive than ten- to twelve-bed dorms. I also do not cook my own meals, but I eat street food and sometimes McDonald's while in a rush. These numbers are basically close to being the cheapest "do everything" cost.

If you are someone who is extremely budget conscious and not in a rush, you can cook your own meals, cut out a ton of museums, and take cheaper transportation. You can also stay in those larger ten- to twelve-bed dorms in hostels, because more beds in a room usually means lower prices. You could even camp in some places if you're up for it. If you're one of these people, you can get your costs down to almost $500 a week in HICs, and $300 in MICs and LICs. That's a huge difference from my costs.

If you are one of these people, the strategies involved are a bit beyond the scope of this book, and I suggest you check out *How to Travel the World on 50 Dollars a Day* by Matt Kepnes, as he does an excellent job of describing where these cost-cutting techniques can be applied.

If, on the other hand, you are someone who wants to have sit-down meals, wants to stay in a real hotel (even if it's a crappy one), and those are the only changes you make but you still do all the sights, you're looking at $2,200 a week in HICs, and $1,500+ in MICs and LICs.

And that's just adjusting for fancier food and accommodations. Of course, there's no limit to where your costs can go with various room upgrades, nice cocktails at lounges, private drivers, etc.

It should be noted again that a huge portion of these budgeting estimates comes from plane flights. By huge, I mean almost a quarter to half of your trip cost in some cases. If you are traveling slower or take minimal long-distance flights, your trip costs will go down dramatically because the flight costs will average out over a much longer period of time and therefore lower your weekly costs. It should also be noted that plane flights are terrible for the environment because of the amount of fuel used, so if you can reduce your flying, you'll also help the environment out.

Also, I should mention, these are estimates that allow you to plan your savings. You are likely to come in under these costs per week while on your trip, but the point is that you don't want to be in the middle of a trip and find out you need another two thousand dollars to finish your trip and you don't have it available. Therefore, these cost estimates are meant to be higher than what your real costs will be. If you keep them in mind as relative estimates, you're nearly guaranteed to have enough money to make it through your trip.

My first seven-month trip, which was about five months of HIC travel with two months of MIC and LIC travel thrown in, ended up being about twenty-five thousand dollars. Using my own estimates, that trip should have been almost thirty-three thousand dollars. My actual costs came in at about 75 percent of the estimated costs, which is good because I didn't get surprised by the rate I spent my funds.

If you already know some of your limits, be it time, budget, or luxury, take the per-week cost estimates and multiply that by your trip length and see what you come up with. Again, don't freak out; you can still adjust things. We haven't even started the real planning yet.

Even the most budget-strapped traveler should be able to travel for quite a while if they go on the cheaper end of things as long as they are willing to make some compromises. And don't forget, you can always work while traveling for more money if you're out for a longer trip and want to extend your trip timeline.

AVOID EXCUSES THAT WILL CANCEL YOUR TRIP

I'm going to mention some things in this chapter that I'm not happy I have to say. However, these things are real and will indeed completely derail any travel dreams you have if you let them. I caution you, though, I'm only telling you the reality. I'm presenting this information because it may be helpful as you decide on the choices you'll have to make about your trip.

Let me start by telling you that if you want to pursue career growth, raise an awesome family, and during both of those you want to be traveling around the world for long periods of time, you aren't going to have enough time in the day to accomplish all those goals.

You're going to need to set priorities on which of these is more important and realize that taking on too much can spread you too thin, which will then ensure none of your goals are fully reached.

Please don't discount what I'm saying. Even if you don't want to hear it, you can't change the laws of nature and give yourself more time to do everything. You have limited time in your life, and if you really want to go on a big, long trip, you may be forgoing other things to pursue your long time on the road. Or you may need to start taking shorter trips and understand that you're not going to reach every travel destination that you'd like.

On a different note, many people want to go on a trip with a buddy (mate) or with a group of friends. Honestly, I'm so thankful that most of my travels have been on my own because it forced me to interact with locals and other travelers. I was able to move around quickly on my own time, which means I got to see more things and eat what I wanted to eat, and I didn't have to worry about someone else's finances and budgeting in addition to my own.

If you want to travel with a group of friends, I want you to think about why. Even if you left for years, it's very unlikely that your true friends are just going to abandon you. Are you going to miss them while you're gone? Video chat can easily solve that problem. Is there FOMO (the fear of missing out) about events or relationships? There will be more events and relationships later. Do you just want to hang out with them more? Well, how is spending a ton of money to go somewhere with them any different than hanging out with them at home? In that last case, you're pretty much guaranteeing that you aren't going to interact with the local area around you much because you'll be in the bubble of your group the whole time.

Unless you think it's going to be easy to get a group trip moving along, I would encourage you not to wait for others to travel with you. Especially because the logistics of doing anything (eating, transportation, even bathroom breaks, etc.) become a nightmare when you have a bunch of people involved. Is it doable? Yes. But if getting your group together is the basis of your trip, it might never happen at all. The more people involved, the more likely someone will back out or won't have enough money, etc.

If you want to travel with one friend, why? Are you afraid for your safety? This isn't really much of an issue, even for lone females (which

I will discuss later). Did some of the reasons for wanting to travel in a group resonate with you in this case? Why?

Unless traveling with a romantic partner, or you just happen to have a really easygoing friend who is ready to do the same exact thing you are, I would avoid waiting for a friend to join you, too.

Really, waiting for friends to get on board with a trip, if they aren't already, may never happen. And this could prevent your trip from happening right out the gate.

The next thing to discuss is how you pay for socializing while you're still at home. How much are you going out to restaurants, bars, movies, shows, concerts, etc.? If you do any of these things and then claim you can't afford a trip that lasts for months, I claim otherwise.

Everyone seems to think that I had a ton of money from my family when coming out of university that allowed me to travel years later. While this does happen with a lot of Gap Year types, I am not one of those people by a long shot. I got out of university with a small amount of debt and no money, and then out of my master's degree with a ton of debt and no money. I did, however, take out a larger student loan than I needed for my master's degree, and part of this was strategically allocated for travel afterward. Then I spent nearly two years drinking crappy beer at home on the weekends because it was much cheaper than going out to bars and restaurants. I didn't go to movies, festivals, or concerts, and the only "fun" money I really spent was on some weekend classes to learn scuba diving. It was easy to save up enough money for a trip this way. How so? Because I wasn't spending twenty dollars a meal and ten dollars a drink while going out for a couple of years. And did any of my friends notice? Not really. Did it affect my dating life? Not really. The only difference was that I wasn't going out and blowing my money on entertainment all the time.

The other big thing that prevents people from traveling on long trips is their job, and this is usually described as a "career" by those with this issue. At first glance, the primary issue seems to be a financial problem. People aren't willing to cut off their income for a while. But that falls into the budgeting category, which usually means the previously mentioned social splurging. Usually when people are having the "I can't leave my career behind" problem, it's because there's a concern that if they aren't continuously working on their career, that somehow they will lose their credibility and won't be able to work in their profession again when they return from their trip.

This thought is one of the biggest fallacies of the current work culture in most HICs. Nobody is directly tracking your career progress and there's no agency taking notes on your performance reviews such that those reviews follow you around from company to company. Plus, almost no one is tracking how long you've been in your field except for maybe the person who initially hires you based on your resume (CV) and interview.

Unless you're specifically being groomed for some high-level position and plan on staying at your company for a long time, leaving your job or taking long periods of vacation, paid or unpaid, is not likely to have any effect whatsoever on your career growth, especially early on in your career.

If anything, in my experience, the effect traveling has had on my career has been a definite positive. I've had whole interviews completely derail because people were so excited to see that I'd been around the world. Yes, you read that correctly. I do list my travels directly on my resume with how long I was out and where I went. To most companies, this shows an ability to be financially responsible, the ability to stay sharp in my profession even when taking a break, and it demonstrates a diverse knowledge of the world along with having a personality beyond sitting at a desk all day. For large international and diverse companies, these are desirable qualities to see in an employee.

When I explained to my bosses what I was trying to do for my first big trip and then quit my job to do so, the executives were so excited to hear my plans that they were almost shoving me out the door so they could start hearing stories and told me right away, "This is awesome! The seat is warm for you when you get back. Let us know!" I took this to mean that they wished they were able to take this trip themselves, but running a company and having families can make that difficult to impossible, so they were excited to see someone else getting the chance to do what they've dreamed of doing, too. Upon my return, I was able to return to that job without any issues, by the way.

The only negative I have encountered is that interviewers sometimes ask me if I'm planning on staying at their company for a while. This is a silly question considering the current state of the world where most employees stay at their companies for only two to four years at a time. What is "a while"? This question is usually easily bypassed, and if the company doesn't want you to work there because you "travel too much," you probably don't want to work there anyway.

Also worth mentioning is that because work has shifted into two- to four-year work stints, getting your old job back in the current work climate may be challenging or impossible. Don't rely on your old job being there for you.

Further, be aware, due to economic factors, location factors, or timing factors, you could very well have a hard time finding a job when you return home and have to spend some time looking around in the market again. This is a very real concern and one you should prepare for, even if you are being guaranteed a job upon returning home.

Most companies will also not look down on you for using all of your time off. This can be quite a bit of time for some people and could be used for a medium-length trip every year.

All that being said, try not to let the fears and concerns covered in this section prevent your trip plans. Adjust things as you can when you realize they're happening. Modify your lifestyle where appropriate. These things will only stop your trip from happening if you let them.

PART 2

PLAN YOUR TRIP

To plan your trip, you first need to decide where you're going to go and how you're going to get to those places. This section will discuss different areas of the world and we'll talk about what appeals to the different traveler archetypes in each area. After going through the first part of this book, you should now be very aware of what you want your trip to be like, know what you want to accomplish during your trip, and have an idea of where your budget and time constraints will be. Knowing all these things will make planning your trip a lot easier. If you still don't feel confident with your answers to these things yet, maybe spend a little more time thinking about them, or keep going through this book to see if you can build a better idea for yourself.

CHOOSE YOUR REGIONS

Chances are, before you even started reading this book, you already had an idea of where you wanted to go in the world and some of the things you wanted to see in those places. Almost everyone, even if their idea of a trip is sitting on the beach relaxing, specifically thinks of a certain area and imagines doing or seeing certain things while there. Maybe going to museums isn't your idea of fun, so when you pictured traveling in Cancún, you visualized the beaches and seeing ancient Mayan ruins. This goes the other way around, too. Maybe you want to go to Central America to see all the ruins and museums, but seeing the beaches isn't really a goal of yours.

Because you already have these things in mind, the purpose of this chapter is to explain some of the various aspects of the different regions of the world. My hope is that you'll find out there are more places you really want to go that you never knew about until now. Starting to travel is fun in this way because you can always find somewhere you want to go next.

The way that I went about collecting the information in this section has been through both reading a lot of guides and also actually experiencing a lot of places. Before I went traveling the first time, I was aware of some popular places that I knew I wanted to see, so I started my research by getting guidebooks for those areas. During my first seven-month trip, I didn't get to go to every place I wanted to visit. So when I came back home, I looked at the rest of the places that I still wanted to go to and started reading through those guidebooks even though I didn't have another trip planned out yet. Once I finished going through all the places I wanted to travel to eventually, it occurred to me that maybe I should look at the guidebooks for the places I *hadn't* thought of visiting, just to see what was out there anyway.

To get started yourself, I highly recommend the *Lonely Planet* guidebooks. For me, the food and accommodations information they provide isn't so useful because I use the internet for booking my accommodations, and I eat on the fly while walking around. But the sites and transportation information is invaluable. I've looked at other guidebook series before and they just don't work for me. I found the information in those other guidebooks too hard to easily parse for what I need. You may have a different opinion. Check out different guidebooks in a bookstore or online before you commit to anything.

If you decide to use something other than *Lonely Planet*, make sure your guidebook of choice has a layout that you find easy to understand and that allows you to quickly find key points and navigation information. What I look for in a guidebook is bullet-pointed site information and really good maps. Those maps are going to be 90 percent of what you're using the guidebook for day to day, so if it's not easy to read, it's quickly going to become annoying, and you're going to miss critical information you may need.

Another thing I like about the *Lonely Planet* guidebooks is that even though a number of their guides are no longer in production, for places like Afghanistan, which used to be really popular as a travel destination in the 1950s–1970s, I was able to find used copies of these guides on Amazon. Through this process, I managed to find a *Lonely Planet* guidebook for nearly every country on earth and I'm only missing a few small island nations. After having used their guides for so much of my traveling and research, it was easy to figure out if I wanted to visit these other places that weren't on my initial travel list.

You may eventually end up doing similarly exhaustive research, but the following regional descriptions will give you a good idea of where to start.

If you have a previous edition guidebook or find a much older, cheaper guidebook, the question arises, "How often are guidebooks updated and how critical is it to have the most up-to-date guidebook?" It depends. For the actual sights you plan on visiting, you could probably get away with a ten-year-old guidebook. For transportation, I'm not sure if I'd want a guidebook more than two or three years out of date. For accommodations, probably two to three years is fine, and for restaurants, you probably want the latest edition. Restaurants tend to roll over operations much faster than say, hotels. That said, however, guidebooks can't possibly display current reviews of accommodations or restaurants because they could never keep up and the book would be huge. We'll talk about websites for these things later in this planning part of the book, but I wouldn't recommend relying on your guidebook for these things. Your main worries with the guidebook are going to be points of interest, maps, and transportation. Those are the things that aren't rapidly changing, and so having a guidebook that's a few years old isn't going to negatively affect you. Some brands of guidebooks update more frequently than others, but if at all possible, I would get the latest guidebook for an area if you don't have anything already. If you're on the extreme budget end of the scale, though, getting a previous edition (within a few years) is very unlikely to negatively affect you.

In my personal experiences, I used a twelve-year-old guidebook in South America and it was totally fine. But then, I got a brand-new South American guidebook for a more recent trip, and even though the book was less than six months old, it didn't contain the information that there was a huge conflict between the north and south villages of Isle del Sol in Bolivia. This conflict negatively impacted my trip, and there was no way any guidebook would have been totally up to date to alert me to that. The point is, most travel information related to sights and points of interest don't change rapidly, and I would have been fine with my old guidebook and probably only would have avoided the issues I ran into if I had read the local news before arriving.

In describing the following regions, I'll also try to mention the archetypes that typically go to specific areas in these regions. For your archetype, you'll probably find some places you never realized that people like you generally go, so you'll have things to consider more in depth. If you find an area like this, I highly recommend getting the guidebook for that area and reading about it more carefully at some point. If I don't list your archetype for a particular region, that doesn't mean there isn't something for you there. Follow your interests if something appeals to you.

The following are the different regions of the world and some very high-level things that are of note there. There won't be too many detailed specifics, but this should be enough to clue you in to each region.

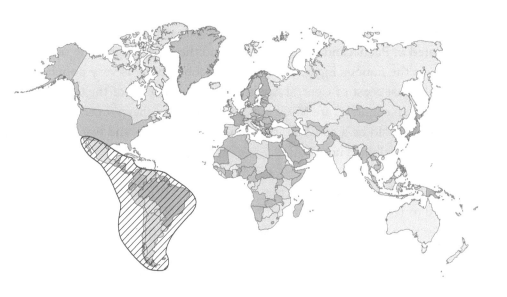

CENTRAL AMERICA/SOUTH AMERICA

This is the majority of the Latin American part of the world. While this area is comprised of predominantly Spanish-speaking countries, there are also some Portuguese, English, and even a few French-speaking countries, too. Even though this part of the world was further populated by Europe in the last few hundred years, there were advanced societies already there when the Europeans arrived. A few of these groups, the Aztecs in the north, the Mayans in the middle of Central America, and the Incas in the west of South America left behind all sorts of structures that still exist. Unfortunately, because of the Christian religious convictions of the European newcomers, many of the artifacts of these native societies, interpreted as pagan, were destroyed or manipulated in order to promote Christian beliefs. For this reason, museums in this region can feel thin compared to other areas of the world. The many ruins, however, are unique to this region and they are amazing. One truly unique feature of the ruins in this region is that you can climb on many of them and stand where the priests used to do human sacrifices and other ceremonies.

Also of note, Mexico has some of the largest pyramids in the world located in Puebla and in Teotihuacán, and these are roughly the same size as the famous Egyptian pyramids. Scuba diving is very popular on the east coast of Central America. In general, most of the Central American countries are MICs and tend to be very cheap for travelers. Safety should be a consideration in Central America and wandering around at night is not advised.

The South American countries are arguably MICs as well, but they tend to feel very European in the larger cities. They also tend to feel safer than Central America. The costs are more expensive than other MICs but are not quite at HIC levels. Cities like Buenos Aires are currently safe at all times of the day and night, but Rio de Janeiro has one of the highest gun robbery rates in the world.

As of recently, Colombia should also be safe to visit due to the disbanding of Fuerzas Armadas Revolucionarias de Colombia (FARC), the group that was fighting the Colombian government. They were the ones creating many of the danger and kidnapping issues in Colombia that most of us have heard about in the past, and they are no longer an issue. I have heard from many people that Colombia is now a great place to visit.

The traveler archetypes I've seen in this region are generally Explorers, Avoiders, Drifters, and Culturists. Some Gap Year people go to this region as well, but they tend to be fewer in quantity than other regions, possibly because this is an area of the world where you can't be entirely carefree due to safety concerns. San Cristóbal de Las Casas in Mexico is a major Hippie spot due to a fairly isolated and predominantly Mayan culture. Also, there are a number of resort spots in Mexico and Belize that are popular with American Retreat types due to cheap cost and proximity to the US. In general, though, the travelers visiting here tend to be here specifically because they want to see the sights and culture or because they are avoiding more popular tourist areas. Many people travel to this region to learn Spanish because they can keep practicing as they continue traveling.

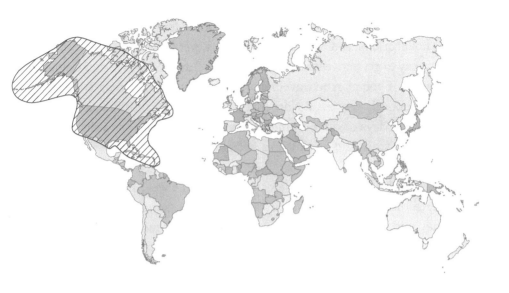

NORTH AMERICA

This region can be broken down into two major subregions: the Caribbean and the US/Canada. The Caribbean is a collection of islands where many of the famous pirate stories took place. The islands themselves contain a few museums and historical sights to see as a tourist. For many visitors, the appeal of these islands are the beaches and related water activities. Because beaches and sights can be seen fairly quickly on many of these islands, many people take cruises to see this area. These cruises rapidly hop between islands, allowing you to explore multiple beaches and countries in a single trip and still have a floating all-inclusive hotel at your disposal. There are a few resorts in this area that are popular for honeymoons and destination weddings by people from the US.

The other major subregion of this area is comprised of the US and Canada and both are great HICs to visit. That said, public transportation in the US is not nearly as developed as it is in other places. I've found that anyone who hasn't been to the US before dramatically underestimates how big the country is, and worse for tourists, we have a low population density compared to Europe. What this means for transportation is that it's not economical to run passenger trains everywhere. Pretty much the only way to get between major cities by land in both the US and Canada is by car. If you plan on traveling to these countries, be prepared to rent or temporarily buy a car. Note that it takes at least four full sun-up-to-sun-down days to drive from coast to coast in the US, and that's with almost no stops and driving on a straight-through route.

Touring the US and Canada could easily take weeks, if not months. Therefore, with their high costs, this area is going to be expensive. That said, both countries have some amazing museums throughout and the people are generally very friendly. Most people coming to the US will have a great trip and will see most of the famous American sights if they hit New York, Washington DC, Las Vegas, and Los Angeles. A side benefit of doing this is that a car becomes unnecessary. Similarly with Canada, check out Toronto, Montreal, and Vancouver.

I've also met people from many countries taking advantage of the youth work visa in Canada called International Experience Canada (not available to Americans, but things change). The folks I know who have worked in Canada have absolutely loved living there.

For the Caribbean, a good portion of people who head here are Retreat and Pensioner folks. For the US, even though it is a popular destination, it does not have the same huge influx of travelers that areas like Southeast Asia and Europe get, so while many Gap Year and Explorer types want to come here, both of those archetypes quickly find there is not the huge hostel selection that other areas of the world have, which drives up trip costs. This, then, tends to narrow down their trip to a few major cities that do have hostels. Outdoorsmen will find that the vast variety of geography and low population density leads to awesome hiking, camping, and sailing opportunities across the US and Canada. The US is known for its national parks and these will be particularly appealing to Outdoorsmen but should be on everyone else's radar as well.

EUROPE

I would imagine that almost anyone reading this book will probably be generally familiar with a lot of things in Europe already. That said, I find most people are more familiar with the UK, Germany, France, and Italy, while most of the rest of Europe is less familiar. Europe has a huge variety of interesting things to see and experience, especially since much of its history goes back to significantly before even Roman times. Incredibly, the Roman structures that do still exist reach from Italy all the way to the north of the UK.

Europe in general, however, is a lot less HIC than people imagine. Many parts can feel like MICs and some parts of Eastern Europe are still recovering from Soviet rule. That said, every single country contains all sorts of interesting things to see. Castles, museums, ruins, history—it's all over the place in rapid succession. It's actually hard to avoid. One thing to keep in mind is that trip costs can be quite high here due to it generally being a HIC area.

So the real question becomes, "What are you trying to get out of Europe?" Pensioners heading there tend to want to see the main sights in the UK, Germany, Italy, Greece, Spain, and France. Explorers go just about everywhere. This area is exactly what Avoiders are trying to avoid, i.e., it's super HIC and full of tourists. Newbs end up here a lot because it feels familiar and is therefore easier to travel to than other travel options. Gap Year folks tend to zip through here to have a few parties and see some of the sights, then move on and spend more time elsewhere in cheaper parts of the world. This is a great area for Drifters because there are endless opportunities for doing odd jobs and just letting the wind carry you wherever. Some Retreat folks head here and usually spend their time mainly in France, Spain, or Italy hanging out and having nice food and drink while they casually explore during the day. Most of Europe is a Foodie heaven because of all the different cultural dishes in close proximity. Get Me Out of My Comfort Zone types may find Eastern Europe interesting to see how Soviet rule affected these countries. Spain is popular with just about everyone.

Also, don't forget about the Scandinavian countries. For me personally, the Scandinavian countries have been some of the most welcoming and nice places I've ever been, and they have lots of interesting cultures and natural wonders, especially wintery ones, to experience. Plus, nearly everyone speaks perfect American English because their languages are difficult for foreigners to learn. That said, the Scandinavian countries are also the most expensive places I've been to on the planet, so there are trade-offs to visiting any location. I think they are worth checking out if you can accommodate them within your travel budget.

EAST ASIA

It's really unfortunate that more people don't visit this area because it's absolutely packed full of awesome things to see and do. Because "East meets West" really only seems to have taken off in the last forty years or so, this area is still a total mystery to many folks. Unfortunately, very little media from this area is consumed globally in the same way as Western media, and the people from this area haven't heavily immigrated to Western areas until fairly recently. This part of the world has history that reaches further back than the Romans, but due to geographical and technological limits over the ages, the East and the West have had relatively little direct interaction outside of trade until the last few hundred years. Due to these factors, the primary travelers you find in these areas are the Explorers because they want to see a little bit of everything. The reason you don't see other archetypes here isn't for lack of things to do; it's because they don't know they should come here!

Overall, all of the East Asian countries have great museums, the countries are safe to travel in, and they are not overly expensive. I highly recommend almost everyone stop by this region at some point in their travels.

Japan is, for me at least, the nicest, most pleasant place I've been on the planet. Whether you're a Culturist or you're generally interested in the culture and history, going to Japan has something interesting for you. Of note, although Japan has a reputation for being an expensive country, in my experience, it is significantly cheaper than Europe, despite charging HIC prices.

South Korea is also quite enjoyable and has many sights and activities packed right into Seoul. Foodies will get a huge kick out of South Korean restaurants and street food.

China has many interesting things to see, but it is also very difficult to get around in without a guide due to the extreme language barrier. I recommend initially taking a tour there unless you plan on staying in major cities and only taking flights between them. China can potentially be a culture shock for many travelers. For this reason, China is a major opportunity for Out of Comfort Zone types due to their different cultural norms compared to most European-descent countries. A note of caution is that while you are safe in China, scams are rampant and pickpocketing regularly occurs with little concern from the authorities.

Be aware that Hong Kong is a major airport stopover hub and is worth spending a couple of days in for almost any traveler. This is because of the ease of getting around and Chinese-related culture but with a distinct Hong Kong style. Foodies will enjoy the dim sum.

Avoiders, Drifters, and Outdoorsman may find East Asia interesting but challenging due to the language barriers and lack of easily accessible maps and trail maps. Explorer types will love the entirety of this area due to its unique cultures. Plus, there's lots of stuff to do. Retreat and Pensioner types may have some interest in the numerous tours and cruises available here. Gap Year folks should stop here but may find there's not the camaraderie and concrete tourist path that exists in other regions.

SOUTHEAST ASIA

When this area of the world comes up, some people who have never traveled before may have mental images from old war movies and TV shows. But that couldn't be further from the truth in terms of what this area offers. Beautiful beaches, cool things to see, resorts, culture, diving, partying, food—this area has a little something for everyone. And it's crazy cheap. Pretty much every single travel archetype will love parts of this area. I have heard nothing but praise about this area ever since I started traveling, and the most negative review of Thailand I've heard was, "It was pretty cool." No matter your archetype, you should consider going to Thailand.

The southern part of Southeast Asia is a little bit different than the northern part, but it's just as awesome. Malaysia and Singapore are both unique in the world because of their blend of Malay, Chinese, Indian, and European cultures. Singapore is also incredibly nice, clean, and safe. The Borneo part of Malaysia has some of the largest and coolest caves in the world to explore. Bali is a notable spot due to it being the only Hindu part of Muslim-majority Indonesia. Eastern

Indonesia and Papua New Guinea are the two main areas that I would urge caution for traveling. Both are remote and rather hard to traverse.

Bali is also a cool place to hang out and became very popular because of the movie *Eat Pray Love*. You will indeed find a lot of *Eat Pray Love* types in the more northern parts of Bali. However, Bali has been popular for a long time as it is to Australia what Cancún is to North America. By this I mean, there are lots of all-inclusive resorts and partying around Kuta in the south. That area can be very hectic and overwhelming in contrast to the north side of Bali.

Certain parts of the Philippines are popular to visit, specifically Palawan for its beaches and cave kayaking. One note of caution: the Philippines have had some political issues in the past few years, so pay attention to current conditions if you do decide to go there.

Thailand, Cambodia, Laos, and Vietnam are very popular with Gap Year types and Explorers because of a well-worn path of cheap things to do and unique sights to visit. Also, there are a lot of hostels and party beaches. Newbs feel comfortable in these core countries as well for this same reason. Thailand is a great place for Retreat types looking to relax. Explorers will also love Borneo and its caves. Foodies will find some amazing dishes in these countries, and be sure to try laksa soup in Malaysia and south Thailand. It's one of the things I discovered on the road that changed my life, and I have sadly never seen it at home. Penang in Malaysia is considered to be a major Foodie hotspot.

SOUTH ASIA

The main frequented spots in this region are going to be India and Sri Lanka. India, by far and away, is the biggest divide among travelers. Having been there, I think I understand why now. Very few travelers come here, but those who do either love it or despise it and usually form this opinion within a couple of days. I think the big problem is that most people don't know what to expect when they arrive in India, and it's a jolt to everyone's system.

India for most people is a land of mystery. We hear about India all the time—moving work overseas, festivals like Diwali, delicious curries, and other Indian food. But few people know what India is actually about. What I came to realize from my own travels is that India is a full-tilt assault on the senses. Everything is loud! Car horns are constantly honking while motorized moped taxis are flying by. The streets are densely packed with people who are moving in every direction in brightly colored clothes. The smells in the air are a mix of exhaust, flowers, and heavily spiced food. Cows are walking past you like a person normally would. Even when you eat, the flavors in the food are bold and powerful. It's very difficult to escape from any of this sensory overload in the cities.

That said, if you aren't scared by the sensory overload, India is absolutely amazing. The people are really friendly and curious about you, the food is delicious, and there's a certain beauty around you in how everyone is working together through the chaos. There seems to be a mutual respect among people and even in all that craziness, people seem to be collectively looking out for each other. It's impressive to watch. Also, if you do go outside of the main cities, things can calm down quite a bit and are not quite so overwhelming. However, you're going to get a dose of sensory overload at some point there, so be prepared.

Beyond this, India is generally safe and cheap. I wouldn't wander around late at night, but I never felt unsafe anywhere I went. However, after having said things are generally safe, I want to add that I'm a tall male, but the news outlets will have you believe India is much more dangerous than it actually seemed. There are always going to be bad people in every country, but the news greatly exaggerates any issues present in any country. That said, female solo travelers will definitely want to keep an eye out for what's going on around them and be sure to wear attire that is respectful to the local values. Meaning, keep your knees and shoulders covered. A good general rule for females is to follow the same level of modesty and precaution as the local women in the area. As long as local women are still out alone during the day somewhere, you should be fine, too.

The biggest hassle in India is scams. Around any tourist sight worth seeing, there are people who are trying to trick you out of your money. But they aren't going to outright steal from you. They'll run some hustle instead. To be honest, I could write an entire book on India alone. For example, getting between cities is tricky—really tricky. This is another country in which I would recommend initially taking a tour, simply because having a guide handle your transportation will save you a lot of stress. Another thing I would recommend is that if you get carsick, you should pack something to help alleviate that issue as nearly all of the roads in India are to some degree unpaved and very, very bumpy.

Sri Lanka is similar to India though much more relaxed. But be wary: they are extremely sensitive to perceived insults and frequently arrest foreigners for offending Buddha. You do not want to end up in jail in South Asia.

The other countries in this region have some really unique and cool sights but are way off the beaten path for most travelers, so there can be little to no tourist infrastructure present.

Explorer types and Out of Comfort Zone types are going to love this region because it's different, it's unique, it's over-the-top, and it's certain to give you culture shock. Dharamshala, where the Tibetan government lives in exile, is a hugely popular Hippie destination and should probably be on any *Eat Pray Love* type's destination list.

One extra note here: Goa in India used to be a major Hippie destination, but this is no longer so much the case. Avoiders can definitely avoid everything staying in this region, and due to extremely low costs, they can be away for a long time. Foodies will love the food here.

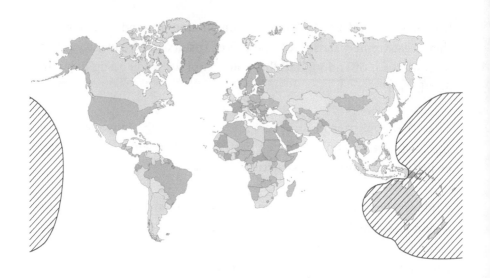

OCEANIA

I'll break this into two areas, the big countries of Australia and New Zealand and then everything else, which is effectively all of the island nations. In both Australia and New Zealand, there are plenty of places to see for all traveler archetypes, there's a well-worn travel path, and there are tons of activities and adventures to try. Plus, the weather is nice and there's partying all around.

Australia is arguably the main destination for most travelers, and I think a big part of this is the Working Holiday program. This program is a one-year work visa that is available to many countries for those under the age of thirty, and the visa itself is very cheap. New Zealand also offers this program, but New Zealand is a bit more laid-back than Australia, and there are not as many jobs available due to the lower population.

The people in both countries are extremely friendly, and the countries are generally very safe. However, because they are both HICs and remote, they are also rather expensive.

Outside of Australia and New Zealand, if you've ever dreamed of chillaxing on some of the most beautiful beaches in the world, you pretty much can't beat Fiji and Bora Bora in French Polynesia. Getting there is likely going to be a major cost, though, which is why closer locales tend to be favored, like Greece for Europe and Cancún for North America.

Australia and New Zealand are two of the most major Gap Year destinations in the world. There are loads of fun things to do and partying all around. Additionally, because of the Working Holiday program, moving to Australia is easy and allows you to work while keeping your travels going. This is about as tailor-made for Gap Year folks as it gets. There are also a few Explorers and Newbs in both of these countries. Retreat types should check out the awesome resorts in the Whitsunday Islands in Australia, and Outdoorsman should check out the amazing hiking opportunities in New Zealand. For the islands in the rest of this area, they are many dream destinations for Retreat types.

AFRICA

This area is the portion of Africa that includes the southern part of the Sahara Desert and then everything south. Because of the distortion caused by most maps, it's not obvious that this region is the largest landmass of the listed regions. This area is comprised of a few higher MICs and then a split of lower MICs and LICs. As such, the sights, ruins, and destinations in this region can be far apart and challenging to travel between and might require being on an organized tour.

Related to that, if you've always wanted to go on a safari, Africa has tons of opportunities for this. Be aware that safaris may not be a show of animals all day long because you're not in a zoo. You're going to be crossing great expanses of national parks looking for animals. But a good safari operator should have experienced guides who know how to track down and watch wildlife.

Be wary that Africa is an advanced travel destination because of the varying quality of infrastructure involved, and it's worth mentioning that you may need to take your safety and security more seriously in some areas. Cities and villages can rapidly change tone from street to street and entering shantytowns, meaning settlements of improvised buildings, is ill-advised as a tourist unless you're with a guide from that neighborhood.

Outdoorsmen will love seeing nature here because of varied landscapes, natural formations, and many opportunities to take guided hikes and camping trips. Explorers will find this area interesting and diverse. Some Pensioners who always had a safari in their travel plans head down here, too. From my own experience, Cape Town's main restaurant and bar street was pretty wild during New Year's Eve, and Victoria Falls is not to be missed by anyone.

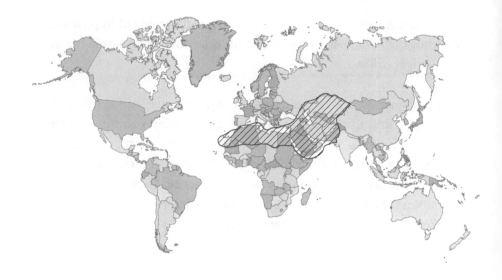

THE MIDDLE EAST, NORTH AFRICA, CENTRAL ASIA, AND SURROUNDING AREAS

The Middle East and North Africa, to include roughly Western Sahara, Morocco, Algeria, Tunisia, Libya, and Egypt, contain loads of sights that hold some of the earliest ruins of human civilization. Many areas also contain significant Roman and Islamic sights. There are so many sights in this region that it would be nearly impossible for me to list them all.

If you want to travel to this region, however, make sure to take current political situations into account. Because of the recent political unrest during the Arab Spring, some countries can have varying levels of stability at any given time. On the other hand, the United Arab Emirates have in recent years become a major traveler destination. That said, other countries have significant issues that fully prevent tourism. Also notable is that a couple of countries in this subregion regularly arrest tourists on claims of espionage. Again, make sure to check the current situation if you're planning on heading to these countries.

Israel is the one country that doesn't really fit into this region but happens to be tucked right into the middle of the whole area. Israel also has some amazing sights, and everyone I've met who's been there has said they enjoyed their visit. That said, because many Middle Eastern countries do not support Israel, having an Israeli stamp in your passport may prevent you from entering other countries in this subregion, and vice versa. If you are of Jewish descent, you can get a free trip to Israel as part of their Taglit-Birthright Israel program.

Central Asia has a bunch of super interesting sights, but the region hasn't been on many tourists' radars until recently because of previously difficult entry requirements. This region used to make up part of the ancient Silk Road, so you can imagine there's a lot of history here. Travel may be a bit more difficult here right now because they're still off the beaten traveler path, and they may not have much tourist infrastructure.

Explorers will want to check out the whole area. Avoiders and Drifters of Jewish descent may find Israel an awesome place to stay for a while, but be aware that staying too long may automatically convert you into a citizen which may automatically get you conscripted into the Israel Defense Forces, aka Israel's military. Hippies back in the 1950–1970s used to travel these areas extensively as part of the "Hippie Trail," but this region's part of that route is no longer the tourist haven it once was.

If you find that an area in this region is inaccessible at the moment but you'd really like to go there, give it a few years. Things can change quickly and those areas may open back up.

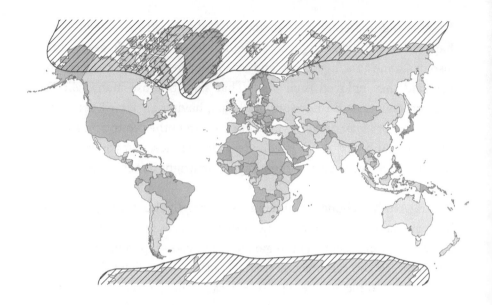

ANTARCTIC/ARCTIC

These regions are a little bit different than anywhere else because, well, explorers only discovered and started exploring Antarctica in 1820, and there are no real cities or man-made wonders down there. For the Arctic, much of the region is constantly moving ice, but there are approximately four million people living in the Arctic Circle with a significant portion comprised of indigenous peoples and mining operations. Both of these areas are amazing to visit because they're pristine, unique, harsh, and for the most part, largely untouched by man.

Traveling to Antarctica is best done by ship, but there are flyover options available. The Drake passage is notoriously rough and some tour operators offer a flight to skip this portion of the voyage. The Arctic can be visited by land and sea, and there are some interesting excursions available. Flyovers are also an option here, and ships will take you over long distances so you can see more.

Traveling by ship will also allow you to go on land excursions during the day, assuming your ship isn't too large. International agreements stipulate that no more than one hundred people from a ship be on land in the Antarctic/Arctic regions at any given time. So the more people on your ship, the less likely you will go on land excursions at all. The ship I was on, the MS *Expedition*, can bed around 130 travelers, which is about the most you could manage and still get people on land. Their trick is that one-quarter of the travelers are out on the water while the other three-quarters go on land, meaning that no regulations are broken, although everyone generally gets off the ship together. Before going to this region, be sure to thoroughly investigate how any potential ship may operate. There are many options available and you want something that's going to meet your expectations.

Because of the harsh environment, the ships that travel here can be fairly spartan, but there are also cruise-liner-type luxury options available. However, those larger luxury ships are unlikely to conduct land excursions. The cost for these trips is incredibly high because of distance and safety, but for the experience, the cost is totally worth it. Going to Antarctica was actually one of the most rewarding trips I've been on just because of how unique, natural, and environmentally extreme everything was. Plus, everyone on the ship really wanted to be there, and due to cost, most passengers were educated professionals who were thirty years old or older and as such, had really interesting stories of past adventures and travels.

These are great trips for Explorers and Outdoorsmen. Also, working on these ships would be great for Avoiders and Drifters. Most people on these ships tend to be Pensioners because of cost and dream destination status.

DESTINATIONS BY ARCHETYPE

We just went through the world regions and, at a very high level, discussed some of the general things of interest in those areas. Now let's look at this directly from the archetype perspective. Look at the locations I recommend for the archetypes you feel drawn toward and do some quick research online for anything you don't recognize and see what these locations have available. In many ways, the countries and cities listed below are also a general list of highlights around the whole world because, in my experience, this is where most people go during their travels. As noted previously, if I don't mention a destination for your archetype, that doesn't mean it's not for you! You can find travel that fits your archetype in most places around the world. The list below is simply a reflection of the most common areas where I've come across larger gatherings of various archetypes during my own travels.

Gap Year

- Australia

- New Zealand

- Thailand, and the rest of core Southeast Asia (Laos, Cambodia, and Vietnam)

Hippie

- Dharamshala, India

- San Cristóbal de Las Casas, Mexico

- Central and South America in general

- The Caribbean Islands

Retreat

- Cancún and Playa del Carmen, Mexico

- Bali

- Fiji

- French Polynesia

- French Riviera

- Italy (Florence and Venice specifically)

- The Greek Isles

Outdoorsman

- New Zealand

- Southern Africa (not South Africa specifically but literally the more southern countries in Africa)

- Antarctica and the Arctic

- The interior of Australia

Avoider

- Central and South America

Drifter

- Anywhere but often found off the main path; Darwin, Australia seemed to have a lot

Explorer

  • Everywhere with points of interest and things to do

Out of Comfort Zone

  • India

  • China

Pensioner

  • Italy

  • Greece

  • Germany

  • UK

  • Spain

  • France

  • Antarctic/Arctic

Culturist

  • Wherever your obsession is

The *Eat Pray Love*

  • Italy for Eat, India for Pray, and Bali in Indonesia for Love
    are popular because of the movie

- Japan for Eat

- Vancouver, Canada for Eat

- Lisbon, Portugal for Eat

- Penang, Malaysia for Eat

- Dharamshala, India for Pray

- North Thailand for Pray

- Kyoto, Japan could also be good for Pray

- Love can happen anywhere

- I would also suggest general travel outside of Europe/US just to experience new things

The Foodie

- Almost anywhere will have some particularly awesome chefs and food to try, but all parts of Asia in particular stuck out to me

- Check out the Netflix series *Chef's Table* to get some ideas

- TheFork.com is a good website for Europe

- Look at Yelp and Google Maps for more ideas and reviews about the area you're going to

The Newb

- Ends up somewhere by accident. If you're reading this book, you shouldn't be this type by the end of this book!

WHERE TO GO WRAP-UP

Now that we've gone through the different parts of the world at a high level, my hope is that you've found some new places you might like to explore beyond the original destinations you were already thinking about.

Before you continue to the next chapter, which talks about more specific planning techniques, get out a sheet of paper, open a Word document, or use a whiteboard, anything you'd like to take notes on, and make a list of countries and/or areas where you're currently thinking about traveling.

After you've created this list, take a look at Google Maps and see where these cities, countries, and regions are in relation to each other. Is there some sort of clear path that emerges to you? If there are a lot of different countries, are there multiple different trip legs that might make sense? If you're planning a short trip that goes to a lot of places, we'll talk about that in the next step, but start trying to think about a route for your trip.

For right now, don't worry about the time factor it takes to travel somewhere while writing your locations down. Your notes will actually help you plan lots of trips into the future as time and budget permit. So for the moment, write down any locations that have given you interest.

With these rough routes in mind, the most important thing you need to do at this point is to buy the guidebooks for the countries you find interesting. One thing to note with *Lonely Planet*'s guidebooks is they offer country- and region-specific books for some areas like Europe. I would suggest you avoid the country-specific guides unless you are a Culturist type for that location or there is no regional guide available. The country-level guides tend to start getting into details about much smaller areas and the more unknown, hidden sights to see. Most of the sights you've heard about are going to be in major areas, so the regional guidebooks, which don't go into as much depth per country, are sure to still have most everything you're interested in knowing about. And this will save you money since you don't have to buy a full library of country-specific books for places like Europe.

As an aside and final note for this section: start reading or watching the news! This may sound totally unrelated to traveling, and it might seem like a strange recommendation, but it's actually critical for your trips and for your understanding of the world and where you want to travel. You don't have to read every article on every news website every day, but I really recommend that you try to look at the news at least once a week and skim over the headlines at a minimum. The reason for this is that countries and regions sometimes have short-term and long-term instabilities and issues. As an example, as part of the mentioned "Hippie Trail," Afghanistan used to be a really popular Hippie and Gap Year destination, but things have certainly changed quite a bit there since the height of its popularity in the sixties.

In my own experience, I was heading through Central America when I was eating breakfast in a hostel one morning and they just happened to have English-speaking CNN playing on the TV in the common room. As I was munching away on my cereal, I was seeing reports of how Honduras just had a military coup. Tourists were trapped in limbo in the country because they weren't being allowed to drive farther into the country, and they also weren't being allowed to turn around and leave. Had I not seen this news on the TV, I would have attempted to cross into Honduras only a few days later and likely would have run into problems. Instead, I just flew over Honduras and continued onward. So keep an eye on the news. It has the potential to alter where and when you might head somewhere. You probably wouldn't have wanted to head into Egypt when they started to have a revolution, right?

DAY-TO-DAY TIME MANAGEMENT AND LOGISTICS

Now that you hopefully have a list of countries and places you're interested in exploring, you need to get more specific. For people traveling for a very long time, some of this may not apply so much. For someone on a tight time restriction, say planning a two-week trip away from work, this information may be critical. Apply as necessary.

Before you continue, go through your guidebooks and research the countries and cities that you're thinking about exploring. Pay attention and take notes on the sights and transportation you are likely to visit and need along your route. Look up how people rank things on TripAdvisor.com, but be aware the general populace may not rate things the same way you would. If you like food, do some research online. Good places to start with are TheFork.com and Yelp.com, but know that information gets sparse outside of English-speaking countries. Get some idea of what the cities contain and what you want to do there. Revisit your initial travel route and see if it still flows well. This ordered list is going to be the starting point for adjusting your plans and getting your trip nailed down.

Before we get directly into the planning, let's talk about some things to keep in mind as you plan more specifically.

WHEN TO SKIP A DESTINATION

Before we really start getting into the day-to-day planning of your trip, it would be wise to cut out anything that doesn't fit into your trip very well. When you look at your list, it may not be immediately obvious that not everything may make sense to visit. This has happened to me a number of times and it will likely happen to you.

One of the reasons this may happen is because a very unfortunate reality of the world right now is that not all places are safe to visit or will *stay* safe to visit. While writing this book, I read a guidebook that had a lot of advice about visiting Syria. That book was written only a few years ago. It only takes a few years and the world can be a very different place. I absolutely do not recommend visiting Syria in the near future unless things dramatically turn around there.

Similarly, I would love to visit Iraq, Iran, and Afghanistan. Some of the deepest histories of the world are in these locations, and all three of these countries used to be a huge part of the backpacker trail known as the "Hippie Trail" from approximately 1955 to 1975. There are many people still alive, probably now senior citizens, who took this popular travel route. Even though it is possible to visit these locations currently, the people I know who have done it recently have had to take precautions at a level that for me wouldn't have been fun.

Look at your list and double-check to make sure that you're not thinking about traveling somewhere that is currently having political issues. Most countries should be pretty easy to figure out. That said, I wouldn't recommend reading the *CIA World Factbook* information to see if a country is having issues as they make every country sound like the plot of *The Walking Dead*. Instead, read the news about that country and check the recent history to see if there is social unrest, war, or any situation where the people are being oppressed. I would also recommend reading the *Lonely Planet* and Trip Advisor website forums as the news outlets are not always the best source of up-to-date information either. For example, notice how Syria hasn't been mentioned for years in the news. However, that doesn't mean things have gotten better there.

Beyond the obviousness of not traveling somewhere with political issues, take a look at what you want to do in each country. For example, if you want to travel in Southeast Asia and rafting through the caves in Palawan in the Philippines is on your list, take a look at the timing in your rough trip route and what else you're looking at doing in the Philippines. Is cave rafting the only thing you want to do there in all of the Philippines? If so, traveling to the caves may not make sense. There's no way to fly there directly, so you're going to have to reconnect through the larger airport in Manila, and it's not particularly known as a nice place. Taking this into account, at a minimum, you're looking at two days of flights, both ways, just to do something that's going to last a few hours. If this is the case, it might not be worth the effort to go to the Philippines. That being said, if you run into this situation during your planning and that destination looks super cool to you, then by all means make the effort! Just know the opportunity costs of doing so.

For example, while I was traveling in France, I tried to visit the beaches at Normandy, but things unfortunately went sideways. I like history and a big part of what I like learning about is warfare and the sacrifice of soldiers in battle. Normandy is one of the most significant places in the world from this perspective. The main problem, though, is that most everything from World War II has been removed in the last eighty years, and Normandy is nowhere near Paris or any other major city. Even going as far as possible by train still leaves you significantly far from the beaches. Every tour company my girlfriend and I talked to was giving us the runaround. We finally started considering just renting a car in Paris and visiting the beaches ourselves. Then we looked at the sights that most of the tours stopped at, and aside from one bunker and a couple of graveyards, almost everything else just looked like land and beaches that could have been anywhere in the world. While the events at these places were and still are truly significant, there's little remaining that indicates that significance. After talking about these issues over a couple of beers, we decided the trip wasn't worth the effort, time, and money and that it would probably be somewhat of a letdown even if we did go because we wouldn't be with a knowledgeable guide.

It would be impossible for me to generalize this idea for any particular area or trip plan without knowing every single detail of your trip and desires. I mention these concepts so you're aware of them, the balancing act that occurs, and hopefully while you plan your trip, you'll be more aware of these ideas and more willing to cut things from your trip if need be.

OVERTOURISM

Right before the COVID-19 pandemic struck, many of the world's famous tourist sights were experiencing unbelievable and unprecedented amounts of what has come to be known as "overtourism." There are a few different definitions for this term, but generally, the idea is that a tourist sight has become overcrowded and unpleasant, and the surrounding area is experiencing negative impacts from so many tourists being there.

This situation had accelerated greatly since the 2008 recession due to many factors, including social media traveling awareness, increased population, and cheaper flights.

In fact, the situation has gotten so bad in some areas that right before COVID-19, some tourist sights had started shutting down to allow environmental recovery time, and other sights were limiting the number of visitors. This was because some areas simply couldn't manage the environmental impact from so many tourists. Other areas were simply experiencing too much wear and tear due to the increased volume of human traffic. Boracay Island in the Philippines and Maya Bay in Thailand are good examples of this if you want to read about how they handled their situations.

Barcelona is another victim of overtourism but maybe not in an obvious way. For Barcelona, many tourists had visited and fallen in love with the city over the years. Eventually, these tourists started deciding to stay longer and longer and this created a huge market for Airbnb rentals. However, the market for these rentals was so large that it significantly reduced the available spaces for rent for locals, and it also drove property prices through the roof. This has gone on for some time, and now, many locals can't even afford to live in the neighborhoods where they grew up. Worse, even if they could afford it, they still might not be able to find a place. With all this happening, tourist buses are seeing their tires slashed and graffiti has shown up in the city telling tourists to "go home." You can imagine that if you were kicked out of your neighborhood because rich foreigners were there for entertainment, you might be upset, too. Barcelona is still struggling with this situation with no end in sight.

Beyond those examples, this overtourism situation can also be time-period specific during the year. I was in Italy over Christmas and New Year's right before the COVID-19 outbreak, and it wasn't exactly pleasant. Italy is crowded even during the off-season because it's so popular, but the holiday period was something else. Every street in Rome and Florence was so densely packed with people that it was difficult to even walk around. Many sights and museums had lines that were hours long. Trains were completely full. It was wall-to-wall people everywhere. If you hadn't booked every single part of your trip months before you left, you weren't going to be doing much while there during this time of the year.

One interesting example of this from that same trip was the sandwich shop Osteria All'antico Vinaio in Florence, Italy. With almost 20,000 reviews and a 4.7 rating on Google, you can imagine this is a *very* popular spot to eat for many tourists. Who, what, why, and how is this sandwich possibly that good, right?! They've literally had to buy up the shops around them and are running lines (queues) out of multiple shop spaces. The crowds were incredible. But was waiting forty-five minutes for a fairly cheap but delicious sandwich worth it? That's going to be up to you. But think about this: the reason so many people are visiting this sandwich shop is that so many people have visited this sandwich shop. It's a weird effect that self-perpetuates and creates its own overtourism. To be fair, I tried the sandwich, too, and it was delicious, but it wasn't worth the wait to get my food. I could have been doing something more meaningful with that time. Being there during a holiday season, in an already overtouristed location, certainly made the situation much worse than normal.

Note that Western holiday periods aren't necessarily the only time for overtourism. Japan experiences a massive influx of people during the cherry blossom season in early April and again when the leaves turn colors in late November. Summers and winters are fairly brutal in Japan, so those are actually the off-seasons for tourism.

The main reason I point this out is to warn you to be careful where and when you book your trip. Popular sights and popular times of year can greatly increase your stress and the need for careful far-in-advance planning. Realize too that public transit may have reduced hours or days off during holiday periods which, when combined with overtourism, can greatly increase your time between destinations.

Many times, if you head somewhere slightly away from the main sights, you can avoid most of these issues. This is why your planning research is important, because you can discover places you want to visit that are not directly in overtouristed areas. Then when you're traveling, you can still see the things you want to see but not necessarily be trapped the entire time in the crushing overtourism of the main areas.

Take all of this with a grain of salt. Because of COVID-19, it may be years or decades before overtourism becomes a problem again. But it certainly will happen again down the line. With more people on earth every year but the same number of tourist sights, the crowding and overtourism problems are likely to get worse in the years to come.

RESPONSIBLE TRAVEL DURING PLANNING

Although I'm writing to you about my philosophies here, I highly encourage you to consider what I'm about to say in this section. There are some destinations around the world that seem very adventurous and different because they're not normal travel destinations.

In some cases, the reason for this is because the countries are run by brutal regimes that imprison their people for almost no reason and who do not allow their people the ability to make a decent life for themselves. In general, these sorts of countries are shunned by the world because they're typically caught up in human rights abuses and the suppression of free speech.

One major reason these places seem different and adventurous is a direct effect of their rejection by the rest of the world. These countries are usually very cut off and people generally do not travel there.

Good examples of this are Myanmar and North Korea.

Unfortunately, if you go to these sorts of places, the money you spend there is likely going into the hands of the government and is thus directly being turned back around into the oppression of the people there.

Can you travel to these places? Yes.

Should you travel to these kinds of places? I would argue the answer is no.

If you're not sure about a certain country, check online and do some research. These countries have been declining in number over the years, but they definitely still exist.

All right, let's get into planning specifics now.

GETTING AROUND DURING YOUR TRIP

Transportation information is critical to planning your trip because much of your transportation, especially long-distance flights, may need to be booked long before you start traveling. Therefore, we should talk about this topic now so you can visualize in your head how you'll be moving around from location to location. It's good to keep in mind that generally, the farther your transportation is going to take you, the more likely you will need to book that transportation in advance.

The main sources of transportation are likely fairly familiar to you already, and there's a good chance you have already taken most of them. Anywhere you go, getting from point A to point B is almost certainly going to take one of the following transport methods. Going from, roughly, long distance to short distance, you have:

- Planes

- Trains

- Boats

- Buses/Cable cars/Transport vans

- Tourist transport vans

- Taxis

- Rickshaws/Tuk-tuks

- Private hire cars

- Metros/Subways

- Walking

- Bike shares

That's really it. Admittedly, I sometimes laugh with the way people fantasize about their future travels, as if they've gone back in time and are going to load their pack onto a couple of donkeys while trying to cross uninhabited mountains somewhere. Unless you're taking a camelback Sahara tour, trekking across the Andes in Peru, or taking another similar tour, you're going to have the same transport as you're currently accustomed to pretty much everywhere on the planet. Even the most non-globalized parts of the world have cars and roads nowadays.

That said, not everywhere is easily accessible by airport. And countries that developed after the car was already commonly used have usually skipped some of the rail development that occurred in other parts of the world. With that said, let's take a closer look into each of these transport methods.

Planes

Absolutely nothing can beat the expediency and price balance of air travel over long distances. If you need to travel long distances, or generally over large bodies of water, you're going to be flying. In relatively newer cities, sometimes you'll find airports closer to the city center. My adult hometown of San Diego is one of these places. The airport is literally streets away from the downtown (city centre), which makes for a pretty cool view while taking off and landing at the airport. But for older cities, like Tokyo and London, and even some newer cities that were concerned about sound pollution, the airport is going to be on the edge or outside of the city. This means you will need to factor in time to and time from the airports you're using. In general, there will usually be some sort of light rail or bus system into the city, but even if there isn't, there should be taxis available. It is very likely that you will need to figure out this transportation choice in advance of your departure, and the *Lonely Planet* guidebooks are an excellent resource for this with their "Getting To/From" subheading which is usually right at the end of the city's section.

One word of caution: in general, the public transportation options to/from the airport tend to be very safe. Taxis, however, are not always so safe. Combine this with the fact that you are holding 100 percent of your travel possessions on you while you go to and from the airport, and this leaves you in a vulnerable position to the rare driver with bad intentions. If you're traveling in MICs and LICs, a lot of accommodations will offer airport shuttles from trusted vendors, and this is a great alternative to using taxis. Plus, taxis are expensive, so many people will want to avoid them if they can, but don't worry if you do end up having to use one. If there are concerns with the taxis at the airport you're going through, there should be a mention in the guidebook. It has happened to me before that the taxi driver has tried to pull off the exact scam listed in the guidebook, so I was easily able to avoid the scam. Please read your guidebook carefully beforehand.

One thing I like to do if I have to use a taxi to get back to the airport is to have my Google Maps ready beforehand so that I can see where we're going. If we're heading somewhere that's not the airport, I'll know immediately. I usually only do this when going to the airport because it's pretty easy to tell that you're going into the city when you're leaving the airport. I'll talk more about this and offline maps when we discuss walking as transportation.

As for actually researching your air travel, I recommend using Matrix ITA (matrix.itasoftware.com) and Google Flights, both built on the same technology, to figure out your options since they are extremely flexible for looking at all possible flight and individual leg options. The "Date Grid" and "Price Graph" functions on Google Flights are powerful and useful tools. A word of warning: Matrix ITA is not very phone-friendly.

Don't be afraid to search a bunch of one-way flights if your itinerary is going in a large loop. Sometimes this can be cheaper, but other times it is cheaper to book all the ultra-long-distance international flights together on a multi-hop ticket and then book the smaller, more local flights individually. Try things out; there are lots of combinations.

The fact that searching like this is even necessary is really tedious and shows a failure on the part of the airline industry to cater to its customers. It is also a byproduct of them trying to maximize profits by exploiting consumer laziness. But if you try out various options, you are likely to save a ton of money. Once you figure out your itinerary, you can head over to BookWithMatrix.com and actually purchase your Matrix ITA flights, or you can usually book directly on Google Flights.

Some companies offer so-called "Round-The-World" (RTW) tickets, and there are also all sorts of buying tricks and credit card point options for saving more money, but I will leave this research up to you since hacking flight costs is a bit beyond the scope of this book.

It is also worth noting that there are more than twenty-four time zones that you can potentially cross. There is one for each hour of the day and then there are actually a few half-hour zones. To further complicate things, some countries observe daylight savings at different start and end dates during the year, and some countries don't have daylight savings at all. Make sure to always check the local time when you land. Because the time zones cover a full day around the world, that means there has to be a line that separates one day from the next. This line is in the middle of the Pacific Ocean and is called the International Date Line. Flying across this line sends you hurtling forward or backward a day on the calendar and this can be incredibly disorienting when you're already jet-lagged and operating on two hours of sleep. If you know you're going to be crossing the Pacific during your trip, double-, triple-, and quadruple-check your timing and dates around both sides of that travel leg to make extra sure of your departure and arrival times and any connections before or after. I've seen a lot of people miss flights and incorrectly book trips because they didn't realize they were losing or gaining a day on this part of their travel. Note: the times and dates listed on your itinerary for plane flights will be the local time in that city for when you are there.

Trains

Trains are a bit different than airplanes but still operate on some of the same basic principles. One of the cool things about trains is that train stations and rail lines take up much less city land than an airport, and so almost universally, central train stations will be right in the center of a city. This makes them attractive options when going from city to city if they're available. Plus, a lot of trains will have toilets and potentially food on board, so it's much nicer than being on a bus.

One thing to be very careful of with all trains is that when booking tickets, you double-check that the train station names *exactly* match the train stations you intend to leave from and arrive into. A good example is Vienna's train stations. Vienna is *Wien* in German. Did you intend to book a train through Wien Hauptbahnhof, Wien Westbahnhof, Wien-Meidling, or Wien-Mitte? Those really are four separate stations in four different parts of the city. Realizing you're at the wrong train station at the last second could really impact your trip, so double- and triple-check your station names and maps during booking and travel.

Most daylight traveling trains have a first and second class, and the only difference between the two is slightly nicer seats and more space in first class. Getting on these trains is pretty easy and unless you're attempting to board a very busy rush-hour train, you should be able to walk up and get your tickets right before you need them. In most places, once you have your ticket, you'll just walk straight onto the platform, but sometimes you'll go through a ticket-checking turnstile first.

Night trains, however, are a very different and much more complicated matter. Night trains are something you should consider for long-distance journeys as they offer a unique experience, save you accommodation costs for a night, and you don't lose any time during the day due to transit.

Depending on where in the world you are, there can be a variety of different classes. The lowest class is usually just seats that are pretty similar to regular rail car chairs during the day. The next class up is usually an open-construction bed cart that a lot of people refer to as the "cattle cart." Beds are stacked three tall and there are no doors anywhere in the carriage. Because there are no doors, and therefore no cabins, the carriage is able to hold more people by adding extra beds against one wall of the carriage. The most expensive beds here will be on the top since you're more removed from all the noise and crowded corridors below. The next class up consists of berth cabins of four to six beds, and this area is typically known as "second class."

Because you have a cabin with a door, these beds are more expensive but are usually much quieter and nicer than the cattle cart. The bed itself is essentially the same, however. The next class up is rooms with two beds, and these may be side by side or on top of each other, bunk style. Sometimes these cabins will include a sink. This is usually first class. And sometimes, rarely, there will be suites that will either have a single or double bed and may have a bathroom in the room.

I personally prefer to be in four-berth cabins, mainly because it's a nice price balance of being not too expensive but also being quiet and having fewer people snoring or possibly stealing your stuff. Whatever you are comfortable with is fine, but note that prices for beds are like the airlines, each jump up in class is significantly more expensive than the previous class, with the seat-only tickets being almost silly cheap.

Tickets for the night train must be booked in advance. This is so important that I'm going to repeat it.

Night train tickets need to be booked in advance, if not well in advance, of your departure date.

There are very limited beds and seats on these trains, and any sort of local holiday or high travel season can make it impossible to find a bed when you show up at the train station right when you want to leave.

Part of the problem as to why these tickets need to be purchased early is that these journeys are pretty long, so looking at flights starts to become an option. Sometimes flights will be much cheaper, but if you factor in time to and from the airport, and the transport costs associated with those, you sometimes end up spending an actual six hours trying to take a one-hour flight, which also burns most of a day. But if you had taken a night train, it may have been cheaper, and you effectively paid for a hotel already overnight, and now you show up in the morning, right in the middle of the city, ready to go.

If they're available, night trains can be an awesome way to save time and money. But nearly everyone knows this, hence why you want to book early.

It should be noted, though, not everyone feels that night trains are so convenient. People who really need their morning showers or who really need a quiet night's rest may feel like they came out of a boxing ring when they arrive in the morning from an overnight train. Be aware if you're one of these people, and weigh the pros and cons of time and money versus comfort and beauty sleep.

One weird thing that causes much confusion for many people is how the on-board ticket check-in and deboarding works on night trains. When you enter the train, the carriage attendant will likely check your ticket to make sure you're in the right carriage, and then you will go in, get your bed ready, and put your stuff away. Once you're on your way, the attendant will come back and collect your ticket, and may or may not also collect your passport if your train is going to be crossing a border during the night. If your passport is collected, don't freak out; this is normal. You will get your passport back before you leave the train. Since the train is an overnight train and prob-ably has numerous stops along the way, people will need to get off the train at different times. The attendant will usually come by and shake you awake about thirty minutes before your stop, but don't count on this. Make sure to set an alarm.

I would caution you that it's during this process of people getting up in the middle of the night and leaving the train where theft occurs. Since everyone else is passed out sleeping, it's easy for someone to grab a piece of luggage and just walk right off the train. Make sure you secure your bag somehow. If you're on the top bunk in a cabin, there's generally an overhead shelf for luggage. If I'm up there, I actually sleep with my head touching my bag. If I'm on the bottom, I unbuckle every strap on my pack so that it's going to make a ton of noise if it's moved. If you are super paranoid, a heavy sleeper, or generally worried, try to cable-lock your bag to something, though in my experience, only the cattle cart has good spots for lashing a cable.

Also, make sure that you are in your proper cart while stopped during the night, as night trains sometimes disconnect and then reconnect carts to other trains going to many different destinations. If you hang out in the food cart all night because you can't sleep, you may find yourself in some unknown destination and separated from your belongings when the sun starts to rise.

As for other things to consider with trains, day trains may have high-speed and low-speed options, with the low speed generally being much cheaper. Night trains always seem to be low-speed trains.

Another major thing to look at during your planning stage is to research if there are any rail passes available. Some countries and areas, like Europe and Japan, have rail passes that you must purchase *outside* of the country. These passes will allow you to travel for free for a certain number of days, and there are usually various options for this. Usually, these passes are only free for during-the-day trains but will give significant discounts for booking night trains as well. As far as I've seen, though, the common requirement for every rail pass is that you can't buy the pass while you are inside the borders of that country. You have to purchase the pass and have it shipped to a foreign country first. Eurail (eurail.com) for Europe is probably the most well-known pass, but you have to be using the trains *a lot* to break even on the pass. Trying to figure out if this pass is cheaper than just buying the tickets while you're there can be very hard to figure out in advance. With Eurail, the night trains are not free but are heavily discounted with the pass. The best pass I've seen is in Japan (japanrailpass.net), where even a single bullet train trip can easily pay for a two-week-long rail pass there, and it's so easy to just walk onto trains going anywhere that it feels almost luxurious, which opens all sorts of travel possibilities. Check where you're going and what path you're taking to see if a rail pass is even an option, because not everywhere has extensive rail lines or offers this type of pass.

Boats

Boats, or ships, are kind of a weird beast. There is some history behind these terms and there is not a clear way to know whether "ship" or "boat" is the proper title for this kind of transportation. Call it whatever the crew calls it, which may differ depending on your location and vessel size. Sometimes boats are your only option, sometimes they're an option but a terrible one, and sometimes they are a fun adventure.

Boat accommodations are kind of like the train accommodations, with shorter trip boats mainly having seats and longer trip boats usually having berth cabins with bathrooms. Some areas have cattle cart beds, but I've personally only come across these while researching the Philippines, and these types of boats seem to be the transport that locals tend to use to get between islands.

If a short-trip boat is available, chances are that's going to be your only route of transportation to get where you're going. In my experience, you usually need to check your larger bags with the crew beforehand and then collect them afterward.

Long-trip boats usually also have a flying option, and many times the flight option will be much cheaper since you aren't effectively renting a hotel room while moving and you aren't on the plane as long. The cattle carts in the Philippines can be super cheap, but they can also take nearly twenty-four hours to get somewhere that would otherwise take an hour or two flight. You'll have to figure out if this is worthwhile to you.

An unusual option that I've heard of a few people doing is grabbing a spare bunk on shipping freighters for very cheap in order to cross oceans. I personally do not know anyone who has ever done this and I have never done the research. However, if you have lots of time and are looking for something new and different, this could be an option.

On ships, it's not uncommon to have a "no doors locked" rule for the entire ship. If this happens, don't be surprised. It's mainly a safety thing, because fire is the worst possible thing that can happen aboard a ship. Having locked doors means more time that a potential fire is burning rather than being put out. Unlocked doors, however, also means your stuff is essentially unlocked as well. This isn't a big deal; you just need to lock up your stuff in your bag. It's not like someone is going to steal your bag during a sea voyage and somehow hide it during the remainder of the trip while you look all around for it. Even if that were to happen, the ship's crew would likely find your bag.

Seasickness is also incredibly common. You have liquid in your inner ear that responds to movement and is a key component of how you are able to balance and feel that cars, boats, or airplanes are moving around underneath you. You also have your eyes, which allow your brain to figure out if things are moving around in your vision. If your eyes and ears don't match up on perceived movement, your body thinks you've been poisoned. That sounds weird to say, but if you think about caveman times, how else would your system start malfunctioning like this? The only way is if you ate some berries or something else that is screwing up your nervous system. So what does your body do? It starts to eliminate anything in your upper digestive tract and puts you to sleep to hopefully allow recovery from the poison you ingested. This is effectively your seasickness response, which makes you violently puke and pass out.

So what do you do about seasickness? Well, the biggest thing is to not get it in the first place. Once you're sick, you're probably going to have to ride it out and that can be really uncomfortable. Trying to keep down medication at that point is going to be hard, and a lot of other remedies are questionable gimmicks that only work for a small percentage of people. If you know you're prone to seasickness, take medication an hour before you even get on the boat, and keep taking it at your prescribed intervals the entire time you're on the boat. If you are going to be on a boat for a long time, scopolamine is a prescription medication that is a wearable three-day patch and works well but can have bad side effects for some people with the most common complaint being extreme dry mouth for the first day or two.

Beyond medications, try to keep your two motion-sensing systems in sync. This means sitting somewhere where you can look at the horizon while you're rocking around. Both your eyes and ears are experiencing the same thing. If you start talking to someone and looking at them, or go below deck where you can't see outside, what you've done is now your eyes are seeing a static non-moving world, while your ears are bucking around on the waves, and so, you get sick.

Buses/Cable Cars/Transport Vans

Buses, cable cars, and less official-looking transport vans are present pretty much everywhere in the world these days. There are lots of varieties of this, so much so that I can't explain everything here, but I'll try for some generalities.

Long-distance buses are usually pretty nice and while "long distance" usually implies going to the next major city, sometimes these cover enormous distances over twenty-four hours or more. Tickets are purchased ahead of time, and these buses usually leave from a terminal. Stops may be taken every few hours, and your larger bags are stored below the bus. Don't put anything valuable in your under-the-bus bags as it's a common scam in Southeast Asia to have some kid hiding below the bus digging through everyone's bags while the bus is in motion.

Mid-distance buses sometimes come in first and second class in which the first class is like the long-distance buses, but the second class is more of a used-by-the-locals option. Usually, these second-class buses are really cheap but are slower, drop off and pick up people frequently, and are packed full of people. You are generally safe on these buses, but you may have people nearly sitting on top of you, and you're almost certain to stick out and be a curiosity to all the locals on the bus.

Short-distance buses and cable cars are usually transport routes within a city, and honestly, even to this day, these are some of my biggest sources of travel stress. Very often, the routes are confusing and hard to interpret in another language. Sometimes the buses will alert you as to what stop you're approaching, but many times they don't. Sometimes you have to tell the driver you want to get off. Sometimes there are stop buttons all over the bus. Sometimes you have to pay with a city-specific pay card, sometimes you have to pay cash, and sometimes they don't give change. Sometimes, rarely, you pay outside of the bus. The point is that buses and cable cars are completely different in different places. The easiest way to deal with this is to ask someone at your accommodation how the local bus system works. In general, I have found that I rarely use these local buses, so it's usually not an issue. Instead, I'm usually in a metro, or if the city is small enough, I just walk everywhere. However, if walking for long periods of time is difficult for you for whatever reason, local buses may be a great option.

Also, be wary, local buses and cable cars can be pickpocket central in certain areas of the world. Move your daypack onto your front and maintain situational awareness if the bus is even remotely crowded.

In some locations, another available bus option is what is known as a "hop-on hop-off" bus. This is a bus with a set route and set stops, but you are actually buying a ticket to go the entire route. At any point, you can get off at a stop and then later on get back on the bus and continue, and this is all on one ticket. These sorts of buses may tour just a single city, may tour a whole country, or may go across multiple countries on a longer route. Your guidebook should let you know if these kinds of services are available where you're headed. These buses are usually pretty nice and are geared toward tourists. They typically have a bus driver or guide who can answer questions for you and may even help you book tours and accommodations. These buses are also a great way to meet other travelers and aren't what I would consider an "organized tour."

Last, transport vans. These are basically vans being driven by a random local trying to make some side cash for taking people around. You likely will need to pay on the spot to get on.

Tourist Transport Vans

Tourist transport vans are sort of like buses, but they're in areas of the world where buses are either nonexistent or very, very slow. These vans are basically tourist buses that are not run by the government or any single distinguishable business. In general, almost all of the tourist transport vans that I have used have been in Central America and were run on a voucher system. You pay for the trip at your accommodation, and then a van comes and picks you up roughly at your departure time. Sometimes they are early or really late arriving to pick you up, so be mindful of this and be ready at least thirty minutes before your scheduled time, just in case. Once picked up, you'll be driven to a meet-up point and your driver will shuffle all of you around to other vans to get you onto the one that's going to your destination. This may happen multiple times during your trip as these vans operate in a big network. Make sure your larger bags come with you anytime you transfer vans. Also, don't stress out if you're just parked on the side of the road for a long time waiting. What's happening is, you're waiting for the other vans to arrive to do another transfer.

Taxis

Taxis. Ugh. I absolutely hate taxis. Not only are they stupidly expensive, but this profession has a tendency to attract less-than-honest people as well. I've had drivers act like they don't speak English and drive me all over the place to get to a destination only to suddenly speak perfectly fluent English when the payment is expected. I've had drivers act like accommodations were shut down when they weren't. I've had drivers agree to an amount for a ride and then change the amount when we arrive. I've had drivers refuse to go across a city saying it's too far. I've also had drivers refuse to go somewhere because it's apparently too close. I've also *frequently* had drivers go on insane racist and sexist rants, which I don't really want to listen to and are highly inappropriate in general. I've had drivers claim they have no change for the bill I handed them when it is literally their job to handle change for their riders. *I hate taxis.*

All in all, taxis come with many scams. Uber and Lyft have been awesome additions to the world, and frankly, with all the issues I've had, I can't wait for the taxi industry to die. If you can avoid taxis, my advice is to do so. Uber is a great alternative where available. Sometimes you're going to be stuck taking a taxi, but just expect these issues, be firm, and try not to get upset. Sometimes you get scammed, sometimes you can do something about it, and sometimes you can't.

If you do need to take a taxi, try to find one through your accommodation or see what the guidebook recommends. Certain companies are known for strict adherence to starting their meters and making sure their drivers are reputable people. If you can find one of these companies, it makes life much easier and most of the issues mentioned will go away.

Sometimes you'll be stuck with a taxi where they will have meters and not use them, or they have no meter at all, and this is where things can get weird. Just about anywhere you go, make sure to agree on a rough price before you enter the taxi. If they're using a meter, they'll give you an estimate, but if they aren't, you can negotiate a price to get somewhere. If you speak the local language and know what the fare should be, you'll get a much better price than someone who doesn't know what the normal fares are there.

Auto Rickshaws/Tuk-Tuks

Auto rickshaws, also called "tuk-tuks," are effectively the same thing as taxis, except they're usually really cheap and have no meter at all. If you haven't seen one, an auto rickshaw is basically a little three-wheeled moped with a bench seat and a little canopy covering. It's like an open-air mini-taxi. All the previous taxi issues apply, but the cheapness of these little carts almost makes up for some of the taxi hassles.

This is a tuk-tuk. It's a little three-wheeled moped with a bench seat in the back and flexible covering over the top.

Rental Cars (Private Hire Cars)

Rental cars (private hire cars) are good for very spread-out areas that don't have some sort of bus tour you can take to get there. This should be very rare. You can either rent your own car or hire a car with a dedicated driver.

If you're traveling to a country that isn't very different from the country where you learned to drive, you may be able to get away with driving yourself. But be aware that trying to park your car may be very difficult or expensive if you're staying anywhere near a city center. If you really want to head to some hard-to-get-to place, try and rent your car, do your trip, and immediately drop your car off again without trying to deal with parking it somewhere urban.

If you're traveling to a country that is very different from where you learned to drive, I highly recommend hiring a car with a dedicated driver. For most people reading this book, those places are going to be countries like China, India, or Italy (really). The driving is so different in those locations, compared to most other places, that it's highly likely you will get in an accident. Having a dedicated driver isn't going to be very expensive, so the cost is worth it for not having to white knuckle the steering wheel every time you get into the vehicle. See the subsection later "Odds and Ends" in the "Safety and Security" section about this driving style issue and why you need to be careful.

In my experience, no tourist area has ever necessitated me renting a car with or without a driver. There's always been some sort of bus, train, or metro available. Worst case, I walk. And I've never felt unsafe enough on public transit that the extra security a private driver would afford me was worth the cost in the end.

That said, there have been a few places that might have been cool to see that required renting a car. For example, the carved-out caves of Allora and Ajanta in India would have been awesome to see, but driving for days to get there and back made the overall rental trip seem like an incredible amount of effort just to see the caves for a few hours. In the end, I skipped the caves. Do what makes sense for you.

If you do plan to rent a car or drive yourself in another country, be careful. Depending on your destination, you may need an international driver's license to rent a car, which I'll talk about more in the

"Get Your Important Documents Together" step of planning your trip. You may also need to buy new or supplemental car insurance.

Also, be aware that when getting your car, the rental car companies love to play games at the counter during the pickup process. They will offer you overpriced and overrated insurance and gas (petrol). It is almost always better to use your own insurance just due to cost. As for the gas, a recent thing I see a lot is the rental companies offering discounted gas on a full tank of fuel. While this initially looks like a great option, what isn't clear is that any remaining gas in the tank is money that goes back to the rental car company. Unless you can time your car return to arrive with literally no gas left in the tank, it's probably more cost-efficient for you to fill up the gas on your own before returning the car.

Metros/Subways

Metros or subways, whatever you prefer to call them, are awesome. Cheap, quick, safe, and usually very clean, most of the time you can't really beat the price-to-value of a metro system. Sometimes these will be above ground and sometimes below ground, but they're all essentially the same. The one thing you really have to pay attention to is the payment system. Prepaid refillable cards are easy to tap and use, but some places use paper tickets or tokens. Paper tickets are sometimes bought in bundles and sometimes bought for individual trips. Tokens are usually one-time use. The cards, tickets, or tokens often have to be fed into or scanned on a turnstile, but sometimes have to be time stamped by machines next to the entrance. Either way, if you have managed to get onto the metro train and haven't swiped, scanned, or time-stamped something, then you forgot to pay for and validate your ticket and this could potentially lead to serious fines if you're caught. Unlike the craziness that goes on with buses, the metro is usually fairly straightforward, and most places have information available in English.

Walking

I think this is fairly straightforward to understand, and believe me, no matter what form of transportation you're using on the larger scale, you're going to be doing a ton of walking while traveling. A lot of walking is going to happen when things are so close together that it just doesn't make sense to hop on a metro to travel one stop or jump in a taxi to go three blocks (three streets over). Because of this, you're going to need to know how to navigate around on foot.

When I first started traveling, smartphones weren't popular yet. And before you laugh at how old I sound, this was in 2009. The iPhone had only come out in 2007, and not only was it perceived as incredibly expensive at the time, but companies were still developing software for these smartphones and they were trying to figure out if this was really the future of phones or not. When I traveled then, I was walking around with a map and a compass. I'm not joking. Things have changed quite a bit, thankfully, and smartphones are not only reliable and capable but can be cheap.

In my opinion, the most important use of a smartphone when navigating a new city, particularly by foot, is Google Maps. That said, you may not have data while traveling which I'll talk about in the "Preparing Your Mobile Devices to Connect to the Internet" section. My pro tip here is that even if you don't have data and aren't on Wi-Fi while walking around, you can still download offline map data while you *are* online (i.e., at a coffee shop, museum, or hostel where Wi-Fi is available). This can be done either by just scrolling around your destination area in advance while on the internet, or by specifically downloading an offline map, which is available in most areas and will capture 100 percent of the map information inside the area you download for use offline.

Because apps change so frequently, I recommend you look up on your own how to download offline map data with Google Maps. To do this, search online for "How to store offline maps in Google Maps." Once the map data is downloaded to your phone, even if you're not connected to any data or Wi-Fi, your map will still work. This is because your phone's GPS will still work because GPS is receive-only and therefore does not require data. It's like a radio. Now you can use the map all day and track yourself using your GPS to make sure you're going to the right places. Combine this with your guidebook map and you're set. You can also use this technique to monitor where you are on buses, trains, and taxis so you don't miss your stops.

A more recent welcome change is that you can plan routes, i.e., getting Google Maps directions—while offline. In the past, you were unable to get directions while offline, but be aware that although offline Google Maps directions generally work within your offline map data areas, sometimes it still can't figure out certain directions without going online. A good example of this is when bus routes are involved and up-to-date information is needed to tell you when to board the next bus. Even if this happens, you can still see where you are, and this should be all you really need most of the time. If you are going to use bus and metro route directions, make sure you get them right as you're about to head out and are leaving Wi-Fi. If you get them and then wait ten minutes before leaving, the information about the next bus or train may be incorrect when you actually leave.

Last for Google Maps, you should also be aware that it's fairly easy for the compass to randomly become uncalibrated when coming out of big buildings and metros. Something about losing and regaining GPS data seems to confuse the compass direction, and while this won't affect where your dot is on the map, it will affect the direction the dot thinks it's facing. Be sure to keep an eye on where the dot is actually moving when you start moving, and don't assume that the directional indicator is correctly aligned with you. If your compass does become askew, select your blue dot and it will bring up a menu with the option to recalibrate the compass. Follow the instructions and you should see your directional indicator realign with your physical direction.

Bike Shares

I should also note that bike shares have really started to pick up around the world, and these may be a great option for you to get around. Just be aware that if you're unable to listen to directions in the direction mode in Google Maps but able to get a ride share bike, you may have to stop frequently to figure out your directions on your phone. Be very careful and get out of traffic first to make these checks. Getting hit in traffic on a bike during your trip is clearly going to ruin your trip, even if you're lucky and don't get hurt. Be careful out there and wear a helmet when possible.

TO TOUR OR NOT TO TOUR

I'm going to revisit this touring topic in the "During Your Trip" section of the book for smaller day-trip-style tours, but this section is about traveling in organized tours for significant portions of your trip.

For some of your smaller tour opportunities, you'll be able to decide if you want to partake in the tour right there in the moment during your trip. But for larger tours, such as those that take you between cities for potentially weeks at a time, you need to book significantly in advance of the tour date.

Should you take these kinds of tours? Well, there are some trade-offs. For some trips, like Antarctica, there's no way to stay down there without booking a bed on a ship for the whole tour, and often this needs to be done at least a year in advance. For other trips, like going through Europe, things are so familiar and easy that there's almost no reason to take a tour unless you really don't want to spend any time looking up train timetables and finding hotels.

The two main questions I would keep in mind with booking tours are, how much do you really want to experience the countries you're going to, and how different are these countries from what you're used to?

If you really want to interact with the culture in any destination you visit, going on a tour is likely going to make it harder to interact with the people in that country. Because you're on a schedule and there's a group of people, you are not going to be engaging with locals and regular merchants on a daily basis. Most likely, you will be bussed straight into and out of anything you do. This is really going to hinder your immersion into another country and its culture. If the country and culture are very different from your own, however, that exact style of trip may be what you need in order to get around comfortably and understand what's going on.

As an example, I took a tour in India and I'm glad I did, because things were so different and transportation was so complicated that I needed a local to explain what was happening around me in order to start seeing the moving parts and how they all fit together. Now that I've done a tour there, I would be confident returning on my own and I'm sure I'd be just fine. But had I not done this first, I probably would have learned some hard lessons and experienced some serious frustrations and scams trying to figure out on my own what was happening and what I needed to do.

I have only done five tours in the whole world so far, two of which were by ship, but I'm glad that I decided to tour where I did. If you want the comfort of less hassle and constant access to someone with a lot of local knowledge, tours are great. If you want to travel cheaply, don't take a tour because there's always a markup and tours tend to bring the group to eat in sit-down restaurants and always stay in hotels. If you want more immersion into a country or culture, going on your own is much more appropriate. If the country is wildly different than what you're used to, a tour guide can help explain all the differences you're seeing. It's all a balancing act.

I should mention that if you do go on a tour, I recommend the company G Adventures. I like them because many of their tours are designed to be fairly flexible while you're actually in a city. I did the G Adventures tour through China and it was great for me because I wanted to see more things than were on the general tour itinerary. When we got to a city, most of the group would go with the tour guide, and I would break off and do my own thing for the day and then meet up again with them for dinner. This flexibility allowed me to see everything I wanted to see but within the larger tour structure. If having the flexibility to wander away from your tour group for a while is desirable, you should check out G Adventures.

TO GO IN GROUPS OR ALONE

Interestingly, many of the considerations for traveling in a tour group apply to traveling with a group of friends outside of a tour. Traveling in a group can be fun and you'll always have company. But if you do travel by yourself, know that you're going to meet lots of other travelers, especially if you book any sort of activities or stay in hostels, where you won't really be alone much anyway. If you want to travel in a group, keep in mind that doing so is likely going to make it harder to interact with the country around you while you're in your group bubble, and it may be more difficult to accommodate everyone's trip desires. One positive of traveling in a group is that sharing the trip costs can make booking transportation and accommodations cheaper per person. On the other hand, groups generally move much slower than individuals because the group can only move as fast as the slowest person. This becomes especially true when getting ready in the morning, eating, and using bathrooms during the day.

Some people really like traveling with only one other person so that they can share the experience of the trip together with someone they know. This can be a friend or a romantic partner, but it's usually more about having a shared experience with someone they already trust.

My recommendation is that if you travel with a single companion or a group that you have an understanding that it's okay to split off and do your own thing from time to time. Compromising is key, but everyone's experience will be better if no one is required to sacrifice their *travel goals* to accommodate someone else's needs.

Overall, I highly recommend solo travel. Even if you're a female traveler, I truly recommend this experience. Trust me, it's not as scary as you might think. Traveling solo just makes everything easier. You can go wherever you want whenever you want. You can take time to meet others on the road. You can eat anything that seems appealing. Most importantly, you can immerse yourself more in the country you're visiting. If you're really concerned about safety for some part of your trip, attach yourself to a group that is doing the same thing as you and you won't have any issues. I've met tons of solo females on the road and I've rarely heard of even minor issues.

Also, one more thing of note is that if you're interested in meeting other travelers or locals, most people are especially reluctant to approach a couple because doing so seems like they're interrupting something. So traveling as a partner duo can surprisingly be some of the most isolating travel. That said, traveling as a couple is totally normal and has its own benefits. I've traveled that way, too, and enjoyed it just as much as traveling solo.

If you're traveling with a good friend and it's just the two of you, make sure you agree on budgeting beforehand. It's not going to be a very fun trip if one person constantly feels like they're avoiding plans and sights because the other person can't afford it. Also, if you connect with someone romantically while on the road, you shouldn't leave your buddy (mate) behind. Make sure before you book anything that both of you have the same general travel plans. Meaning, you mostly want to do the same things and that you both want to go to the same places for the same reasons.

Some people may also like to travel with an expert for their destination. Regardless of how you find this person, whether they are your tour guide or a friend, traveling with an expert completely changes the dynamic of your trip. My warning here, though, is because the expert is looking through the eyes of someone who knows the ins and outs of everything you're doing, it becomes very easy for you to miss out entirely on why certain decisions were made, why certain sights were visited, or how you managed to get to someplace. Have you ever gotten into a car as a passenger to go somewhere you've never been, but then you get there and you have no idea which route you just took? It's the same thing. Because you're not actively engaged in making the trip happen moment by moment, you lose the context of what's going on. This can leave you with the feeling that you never really got to see the culture somewhere because you didn't have to figure it out yourself. This may totally work for you, but I recommend you be careful with this and spot it when it's happening so that you can make a choice to venture out on your own or be more engaged if you need to.

Is there a single answer in this section for who you should travel with? Not at all. Do what feels comfortable and natural. Just make sure that if you do travel with others that you're on the same page about what you want out of your trip. And don't be afraid to travel solo.

If you do travel in a group, the app Splitwise is an excellent tool for splitting costs and tracking who owes who money. I highly recommend this app and it also allows for inputting money owed in currencies beyond just USD, so it's great for international trips.

HOW TO DETERMINE HOW MUCH TIME TO SPEND SOMEWHERE

Most people don't just travel all willy-nilly and show up in places with no idea why they're there. Usually, most people have an itinerary of nature, museums, and/or activities in mind that has led them to their destination to begin with. That said, how do you figure out how long you should stay in a location before you've actually been there? This can be tricky in the beginning but gets really easy with practice and experience.

Even travelers with all the time in the world (Gap Years, Avoiders, and some others) still have a plan they're roughly attempting to follow. The difference between these travelers versus the strict-schedule travelers is that these travelers will take diversions or stay longer in some places as they discover things while they're traveling. For example, they may plan on going straight from Sydney to Brisbane in their rough plan for Australia but find out through word of mouth that there's actually a really good surf school in-between the two cities (there really is, by the way, called Spot-X outside of Coffs Harbour). They may stay a couple of weeks at this school learning to surf even though it wasn't in their plan. Then, after they feel they've gotten their fill at the surf school, they'll continue on to Brisbane.

Typically, only the Drifter types will truly go wherever the wind takes them; almost everyone else has some rough plan they've made. I bring this up because everyone in their rough or specific planning will want to gauge the minimum time they want to spend in one location. This helps roughly plan the itinerary for the greater trip as well, which then affects the trip's budgeting and timing. We'll discuss both of those shortly.

In order to gauge your minimum stay in a location, you need to open up your guidebook and look at the location in question and figure out what you want to do there. Then keep these principles in mind:

- Anything that requires a vehicle-based tour is going to require a whole day.

- Any hike or national park tour is probably going to need a whole day.

- Any class or food tour kind of thing is going to use a half or a whole day.

- Scuba diving trips, unless shore dives, are going to require a whole day. They start early, but you're going to be tired afterward.

- Any activity you partake in that is not a vehicle tour (skydiving, zip-lining, kayaking, etc.) will need at least half a day.

- Any sit-down restaurant kind of meal is going to use two hours out of your day, but because most activities shut down at 5:00 p.m. (17:00), you can go to restaurants for dinner without losing time for other activities.

- On average, and this is purely based on my conversations with others and is not a precise or researched number, most people can get through two to three museums per day if they're close together and there are minimal breaks. If you read every little thing and like staring at artwork, this may be closer to one to two museums per day. If you're not impressed with much or don't read everything or sit down to dwell on things, you can probably get through roughly four museums in a day depending on museum size and distance between them. For the people who fly through museums, many museums in MIC and LIC destinations are small and centrally located, which can make five to six museums possible. But in some places like London where the museums are huge and spread apart, you will likely be closer to two to three museums, even if you're really moving. Places like the Louvre and the Vatican are basically a series of museums connected together and they are going to eat your whole day regardless of pace. Possibly multiple days for some people who are really interested. Be aware that you may need to book tickets to famous museums in advance if you want to avoid waiting in long lines (queues).

- City squares, cathedrals, churches, mosques, temples, etc., you can pack a lot of these into a day. The main limitation here is distance and how fast you can walk. Fifteen to twenty minutes is probably how long you will spend in most of these types of locations mainly because they're small. That said, something like the Philosopher's Walk in Kyoto, which is around twenty to thirty gardens, temples, shrines, and other amazing sights, is hard to get through in less than two full days, even if you're really moving. There are just too many things to see, foods to try, entrance queues, and it's a significant walk.

Here's a rough example for the Philosopher's Walk. Your day won't nearly be this neat if you do the walk, but it's a rough calculation: thirty stops at twenty minutes each = 600 minutes or ten hours. If you add in time walking between stops and stopping for lunch, you easily have sixteen hours for two full days. It would probably be *much* more comfortable over three days so that you're not rushing.

As you start traveling, you'll figure out really quickly what your pace is for things like museums and places of worship. This pace will help you plan, without even having stepped foot in a city, what the minimum amount of time is that you will need to visit the sights and activities on your list.

Keep in mind, though, this is the minimum time required. This is because lingering somewhere can be just as, if not more so, educational and fun than visiting the tourist sights that are listed in most guidebooks. If you really love the French language and think Paris is really romantic, then spending three days there just seeing art museums isn't going to be enough time for you. Spend more time there. Walk around, hang out, eat, and explore.

Once you get past the sights and start interacting with locals more, you really start to learn about cultural attitudes, how people live and think, and see the way the world is connected. Unfortunately, you can't really plan this kind of exposure; it just happens on its own. Either slowing down and allowing some extra time to freely explore, or intentionally spending some time going to non-touristy locations, is going to be the only way you get this experience. Balance this into your schedule and keep in mind that just seeing the tourist sights won't fully expose you to the culture and people.

If you can, work in a bit of "nothing planned" time into your schedule and then just go out and wander and explore the locale you're in. I promise you, your trip will be enriched. Things will start happening that you'll quickly realize there's no way you could have planned.

HOW MUCH TIME IT TAKES TO TRAVEL BETWEEN LOCATIONS

Before you start planning things out on a calendar, consider transportation timing. If there's one major mistake I see newer travelers make, it's severely underestimating the time it takes to get from point A to point B.

The following story is something I come across all the time, and until you've completed your first trip, this is a really easy mistake to make. A friend of mine was asking for help planning a trip to Europe a few years ago, and she had nearly twenty cities that she and her boyfriend wanted to visit in the one month they had available to take their trip. These cities spanned over England, France, Germany, Switzerland, and Italy. If you ignore the details of what they wanted to do in these cities and just purely look at the timing involved, thirty days divided by twenty cities is a day and a half per city. Even if Star Trek teleporters really existed, this would have been an incredibly rushed trip.

Worse, if you include the time just in the airplane flights to Europe and to North America, they had even less time. Eventually, after a few revisions, they trimmed their trip down to about ten cities. Even with trimming their trip, when they got back, they said their trip still felt incredibly rushed. They spent around two days in almost every location, and after weeks of doing this, you can imagine it starts to feel exhausting. Every other day, they were switching hotels, having to relearn a new city, find the next train station, etc.

Be careful with your planning if you have limited time.

Most of the planning problems that arise in this regard are because many new travelers assume high-speed rail is readily available and that airports are centrally located in all cities like they are in a lot of US cities. In almost every part of the world, however, neither is true. This means huge hour-long trips to get to airports, and trains that are moving at around 60 mph (100 kph) over long distances. High-speed rail, at 180 mph (300 kph), sometimes operates internally within countries, but it's rare to see a high-speed line between countries. Beyond that limitation, in many places rail won't even be an option, so you'll be sitting on a bus and might be in traffic for hours.

Think about a flight this way: you're close to the center of some city because that's where all the tourist stuff is, and you need to catch a flight to your next city. To do this, you need to get to the central train station to get the rail line to the airport. It takes anywhere from fifteen minutes to half an hour to get to the central station. Then you need to take a twenty- to sixty-minute trip to the airport by train. Add to this that you need to be at the airport probably two to three hours early. When the time arrives, you take your flight. At your destination, you probably need to collect a checked bag. Finally, you need to unwind the getting-to-the-airport process and get to your next lodging, so thirty to ninety minutes again for that. If you add this all up, even a sixty-minute flight has now taken you potentially seven hours to complete on the long end. This isn't even factoring in eating, showers, etc. Anytime you take a flight, regardless of how early or late it is, just assume that you are burning that entire day just on air travel.

Trains are not much better over long distances. You cut out a lot of the airport issues, but you're still losing most of your day. Most things you want to do start early or close at five in the afternoon, so even though you may still be able to stroll through a city late at night, any long train trip is probably going to also consume a "functional" day of your overall trip.

You can potentially avoid losing most of your day with shorter train trips if you leave really early and get to your destination just as things are opening. Similarly, if you can start a shorter trip around dinner time, you can have that day to do stuff and then get on your train.

Also, overnight trains are an option sometimes. If you are taking an overnight train, these tend to leave very late at night and arrive very early in the morning, so you get the benefit of a free bed during your train trip and don't lose a day traveling in the process. But you get no shower and have a crappy bathroom, so it's a trade-off.

Factor all of this into your trip planning and be realistic. Look at your guidebook and look at the cities you want to visit. In the back of those cities sections in the *Lonely Planet* guides, you will find a "Getting To/From" section, which will show you how to get to the airport and sometimes includes rough guesses of transit time to other common destinations from that city.

If you have to cut deep into your plans because transit time eats up a lot of days, split your trip into multiple trips or cut your destination list down to the things you care about the most.

Take some time and figure out how to get between the cities in your tentative travel plan and adjust your overall destination list as makes sense. Which leads into the next topic.

SAMPLE ITINERARIES

Here are a couple of examples from my own travels that will show you how to put all your trip planning research together into an easy-to-follow itinerary. I know a lot of things to consider have been presented so far and you'll see how this all fits together in the following two examples. Both of these examples are the real-life planning steps I went through for two of my fixed-duration trips in which I had limited vacation (holiday) time and was trying to work around a normal nine-to-five workweek to maximize my time off. If you're putting together a much longer trip, this level of somewhat rigorous planning may be unnecessary, but these techniques will still be necessary on a shorter scale as you travel around. In that case, planning the early portion of your trip itinerary is a good place to get started for your overall trip.

EXAMPLE: SOUTH AMERICA

This trip was slightly unusual because I was finishing one trip in Washington, DC, and then roughly three weeks later, I had a prescheduled event to attend in Hawaii. At the time, I lived in San Diego. Because I had the ability to keep traveling between these two dates and I hadn't been to the central part of South America yet, the twenty-three days available seemed like the perfect time to visit South America. My general plan was to go from Lima, Peru to Rio de Janeiro, Brazil and see the key sights between these locations.

When I first started to plan my travels to this area, I had looked at doing the G Adventures tour, called the "Southern Cross," to see these spots. But after traveling through Central America already, getting around in South America seemed like no big deal, and there were a number of things on the Southern Cross tour that I wasn't specifically interested in seeing. So I decided there was no reason to pay someone else to take me around and that the trip should be easy to do on my own.

After researching the *Lonely Planet South America* travel guide, I figured out the list of cities that I wanted to visit and decided it seemed to make the most sense to see them in this route order:

- Lima

- Cusco

- Puno

- Copacabana

- La Paz

- Uyuni

- Potosí

- La Paz

- São Paulo

- Foz do Iguaçu

- Rio de Janeiro

The reason that La Paz shows up twice on my list is because my *Lonely Planet* guide had listed that getting between Bolivia and Foz do Iguaçu would take an immense amount of time by road, so because La Paz is the main airport in Bolivia, that seemed like the logical place to return to in order to fly to Brazil.

Additionally, my flight searches revealed that getting to the waterfall Foz do Iguaçu requires going through a major city in Brazil. It's possible to get to the falls from the Argentinian side, but that requires going to Argentina, which was significantly out of the way for my itinerary. Taking this into consideration, I had to go through São Paulo to get to Foz do Iguaçu.

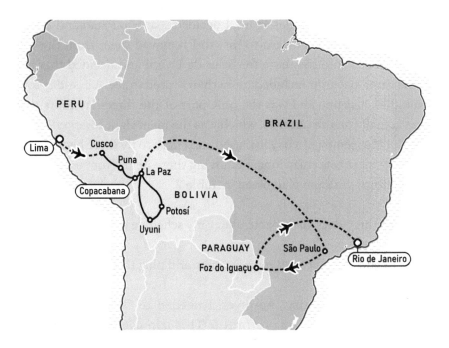

Map 1: My initial planning route through South America. Notice this route flows across the continent, within the limits of transportation, without zigzagging or doubling back.

Taking these transportation limitations into account, if you look at Map 1, you'll notice these cities are in logical order geographically and could be visited either in this order or the reverse order.

After doing more transportation research between the guidebooks and flight searches, I then began to add in my guesses on the transportation times and days I would need per city. I ended up with the list in Table 1.

This plan, unfortunately, required more days than I had available. I only had twenty-three days total to do my trip. So I had to make some changes.

At this point, I started asking myself what really mattered to me. After looking at the cities again, I decided that São Paulo and Potosí just weren't that important to me, so I removed them from the list. I also looked into the tours for Salar de Uyuni and decided that the basic three-day tour included more than I cared to see. A one-day tour would be just fine and was the only part of the three-day tours that was actually on the salt flats, which was the main sight I wanted to see there. I also removed a day in Cusco and chose to fly there because the bus trip there was crazy long. Removing these items from my original plan left me with the plan listed in Table 2.

Twenty-three days was doable under my schedule constraints.

Now I needed to get even more specific and plug this into a calendar.

Before I could do that, however, I needed to figure out if I was starting my trip in Lima or in Rio. This trip could easily be done in either direction, but I wondered if maybe there were different costs associated with flying into and out of different airports, so this is what I needed to check. To determine which direction I was going, I started to research flight options and costs while keeping in mind that my final destination of Hawaii also complicated the

FROM	TO/AT	DAYS	TRANSPORTATION
Washington, DC	Lima	1	Flight 9 hrs direct
	Lima	1	
Lima	Cusco	1	Flight 1.5 hrs or Bus 20+ hrs
	Cusco	3	
Cusco	Puno	1	Bus 6-7 hrs
	Puno	1	
Puno	Copacabana	1	Bus 3-4 hrs
	Copacabana	1	
Copacabana	La Paz	1	Bus 3-4 hrs
	La Paz	1	
La Paz	Uyuni	1	Bus/Train 11-12 hrs
	Salar de Uyuni Tour	3	
Uyuni	Potosí	1	Bus 3-4 hrs
	Potosí	1	
Potosí	La Paz	1	Bus 8-9 hrs
La Paz	São Paulo	1	Flight 5 hrs
	São Paulo	1	
São Paulo	Foz do Iguaçu	1	Flight 1.5 hrs
	Foz do Iguaçu	1	
Foz do Iguaçu	Rio de Janeiro	1	Flight 7 hrs
	Rio de Janeiro	4	
Rio de Janeiro	Honolulu	1	Stop in LA, 2 flights, ~ 24 hrs

Total Days: 29

Table 1: My initial guesstimation on the required days needed for transportation and touring for this trip. However, I did not have this much time available.

FROM	TO/AT	DAYS	TRANSPORTATION
Washington, DC	Lima	1	Flight 9 hrs direct
	Lima	1	
Lima	Cusco	1	Flight 1.5 hrs
	Cusco	3	
Cusco	Puno	1	Bus 6-7 hrs
	Puno	1	
Puno	Copacabana	1	Bus 3-4 hrs
	Copacabana	1	
Copacabana	La Paz	1	Bus 3-4 hrs
	La Paz	1	
La Paz	Uyuni	1	Bus/Train 11-12 hrs
	Salar de Uyuni Tour	1	
Uyuni	La Paz	1	Bus 10-12 hrs
La Paz	Foz do Iguaçu	1	Flight 10 hrs
	Foz do Iguaçu	1	
Foz do Iguaçu	Rio de Janeiro	1	Flight 7 hrs
	Rio de Janeiro	4	
Rio de Janeiro	Honolulu	1	Stop in LA, 2 flights, ~ 24 hrs

Total Days: 23

Table 2: My modified itinerary that included only the most important things I wanted to see.

itinerary. Flying from South America to Honolulu is not a standard path and almost certainly was going to require at least a single stop in the US.

As it turned out, the flights from Washington, DC to Lima were slightly more direct than they were to Rio. And the flights from Rio de Janeiro to Los Angeles were slightly more direct, too. The costs were nearly identical as opposed to going in the other direction. After searching a bunch of flight options as individual legs and combo tickets using Matrix ITA, the cheapest flight itinerary looked like this:

- A multi-leg ticket from Washington, DC to Lima and then from Rio de Janeiro to Los Angeles

- A multi-leg ticket from Los Angeles to Honolulu and then from Honolulu to home in San Diego to wrap up the trip

- A one-way ticket from La Paz to Foz de Iguaçu with layovers in São Paulo because there's no direct international flight to the falls

- And a one-way ticket from Foz de Iguaçu to Rio de Janeiro, again with a layover in São Paulo because no direct options were available

Booking the tickets in just about any other combination resulted in dramatically higher prices. Experimenting with flight leg combinations can save you a lot of money. One thing to note is that I couldn't manage to fit the flight into Hawaii onto the last day. I was originally attempting to arrive at night in Honolulu, but I couldn't make it work with the flights available, so instead I was going to leave early on the twenty-fourth day and arrive in Hawaii just before noon.

The next step now was to plug this into a calendar. I really like using WinCalendar.com for this phase of planning because the calendars it generates are capable of being opened in Word and you can type notes into the individual days.

I had the option of leaving on September 27 or 28, but my October 20 date was a hard deadline. If I wanted to leave on the 28th, I would have needed to cut out another day from my trip, which I didn't want to do. Plugging everything in resulted in Calendar 1.

The highlighted days indicated a tour needed to be booked for those days.

Once I saw this all fit together with my timeline, I started to book flights. Then I started researching bus options between the more localized spots. As it turns out, there were dedicated tourist bus companies that would get me where I needed to go. After I had this plan together and my transportation booked, I then booked all my accommodations based on my calendar. We'll talk about booking things in the "Preparing for Your Trip" part of the book.

At this point, my trip was pretty much set and ready to go.

Now that we've gone through one example, let's check out another one for Europe.

EXAMPLE: EUROPE

My girlfriend was joining me for this fairly straightforward Europe trip, and it also had limits as to how much time we could spend there. I had previously seen other parts of Europe, so this trip was partially dedicated to the west end of Europe which I had not visited before. This included Switzerland, France, Spain, and Portugal, as well as hitting two prior destinations for me including Germany and Austria for family and fun. All of this trip was new to my girlfriend.

SUN	MON	TUE	WED	THU	FRI	SAT
23	24	25	26	27 Fly from DC to Lima 9 hours	28 Tour Lima	29 Fly Lima to Cusco 1.5 hours
30 Tour Cusco	1 Machu Picchu 1 day tour	2 Sacred Valley tour?	3 Bus Cusco to Puno 6–7 hours	4 Tour Puno and Floating Islands	5 Bus Puno to Copacabana 3–4 hours	6 Tour Copacabana and Isla del Sol
7 Bus Copacabana to La Paz 3–4 hours	8 Tour La Paz	9 Bus/Train La Paz to Uyuni 11–12 hours	10 Salt flat tour, Salar de Uyuni 1 day	11 Bus Uyuni to La Paz 10–12 hours	12 Fly La Paz to Foz do Iguaçu 10 hours	13 Tour Foz do Iguaçu
14 Fly Foz do Iguaçu to Rio de Janeiro 7 hours	15 Tour Rio de Janeiro	16 Tour Rio de Janeiro	17 Tour Rio de Janeiro	18 Tour Rio de Janeiro	19 Fly Rio de Janeiro to LA 15 hours	20 Fly LA to Honolulu 6 hours

Calendar 1. My finalized itinerary for visiting South America. The highlighted days had tours that needed to be booked.

One of the big considerations for this trip was visiting Oktoberfest in Munich. Because that lasts for just more than two weeks toward the end of September, that pretty much set the direction of travel for this trip.

In my initial pre-travel research, done years before planning this trip, I had wanted to visit a lot of cities in both Spain and France, but when this trip opportunity finally came up and I looked at the *Lonely Planet* guides again, I realized that many of the cities I had previously researched didn't actually contain much I was interested in seeing. So after discussing with my girlfriend, those cities were removed, but even with their removal, this trip looked fairly tight. I knew I was going to need at least three days in Paris and that Munich and Vienna, with loads to do including Oktoberfest, were going to be at least two days each.

For a roughly three-week trip, if those three cities were the only places we visited and if the estimated travel days were added, that was already twelve days including the time zone shifts. Two days to fly, two days in Munich, one day for a train to Vienna, two days in Vienna, one day for a train to Paris, three days in Paris, and then one day to fly back. This was already about half of the roughly three and a half weeks I had available, so the rest of everything needed to be concise. I wasn't going to be visiting another twenty cities in the remaining week.

I decided to only visit Barcelona and Madrid in Spain and then leave Europe from Lisbon. I also kept my Switzerland plan tight and added only Zurich and Geneva to the list. I passed these ideas by my girl-friend and she was also cool with this rough plan.

Just roughly throwing my city list onto a calendar and guessing at how much time I needed in each spot resulted in the preliminary itinerary shown on Calendar 2.

SUN	MON	TUE	WED	THU	FRI	SAT
24	25	26	27 Fly out of LA	28 Fly into Frankfurt and then same-day train to Munich	29 Munich	30 Day trip from Munich to Berchtesgaden
1 Vienna	2 Vienna	3 Salzburg	4 Zurich	5 Geneva	6 Monaco	7 Paris
8 Paris	9 Paris	10 Nice	11 Barcelona	12 Barcelona	13 Ibiza	14 Ibiza
15 Madrid	16 Madrid Night train to Lisbon	17 Lisbon	18 Lisbon	19	20 Fly home	21

Calendar 2: Our initial itinerary for this trip to Europe. The non-highlighted days were my original guesses on time needed in the main cities we wanted to visit, but that left some days available still, so the highlighted days were things between the main cities that we were interested in seeing and were already along our route. The 19th was an extra day at this stage of planning.

At this point, this was already a fully loaded schedule. The reason I didn't initially list the dedicated travel days on the calendar that I mentioned before is that all of these locations are fairly close together. It seemed likely that the trains between cities could be taken either early or late so that the day was left to explore. If that worked out, the transportation time for this trip wouldn't require extra days. The 19th is blank because there was an extra day available in the trip. So I thought that maybe I would add back one of the cities I had removed.

Next, I started researching trains between these locations. Since Europe has the very useful Eurail pass and because these locations were fairly close together, there was no need to take flights internally within Europe. The Eurail pass would cover everything train related.

However, my initial assumption that we'd be able to travel without losing a day between cities turned out to not be the case. The reality was that getting between Vienna, Salzburg, and Zurich was a little challenging. The available trains only left at inconvenient times and getting from Salzburg to Zurich took a long time. But I noticed that there was an overnight train from Vienna to Zurich, so that was a better option overall. Taking advantage of that night train changed the order that the cities would be visited in, even though on Map 2 it looks less convenient. Also on Map 2, I realized in Calendar 2 that I made two geographical mistakes, one in assuming that Nice was much farther west than it really is. Monaco and Nice are right next to each other, so it made more sense to visit them together. The other mistake was in doing a day trip from Munich to Berchtesgaden because that trip effectively transfers in Salzburg, so that should be done while staying in Salzburg.

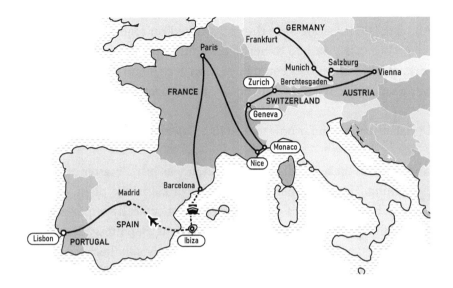

Map 2: My initial transportation-driven route through Europe. Again, attempting to avoid zigzagging and doubling back.

Then it turned out that going to Ibiza takes a long time by boat. Going by plane was an option, but it was going to be a hassle and was fairly expensive. The only reason I really wanted to go there was to see the legendary partying scene, and after some thinking, that just didn't seem like a worthwhile reason to go through so much effort for only a day and a half there. So Ibiza got removed from the original plan.

It also turned out that some of the train travel times between cities *were* only a few hours long because high-speed rail was available, meaning that they could be done very early or very late in the day and not disrupt the nine-to-five core hours to see and do things.

Further, an extra day was gained from removing Ibiza but was eaten by getting from Zurich to Geneva. The reality was that the train trip was much longer than I would have guessed. Instead of losing most of a day to train traveling, a stop in Gruyères was added to at least do something besides sitting on a train all day.

All of these decisions were things I worked on together with my girl-friend because I wanted to her to have the trip she wanted as well. All sorts of different places could have been added and removed, so there was a lot of discussion in putting all of this together.

Updating the calendar now looked like Calendar 3.

Now with all these details mapped out, it was just a matter of booking everything. However, that too threw a wrinkle in the plans. It turned out that booking hostels during Oktoberfest typically requires a mini-mum of a three-night booking. That meant Berchtesgaden needed to be a day trip from Munich, but that's totally silly because going to Berchtesgaden basically takes you to Salzburg anyway. This added some "unnecessary" train time to our trip, but wasn't overly interrupting to our plans. Because of this change, we also decided to stay in Salzburg on the next night so that our day in Salzburg wasn't a rush. That left us with the plan shown on Calendar 4.

As mentioned previously, our Normandy plans were interrupted because of a number of tour operator cancellations. Instead, a day trip to the Palace of Versailles was put in its place on the calendar only the day before we were scheduled to go there. You'll find out during your own travels that you can plan as much as possible, but your plans may change *while* you're traveling.

One last thing learned from this trip. After leaving Paris for Barcelona, I noticed a lot of the train stations we were stopping at on the way looked really familiar, and sure enough, looking on Google Maps, it turned out we had gone straight down and slightly east to the coast, almost all the back to Nice before we cut over toward Barcelona. I had assumed that the route from Paris to Barcelona would have been more to the west. Because of this, it would have been more efficient for us to go from Geneva to Paris and then Paris to Nice, but it was obviously way too late at that point. I totally messed that up, but did it hurt our trip? Not at all. Everything still went as planned; we just had a few extra hours on the train. Live and learn.

SUN	MON	TUE	WED	THU	FRI	SAT
24	25	26	27 Fly out of LA	28 Fly into Frankfurt and then same-day train to Munich 3 hours	29 Tour Munich and Oktoberfest	30 To Berchtesgaden Stay in Salzburg 3 hours
1 Tour Salzburg Evening train to Vienna 3 hours	2 Tour Vienna	3 Tour Vienna Night train to Zurich	4 Tour Zurich	5 Train to Geneva with a stop in Gruyères All day	6 Tour Geneva	7 Train to Nice 6–7 hours
8 Keep room in Nice Day trip to visit Monaco	9 Tour Nice Evening train to Paris 4 hours	10 Day trip to Normandy 2 hours there 2.5 hours back	11 Tour Paris	12 Tour Paris	13 Tour Paris Evening train to Barcelona 5–6 hours	14 Tour Barcelona
15 Tour Barcelona Evening train to Madrid 3 hours	16 Tour Madrid	17 Tour Madrid Night train to Lisbon	18 Tour Lisbon	19 Tour Lisbon	20 Fly home	21

Calendar 3: The finalized itinerary for visiting Europe for this trip. This is a bit of a departure from where this trip plan originally started.

SUN	MON	TUE	WED	THU	FRI	SAT
24	25	26	27 Fly out of LA	28 Fly into Frankfurt and then same-day train to Munich 3 hours	29 Tour Munich	30 Day trip to Berchtesgaden Stay in Munich
1 Early morning train to Salzburg 3 hours Tour Salzburg	2 Early morning train to Vienna 3 hours Tour Vienna	3 Tour Vienna Night train to Zurich	4 Tour Zurich	5 Train to Geneva with a stop in Gruyères All day	6 Tour Geneva	7 Train to Nice 6–7 hours
8 Keep room in Nice Day trip to visit Monaco	9 Tour Nice Evening train to Paris 4 hours	10 Day trip to Normandy 2 hours there 2.5 hours back	11 Tour Paris	12 Tour Paris	13 Tour Paris Evening train to Barcelona 5–6 hours	14 Tour Barcelona
15 Tour Barcelona Evening train to Madrid 3 hours	16 Tour Madrid	17 Tour Madrid Night train to Lisbon	18 Tour Lisbon	19 Tour Lisbon	20 Fly home	21

Calendar 4: The actual finalized itinerary once everything was booked.

WHEN TO MAKE EXCEPTIONS DURING PLANNING

There is a really good chance that if you have limited travel time for your trip that you're going to have to cut some things out of your trip just like I did in my examples. This can be really hard. Some things may seem obvious to remove, and other things may pain you terribly if you have to miss out on them.

Trying to nail down your day-by-day plan for a trip can be difficult. What I'm about to say is meant to be a guide and not the rule of law. Like many things in this book, your own desires and expectations for your trip are going to greatly influence what is worth your time and what is not.

In my experience, I personally found the Terracotta soldiers in China to be a huge letdown. The pictures you can see online are pretty much exactly, if not better than, what you can see in person due to the fact that you can't get anywhere near the soldiers in person. That said, if this is something you have dreamed about seeing, or something you researched a lot, then it's still worth going to see.

With my previous travel experiences in mind and because I'm limited on money and therefore time, these days I usually play the "Is this sight going to look the same in person as it does in pictures online?" game a lot. I try to choose to travel to see things that I really feel will evoke something in me by being there. For example, I visited Victoria Falls in Zambia, even though it was significantly out of the way for my trip to Southern Africa. The sounds, the feelings, having to swim across a waterfall and not get sucked over the edge (seriously), the experience was something you cannot get by looking at a photo. Because of that, the falls were an absolute must for my travel adventures and I'm glad I went out of my way to go there.

All of your planning is a balancing act, especially if you have to decide on all the details of your trip before you leave. Checking photos and videos online can also help you figure out if you really want to do something and how much of a priority it is to you.

The best advice I have for someone who finds they don't have enough time for everything in their trip is to ask yourself, "Can I go back later, and if not, is not doing that one thing on my trip going to bother me for years to come?" If the answer is yes, then I recommend that you figure out something else to cut that you won't mind skipping. The important thing is to focus your travels on the things you really care about first, and then do everything else.

TRIP TIMING AND BUDGET TWEAKS

Budgeting and trip timing are somewhat related, which is why I'm going to talk about both of these together. If you travel during the tourist off-season for a particular destination, you can potentially save a lot of money on airfare, rooms, and even tours depending on what you're doing. Thus, knowing when and how the off-season works can be pretty important.

One thing that caught me off guard when I first started traveling was how global weather works. Having spent my time growing up in Texas and Germany, I was accustomed to four seasons with winter in January. This may also be what most of you are familiar with, too, but it turns out there's more to weather than this.

The somewhat obvious part was that the seasons are flipped in the southern hemisphere. Winter is in July and summer is in January.

What I didn't understand was how the equatorial areas work. It turns out the equator doesn't have seasons like most people know them. The equator has two seasons made up of a six-month period of hot, dry weather and a six-month period of hot, rainy weather. And I mean that literally it rains almost continuously for six months straight. These seasons are usually referred to as the "wet" and "dry" seasons. In some parts of the world, you will hear the wet season called "monsoon season" or "hurricane season" depending on location.

What further surprised me with this, though, was that wet and dry seasons are different all over the equator. Weather and wind patterns around any given region are different, and so the wet and dry seasons are at different times of year for each area.

What was also more surprising to me was that these two kinds of seasonal systems blend into each other slowly. I lived in San Diego for quite some time, and people all over the US know about San Diego for its amazing weather because it's so mild. You barely need a light jacket to stay warm all year round. That said, the winters are also rainy but not continuously, and the climate tends to be quite dry.

If you think about this, San Diego has weather that is effectively in-between the four-season and two-season systems. Instead of having winter, it just kind of cools off. But instead of having crazy multi-month-long storms, there are some scattered rain showers in winter. Essentially, it has both seasonal systems, but it's comparatively milder to both. If you look at a map, you'll notice San Diego is pretty far south in the US but isn't quite equatorial. San Diego literally has a blend of both seasonal systems due to its latitude. Cape Town in South Africa happens to be located at a similar latitude and proximity to the ocean as San Diego, and no surprise, it has similar weather for this same reason.

So as you're putting your trip together, think about what time of year you want to go somewhere. Do you care about traveling in pouring rain or heavy snow for your entire trip? If either is an issue, you need to find out the weather patterns for that specific area and plan accordingly. Using climatemps.com and searching by city is a great place to start. If they don't have what you need, search Google images for "[city name] weather averages by month," and then look at the images to get the information you need. This works for any area but will be critical for the equator due to the irregular seasonal patterns across regions there. Winter is a bit more obvious in zones with four seasons, but the length of winter may not be so obvious.

As mentioned, traveling during the off-season in any region will save you a lot of money. The tourist season for locations with four seasons is typically the summer. Kids are out of school, the days are long, and it's warm, so everyone goes to these spots. Winter, except for the major holidays, is the off-season simply because it's uncomfortable and dark, with really short days. The spring and fall ramp up and down between busy and not busy. These are sometimes called the "shoulder" seasons for tourists.

For the equatorial regions, the high tourist season is usually right toward the end of the wet season and lasts about four months. The end of the dry season can be exceptionally warm in some areas, and this heat drives tourists away. Then heavy rain comes in fairly quickly. Most of the cities I've looked at in these regions have about a six-month extra-hot/wet period that would be considered the off-season. The transition periods are relatively quick.

For someone on a shorter trip, their trip may only be located in a few closely packed regional areas. For someone on a longer trip, spanning multiple continents and regions, they may cover a lot of areas. Hopefully, you have a relative guess at how long you want to stay in each area by now and have some logical path in mind. Take this path and time period and start looking up the weather for when you think you want to go on your trip. You may find every destination on your list has nice weather, or you may find that you want to offset your trip a little bit due to consistently bad weather along your route.

If you're on a long trip, there's a good chance that one or two places may likely have poor weather when you want to be there. You're going to have to ask yourself if you really care and if shuffling your whole trip around is worth missing some bad weather. Don't be afraid to zigzag a little if you need to; just be aware you're going to be paying for it in related transportation costs.

Similarly, if you're on the extreme budget end of the spectrum, shooting for these "bad" weather time periods is probably exactly when you want to be in those places. Cheaper rooms will be available, flights will be in less demand, and tours will be less crowded, meaning cheaper options. Essentially, it's a little rain and maybe cold weather for major savings. Just pack accordingly.

For people taking shorter trips, your normal at-home day-to-day life may be something you have to plan around. Are you taking a break from work or school? Do you need to be back home before a certain date for a wedding or other major life event? Is your giant work project finishing in March? Do you have to wait for your kids to go on break from school? These are definitely things that are going to affect when and how long you can travel. If these sorts of restrictions apply to you, it may be a balancing act of figuring out the best way to work tourist season, trip length, and weather to your advantage. Maybe one of those is more important than the others. You'll have to figure out how these affect you.

Once you do figure out when your trip will align with your life, then you need to figure out how this is going to affect your budgeting and your packing requirements. Traveling during the winter through Europe is going to reduce your trip cost, but it's also going to require extra layers and probably a coat or fleece in your pack. Notably, some areas of Europe are quite popular in winter, particularly around the holidays, so keep that in mind, too. Think Christmas markets in Germany and Christmas masses at the Vatican.

Also, be careful that you don't plan to do tons of outdoor stuff when it's wintertime and the days are short. That's going to seriously mess up your activity plans. Many outdoor adventures close earlier, are unavailable, or are less enjoyable with shorter, colder, more weather-impacted days.

Last, check your guidebooks for information about how different islands operate during the off-season because many businesses may shut down during these times. Places that are known for this are the Caribbean and Greek Isles. Everyone goes here for sun and beaches, so when the conditions aren't favorable, there are few tourists around and therefore there is no reason for the locals to keep everything open and running. Be aware that places close to the equator may be in hurricane season during their off-season.

If the weather is notoriously severe in an area when you're planning on heading there, be prepared for canceled flights, missed boat connections, power outages, etc. All of that is obviously going to affect your trip.

Therefore, although there is a massive cost-saving and crowd-reducing advantage to traveling to places during the off-season, there are some major trade-offs that may not make your trip enjoyable at those times.

I said this previously in the budget estimating section, but also remember that the slower you travel and the more localized your travel, the more you will avoid the incredibly expensive long-distance flights. Minimizing the number of long-distance travel legs you take will drastically reduce your trip costs. So if you can stick to one geographic area or take more time for your trip, you can reduce your per-week costs quite a bit.

RESORT-STYLE TRIP ADVICE

If you're planning on taking a luxury cruise or staying in a resort during your trip, be careful to do some research into the "style" of the resort you're thinking of booking. Resorts can have some specific personalities or have time periods where they try to cater to different kinds of travelers. For example, some resorts may advertise themselves as being "family friendly," or "adults only," or have weeks or months when either of those could be true. Make sure you book something appropriate for your desired trip because booking the wrong resort or a resort at the wrong time could potentially ruin your trip. Imagine if every room at the resort has kids that are running around screaming when all you wanted to do was relax in silence. Also be mindful that resorts may have cheap room prices or packages but then have hidden "resort fees." One place this is common is in Las Vegas, Nevada, where casinos have relatively cheap rooms per night, but they charge additional fees and taxes when you arrive. Also, you may be required to purchase a meal plan or spending package per day to book a resort or cruise, which should be factored into your cost.

DRAFT YOUR ITINERARY

You've heard a lot of things at this point to help you begin to plan out your trip. Now is the time to sit down and actually plan your trip down to the last major detail if that fits your *travel style*. Get a calendar out for when you want to do your trip, or do more research to figure that out, and then start writing down city names on days and figure out your transportation by grouping locations together that make sense. If you're on a long trip and don't need to strictly manage your time that much, at least plan your rough course and figure out time requirements and budgets per region.

If you find you don't have enough time to do everything you want, you will need to cut things out, spend less time somewhere, or adjust things as needed according to your individual desires.

But don't actually book anything yet! Right now, you're just getting your tentative plan together. You'll start to purchase many things after you read the next part of this book.

Once you get your plan carefully laid out, whether specific down to the day or a general plan you intend to follow, you should revisit the "Rough Budget Calculations to Keep in Mind" section from earlier and look at the budgeting estimates that were laid out there. This is now going to be your budgeting target for your trip.

If you are intentionally traveling in the off-season somewhere, you can probably take 10–20 percent off the estimates and work with that number.

With this budget calculation completed, you need to make sure you have enough money. Unless you're rich, have been given money to travel, or have already been saving for a while, you may need to save up some money before your trip.

I'm not going to get super crazy or in-depth about this, but if you're struggling to figure out how to save to make your trip happen, take a look at your at-home life. I guarantee there are parts of your life where you're either indulging or taking the easy route, and these are opportunities to save more money to get your trip funded.

Do you drink coffee? Make it yourself. Do you drink alcohol? Stop buying drinks at bars. Do you eat out? Cook at home. Do you pay for a gym membership? Find a cheaper gym or exercise at home. You can find countless books and blogs that can get you started down this path.

The blog *Mr. Money Mustache—Early Retirement through Badassity* and the book *The Life-Changing Magic of Tidying Up: The Japanese Art of Decluttering and Organizing* by Marie Kondo are great places to start. I know a book on organizing sounds like a weird budgeting recommendation, but learning minimalism will actually save you a tremendous amount of money in the long run, not to mention it will vastly increase your packing skills to help with your travel while also decreasing how much you want to pack. So give it a shot.

For those attempting to take long trips where you will likely not keep an address at home while you travel, be careful to budget in a safety net and figure out a return plan that will allow you to reintegrate into society when you get back. It may take you some time to find another job, settle down in an apartment (flat), and get mobile in a vehicle again…all that kind of stuff. You don't want to come back with five dollars to your name and then try to figure out how to get stable again.

If you find out that you simply can't budget your life to meet your trip costs, you're going to need to adjust your itinerary. Pushing the trip further out to save more money or shortening your trip are both good options. Can you shift your trip to the off-season to save on costs? If you're stuck, revisit the Trade-off Triangle Exercise and see how you might be able to make some changes.

Saving and budgeting your at-home life is one of the hardest travel steps for most people. Planning your trip is a ride down fantasy lane, but this is really where the rubber meets the road. How bad do you want to travel? How much does this really mean to you? Are you willing to sacrifice some bar tabs and restaurants to go on your trip? Do you really need that sports channel cable package?

If you're struggling to stick to the plan, I suggest hanging something up on your wall with some internet pictures relevant to your trip, along the lines of the book/movie *The Secret* and its "vision board" concept, so that you have a reminder of why you're skipping out on some things every week and trying to live cheaper every day. Stay focused on your goal and you'll get there. I did it, and you can do it, too.

PART 3

PREPARING FOR YOUR TRIP

By now, you should have your trip completely planned out whether that be down to the day for a short trip or roughly enough to know your general route and stops for a long trip. Either way, you should know the details of your trip inside and out. You know where you're going, how long you have, and what your goals are. Even though getting this plan together was probably the majority of your trip preparations, there are still many things you need to do before you leave. That's what this part is all about.

I have put Part 3 together in the order things should be worked on for your trip based on how long they take to complete. By that I mean, the next section is the first thing you need to work on because it takes the longest amount of time to complete. The last section is the stuff that you'll need to worry about right as you're leaving on your trip.

Saving up money is likely going to be the longest thing you need to work on, which was discussed previously at the end of Part 1 "Preplanning for a Better Trip," but that's more of a passive trip preparation, so it won't be discussed again here.

The next sections will describe how to get your body ready for traveling, how to get your important documents ready, and how to prep your bank accounts for use while traveling. Then we'll discuss packing and also cover the details on how to get your life at home ready for being away.

This part is essentially meant to be a to-do list to prepare for your trip once you have a trip plan in place. My suggestion is to read through this once right now to get an idea of what's ahead in your trip planning and then come back and reference Part 3 again as necessary when you really start making these things happen.

PREPARING YOUR BODY FOR TRAVELING

This section title sounds like a strange topic for travel, but this is a very necessary and real thing. If you've never traveled far and wide before, this is the step of preparing for your trip that is going to take the longest, mainly because of vaccinations, so I suggest starting on this before you worry about anything else.

After that, we'll talk about malaria, and you should talk with your doctor about this disease during your travel vaccinations visit.

Your physical fitness is a big consideration as well and it's something you should be consistently working on until you leave for your trip.

VACCINATIONS

In my experience, people forget about this step until the last second, and it usually results in a panicked emergency visit to the doctor's office to make sure they can still take their trip. Don't be this person.

Most of the people reading this book will likely be coming from countries that have good medical institutions and medical care and will probably have received a number of vaccinations in their childhood. These are great for daily life and domestic travel, but unfortunately, in many parts of the world, these standard childhood vaccinations aren't enough.

Sadly, most of the people who live in the places that necessitate these extra vaccinations don't even have a chance of getting the vaccines you're getting, but that's another topic entirely. I mention their lack of vaccinations because vaccines stop the spreading of disease. If everyone in a group or society is unable to contract a disease, that disease will not spread. If this were the case, you could visit these countries without getting any additional vaccinations and would probably be fine. No one there would be able to spread the disease to you. But because the locals in many places aren't vaccinated, a disease can move freely through the population. This means that if you aren't vaccinated, you're just as likely as any of the locals to catch something.

So what to do? Well, you're going to need to head to your doctor and do a "travel clinic" visit. Because you're the one opting to go traveling and most of the medical concerns that arise from traveling are things you would never face at home, the travel clinics in many countries are not covered by any sort of insurance, and you will have to pay out of pocket in order to make this visit. Since the main point of this visit is to get a bunch of vaccinations and each one of these has a cost, this doctor's visit can potentially be very expensive because certain vaccinations are not cheap. I think my total travel clinic cost was close to $1,000 by the time I was done. Thankfully, most vaccinations last for ten or more years, so this initial investment lasts for quite some time.

In general, you will want to get the following vaccinations no matter where you are going during your trip:

- Tetanus, Diphtheria, and Pertussis (TDaP)

- Measles, Mumps and Rubella (MMR)

- Hepatitis A and B

- Seasonal Flu Shot

Theoretically, you should have been vaccinated already as a kid with TDaP and MMR, but these typically require a booster shot during adulthood, so double-check your records regarding these and talk to your doctor.

Then, if you are traveling to the following regions, you will also want to get these additional vaccinations:

- MICs and LICs: Typhoid

- Equatorial areas if you plan on being exposed to farming or livestock: Anthrax

- South America or Africa (think equatorial areas on these continents): Yellow fever

- Africa or South Asia: Polio booster

This is not a complete list, but those are most of the common extra travel vaccinations. Your doctor will be able to explain all of the options and what you need much better. Be aware, there are vaccinations like rabies and Japanese encephalitis that are ridiculously expensive. You should chat with your doctor about your odds of getting a particular disease, which will help you determine if you can safely skip a vaccination and potentially save money. Hepatitis A and hepatitis B are worth getting even if you aren't traveling abroad since they're easy to contract and are both STDs (STIs). Yellow fever is a required vaccine in many countries and you should find out if that's applicable to your trip's destinations. Many countries in those regions will not let you into their borders without proof of a yellow fever vaccination.

To read more about various vaccinations and recommendations by country, check out the Traveler's Health Centers for Disease Control and Prevention (CDC) website at cdc.gov/travel.

Make sure that you get an International Certificate of Vaccination booklet, pictured at the end of this section, during your visit and have every vaccination you received logged into that booklet. If you need more than three shots (jabs) for your trip, which can easily happen, you will have to come back another day to receive the rest. Receiving too many vaccinations at one time can cause some nasty side effects and even death. The hepatitis B vaccination is a three- to four-shot series that has to be administered over a six-month period. That's why you need to start this process really early before your trip.

If you have any concerns about vaccinations, check out the history of how the "anti-vaxxer" movement got started in the two-part series by the Khan Academy on YouTube, called *Vaccines and the Autism Myth*. Be aware also that not receiving certain vaccinations, and therefore not having them in your International Certificate of Vaccination booklet, will prohibit you from entering some countries.

In addition to vaccines, your doctor should give you a prescription for antibiotic pills for emergencies, and I'll talk more about that in the "Medical Issues and General Hygiene" section.

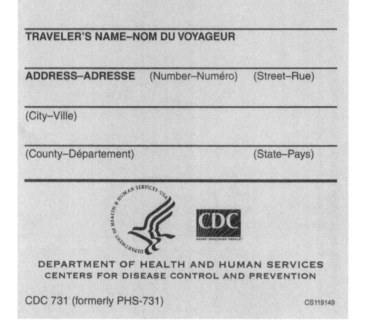

INTERNATIONAL CERTIFICATE OF
VACCINATION OR PROPHYLAXIS

AS APPROVED BY

THE WORLD HEALTH ORGANIZATION

CERTIFICAT INTERNATIONAL DE
VACCINATION OU DE PROPHYLAXIE

APPROUVÉ PAR

L'ORGANISATION MONDIALE DE LA SANTE

TRAVELER'S NAME–NOM DU VOYAGEUR

ADDRESS–ADRESSE   (Number–Numéro)   (Street–Rue)

(City–Ville)

(County–Département)   (State–Pays)

DEPARTMENT OF HEALTH AND HUMAN SERVICES
CENTERS FOR DISEASE CONTROL AND PREVENTION

CDC 731 (formerly PHS-731)   CS119149

Your International Certificate of Vaccination booklet should look very similar to this and be bright yellow.

INTERNATIONAL CERTIFICATE OF VACCINATION OR PROPHYLAXIS
Certificat international de vaccination ou de prophylaxie

This is to certify that
Nous certifions que (name – nom) _____   (date of birth – né(e) le)   (sex – de sexe)   (nationality – et de nationalité)

whose signature follows
dont la signature suit _____

(national identification document, if applicable – document d'identification nationale, le cas échéant)

has on the date indicated been vaccinated or received prophylaxis against
a été vacciné(e) ou a reçu une prophylaxie à la date indiquée   (name of disease or condition – nom de la maladie ou de l'affection)

in accordance with the International Health Regulations.
conformément au Règlement sanitaire international.

Vaccine or prophylaxis Vaccin ou agent prophylactique	Date	Signature and professional status of supervising clinician Signature et titre du professionnel de santé responsable	Manufacturer and batch no. of vaccine or prophylaxis Fabricant du vaccin ou de l'agent prophylactique et numéro du lot	Certificate valid from: until: Certificat valable à partir du : jusqu'au :	Official stamp of the administering center Cachet officiel du centre habilité

Inside the booklet: internationally tracked vaccinations go here.

OTHER IMMUNIZATIONS/PROPHYLAXIS RECEIVED
Autres vaccinations/prophylaxies reçues

This space is provided to record immunizations/prophylaxis that are not required for entrance into any country but have been obtained by the traveler for additional health protection (immune globulin, malaria, measles, etc.).

Inscrivez dans cet espace les vaccinations ou prophylaxies non obligatoires pour l'admission dans un pays, mais qui ont été effectuées pour une protection accrue (immunoglobulines, paludisme, rougeole,...).

Date	Vaccine/prophylactic drug Vaccin/médicament prophylactique	Dose	Physician's signature Signature du médecin

Also inside the booklet: put all your other vaccinations here so you can keep track of everything and know when you need boosters in the future.

MALARIA

One sore subject area in regard to travel health is malaria. The reason this is a sore subject is that there are many conflicting opinions about how to prepare for and deal with malaria. Malaria is a parasitic disease spread by mosquitos. I'll also talk more at length about malaria in the "Medical Issues and General Hygiene" section because you likely won't need to take malarial pills for your whole trip, but there are some things to consider.

I mention it here, though, because it's going to come up during your travel clinic. Unfortunately, there's no vaccine for malaria, so that's out. The only option to prevent malaria is to regularly take pills while you're at risk, but all of the pill options have nasty side effects, so that isn't really a great option either. The thing to consider is that many people live in malarial-infested areas and take nothing for malaria. So if everyone in the malarial areas isn't taking any malarial pills, should you? Well, you're going to have to talk with your doctor about this based on where you're planning to travel.

If you're planning on being deep in the jungle around the equator for a few weeks, taking a malaria pill every day may be worth it, but if you're only going to be in huge cities in malarial warning areas, maybe you don't need it. This is mainly because urban areas don't have as much standing water for mosquitos to grow, and urban areas are aware of the malaria problem and so try to stop mosquitos from growing in the first place. Jungle areas will not have these kinds of controls. Again, this is a conversation you'll need to have with your doctor. It should also be noted, malarial pills do not prevent malaria; they only reduce the chance of contracting malaria.

PHYSICAL FITNESS

I can absolutely tell you, with 100 percent certainty, that the more in shape and fit you are, the more you will enjoy your trip.

No matter what, you are going to be carrying and lifting your bags, even if they have roller wheels. You are also going to be walking significant distances and likely up and down stairs. You may also be hiking, swimming, climbing around in caves, etc.

The more fit you are, the more you will be able to tolerate these kinds of activities. Then you can do more of them and not be sore and tired for days afterward, thus maximizing your fun time while on the road.

This is not to say that someone who is on a cane, or has a broken collarbone, or has some other physical limitation can't travel. Far from it. But the more capable and enduring you are, the more you'll be able to do without getting exhausted.

In my opinion, the single best thing you can do for travel fitness is rucking. If you haven't heard of rucking, it's where you take a backpack, and it doesn't need to be large, 20 L is plenty big, and put weight in the pack, between 10–50 lbs (5–20 kg), and just go walk around. Trust me, you'll be exhausted after 2–3 miles (4–5 km) of walking around with a 30 lb (13 kg) pack if you've never done it before. Your eyes will feel like they're popping out of your head, you'll be walking slowly, and your shoulders and neck will feel like someone is ripping them off your body. However, within a few weeks of rucking, you'll adjust pretty quickly and it'll feel like nothing. Luckily, rucking is easy to do because you can do it while you get groceries, go to the bar, and go to work. Just load up a pack and carry it around. I wouldn't recommend starting at 30 lbs (13 kg), though. Instead, start at 10 lbs (4–5 kg) and work your way slowly up from there.

You can do all sorts of other types of workouts as well—anything will help—but rucking is pretty much exactly what you're going to be doing on your trip anyways. In sports literature, they call this "specificity," i.e., the idea that your workouts are very similar to what you do in a competition. Therefore, the benefits of the workout directly improve your competition performance, which is exactly what we want here. This is called the specific adaptations to imposed demands (SAID) principle. Basically, your body will specifically adapt to rucking, i.e., the imposed demand, and this is the closest thing to what you're going to be doing while traveling, so the adaptions your body makes will carry over right into your travels.

If you plan on trekking during your trip at all, rucking is literally what you will be doing, so rucking before your trip should be mandatory training for you, and working your way up to off-road hikes with 30 lbs (13 kg) for women and 50 lbs (22 kg) for men would be wise.

You can find all sorts of information on rucking through a company called GORUCK at goruck.com. They also have extensive information on how to use your ruck as a full gym in and of itself, which is nice, too.

If rucking doesn't sound like something you'll be interested in, any sort of exercise is also great. Running will give you many of the same fitness improvements, and so will things like CrossFit and group exercise classes. I would highly recommend you do *something*! Anything is better than nothing, and working out is not a one-size-fits-all area for people.

Sports physiology and training is a complicated topic area that carries with it risks of injuries. I only briefly mentioned a few things that may be helpful for your travel, but if you're considering any kind of training, seek out knowledgeable people who can help you learn to perform movements properly and safely if you aren't completely sure how to go about a certain style of exercise.

GET YOUR IMPORTANT DOCUMENTS TOGETHER

Another series of steps you should also do well in advance of your trip is getting your passport, your visas, and maybe an international driver's license. I would try to do these at least three months before your trip, though I recommend six months before, if possible.

PASSPORTS

There's no way around getting a passport for international travel. It's required for crossing borders and you're going to need your passport number in order to book many of the major transportation legs that make up your trip. You will also need this number to book longer tours in advance. Luckily, they're pretty easy to obtain, although in many countries, it requires an appointment and then some processing time to get your first passport.

What is a passport? Well, a passport is effectively an international identification (ID) card. Your local identification cards like driver's licenses, insurance cards, etc. are valid only in your country of residence. The moment you walk outside of your country's borders, no one else will recognize or accept any of those documents. The passport is the only thing that everyone recognizes among all countries. Inside your passport, there are blank pages. These are for your "visas," which we'll talk about next.

Many countries require passports to have at least six months of validity left and at least two full blank pages for entry. I suggest buying an "extra pages" passport, if that's an option, just to help avoid running into this problem especially because many passports only have twenty pages and many visas take up a full page. So twenty pages can fill up in a single long trip fairly easily, especially if you find yourself crossing and recrossing borders to get to new places, which can happen in regions like Southeast Asia.

VISAS

A visa is a stamp or sticker placed in your passport that shows you have been given limited permission to enter a foreign country. Even within a single country, there may be many different types of visas, including but not limited to student visas, tourist visas, and work visas. Different visas will have different permissions.

For example, a tourist visa may allow you to stay in a country for up to ninety days but will not allow you to work and will not allow you to apply to live in dwellings (apartments, houses, etc.) in that country. A student visa may allow you to apply for dwellings and have a four-year limit, but may allow for three months of work during the summer each year. A work visa may be valid for two years and allow for both work and dwelling. These visas can be very different between countries, and there may be many multiple types of these visas within a single country.

Some visas can be obtained on arrival, and "obtained on arrival" is actually the technical term frequently used for this, whereas other visas may need to be applied for in advance of attempting to enter a country. Usually, this will mean leaving your passport with that country's embassy for a few days while they get your visa together. Your passport will be returned with something inside that shows you have been approved for a particular visa type. Then, when you enter the country, your visa will be stamped and effectively consumed (activated) at that time. Many countries also stamp you out of the country to show that you really left. Be aware that if you arrive into the interior of a country, i.e., not at a border, that does not have an obtain-on-arrival visa, you may end up in serious trouble and may be fined, imprisoned, or immediately sent back outside the country.

If you are on a particularly long trip, you may not be able to apply for some visas before you leave, because most visas have a certain validity period that may not fit into your timing. For example, you could apply for a visa and get your passport back, but the visa must be used within six months and you aren't going to be in that country for another seven months. What to do? You're going to need to apply for your visa at that country's embassy somewhere along your trip route. Note that doing this can be quite disrupting to your trip as it can take days, possibly weeks, to get your visa together. In the meantime, you'll have to keep revisiting the embassy and be doing little else while you wait. I highly suggest avoiding the visa application process during your trip unless you absolutely must.

Do note that you can be denied a visa or entry to a country for just about any reason. I know someone who almost got turned away at entry because they made a joke about the weather. Seriously. Border officials are notoriously some of the crankiest people in the world, so do your best to act polite and be agreeable. You will always need to remove your hat for officials, but sometimes you can leave glasses on. Take your hat off in advance of standing before the border agent. If something weird happens—for example, the border official starts interrogating you as to why you want to come to their country at all—be calm and let them run the show. They don't care how long you've been traveling and how tired you are. If you're rude or impatient to a border agent, you are almost assuredly going to have some problems.

Also note that while taking international transportation, like airplanes, if you are headed somewhere that will not grant you a visa upon arrival, the airline staff will check for the proper visas for your destination before you ever board the transportation. So make sure all your visa details are correct ahead of time. If you are unable to show you have the correct visas, you will be denied boarding onto the transportation.

Some countries are very strict with their visa requirements. Russia, in particular, wanted to know all the details of my trip, including everything down to my hotel's phone number, but then they say in the visa application not to book anything until the visa is finalized. Well, how can I know where I'm going to stay if I don't book it first? Then, when you are there, any location you stay at for more than three days requires that you officially check in and get paperwork to prove you were there. All of these check-in slips are supposed to be presented upon leaving Russia. However, the border official I talked to literally just dumped all the paperwork onto the ground behind him and then stamped my passport. Craziness.

If you need to send your passport to an embassy for your visa application, sometimes this application and your passport have to be physically taken into the embassy because there is no mailing option. This can be frustrating if the embassy is far away from you. Thankfully, services exist that will help you with this by taking the passport and application in for you. I personally use VisaHQ in the US and they have been great. Plus, their website lists all of the up-to-date visa requirements for all countries, so use them to check out your travel list and figure out what visas you'll need. Note that a single country may have different visa requirements depending on your citizenship and possibly the country in which you reside. Mongolia, for example, requires a pre-trip visa application from citizens of the UK but processes visas on arrival for citizens of the US. VisaHQ will also make this clear for you even if you're a citizen of a country other than the US.

INTERNATIONAL DRIVER'S LICENSE

Many countries will recognize your home driver's license as proof that you know how to drive, but some countries will only accept an international driver's license. These international licenses are not hard to obtain, but they do cost a fee. I have personally never needed one of these licenses, but I also don't rent (hire) vehicles for the most part, which also means I don't even have one of these licenses, because I'd rather save the money. Make sure you check your destination country's requirements in advance if you plan on renting a car.

INTERNATIONAL STUDENT IDENTITY CARD

An International Student Identity Card (ISIC) is something a lot of travel agencies push. This is designed to be an internationally recognized way of proving that you're still in school. However, most travel agencies sell these to anyone since there's no actual verification of anything on the card itself. Supposedly, these cards offer discounts all over the world, but in my experience, I've only seen a few countries recognize them as being valid at all. I personally think this is kind of a scam, but it's not super expensive, so it's up to you. You'll have to get a rundown of where the card will get you discounts and see if this overlaps with your itinerary.

Even if you don't get the ISIC card, if you are a student, take your student ID with you. Many locations you'll visit do offer student discounts even if they don't recognize the ISIC card.

PREPARING YOUR MOBILE DEVICES TO CONNECT TO THE INTERNET

Technology is awesome. Arguably even more awesome is how fast technology spreads now compared with a hundred years ago. Even when I first started seriously traveling in 2009, Wi-Fi was already readily found in almost every city I visited. There were only a few exceptions, even in poverty-stricken areas. Now, however, with smart-phones almost everywhere in the world, getting internet on the road has become easier than ever before.

When you travel outside of your home country with a mobile phone, typically, at least in the US, your phone is "locked" to a certain mobile carrier and you have some connection plan with that carrier which will go into roaming mode when you leave the US. Most plans that I'm aware of allow you to connect to foreign networks for free so long as you don't make calls, don't send any texts, and don't use any data. If you receive calls and don't answer, or only receive texts, you will not incur any roaming charges. When you receive calls, send texts, or use data, you have likely now incurred some sort of roaming charge. Don't assume your plan follows these rules, though. There may be all sorts of options for international add-on plans, or in my case with AT&T Prepaid, my phone plan didn't allow me to even connect to a foreign network.

Depending on your plan, your carrier might charge your calls by the minute, by the amount of data used, or some similar metric. Sometimes they have agreements with other countries in which you instantly incur a ten-dollar fee, but then your normal at-home plan rates apply for the next twenty-four hours. Check with your carrier to know what penalties and charges you are going to incur while roaming so you don't come home to a $1,000 bill.

The better way to use mobile data is to get your phone "unlocked." In the US, if you are on your carrier for six months and own your phone outright, you can ask them to unlock your phone. This allows you to put another carrier's SIM card in the phone and use the other carrier for service. Once your phone is unlocked, you can buy a local SIM card and use that while traveling. If your phone isn't unlocked, it simply won't connect to the network through the new SIM card.

Each time I get a new phone, I hang on to my last phone for traveling. I don't really care about losing my old phone like I would my new phone, so the old phone is perfect for carrying around when I travel. The only problem with this is that the older phone tends to be slower than a more current model, so you either need to be patient or just use your new phone. This can also be a slight bummer if you're using your phone as a camera because the older model's camera quality is probably not as good.

Something to make note of is that there are two main types of mobile phone networks: CDMA and GSM (you don't need to know what these stand for). In general, only the US has CDMA networks, and the main providers are Sprint and Verizon. Pretty much the entire rest of the world uses GSM. If you have an older CDMA phone, sorry, you're out of luck and your phone is likely not useful to you outside of the

US. If you have a GSM phone, note that some countries use different GSM frequencies for data transfer. This means that your phone will still work around the world, but you may not have access to the fastest data transfer speeds depending on the carrier you're using and your phone's make and model. Don't worry, it will still work; it may just not be lightning quick when using data.

This all said, 4G and 5G networks are moving to a new standard that is universal for data only. If you have a 4G CDMA phone, you may or may not be able to use your phone internationally for fast data depending on where you go. If you have 5G, you should be generally more compatible, but most places don't have real 5G yet and few phones operate on all the 5G frequencies. The point here, as of writing this, is that you need to check with your phone provider to make sure you can use your phone internationally, and make sure you get the phone unlocked before you leave. If this requires six months, you should start this process now.

If you're outside of the US, these things should be significantly easier for you, but check with your normal carrier anyway about their plans and unlocking and all of this stuff.

Assuming you are able to use your phone abroad, local SIM cards are great. In Europe, a 1GB to 5GB data SIM can be purchased for $90 or less, and this data will work across almost all of Europe. In Malaysia, I got a 1GB data SIM for something like $5.

Once you have mobile data, then maps, news, etc., are all at your fingertips anywhere you go.

Maybe you don't have an unlocked phone, or you don't want to pay for mobile data since you don't really need it to get by, and that's fine. As previously mentioned, Wi-Fi is almost everywhere, too. Accommodations will have Wi-Fi almost 100 percent of the time. However, if you're in a hotel, they may charge some fee to get onto their Wi-Fi, which is disappointing considering hostels nearly always have free Wi-Fi. One small annoyance is that in some hostels, the Wi-Fi may only work in a certain area of the hostel, usually the common room or lobby. This happens quite a bit, and it's normal since having a ton of routers and Wi-Fi extenders costs a lot of money, so you might not be able to lie in bed and cruise the internet. Beyond your accommodations, cafés, Starbucks, and McDonald's almost universally have free Wi-Fi as well. Many museums also have free Wi-Fi for the purpose of allowing you to take self-guided tours through their apps. The main things you need to worry about when you're traveling are email and maps, so don't forget to handle these while you're on Wi-Fi. Gmail has a nice app feature that when you get on Wi-Fi and open the app, you automatically sync up, and then you can work on your emails while you're offline. Any emails you send will be queued up and sent as soon as you get on Wi-Fi again. Also, as mentioned in the transportation section, offline maps work great since your GPS still functions even without data.

One of my favorite "discoveries" while traveling was figuring out that Shazam has an "offline mode." I have heard all sorts of awesome music in places I wouldn't have guessed, and trying to figure out what's playing can be impossible if you don't speak the language or there aren't lyrics. If you open Shazam normally, it tries to connect to the Shazam service, but if you're offline, this will fail and you can't Shazam anything. However, if you change your settings while online to "Shazam on app launch," or add the widget to your phone's home pages, Shazam will start up immediately recording. If you're offline, it will record fifteen seconds of music and then give you a notification that a recording was stored for later use. Once you're online again, all the recordings will be uploaded and you'll find your music. Awesome!

It should be noted that these days, due to terrorism tracking laws, many countries require a two-factor email sign-in to access Wi-Fi (meaning one of those codes or emails you have to click on to verify that you are really the owner of your email address). The Wi-Fi itself is free, but theoretically, the Wi-Fi provider is supposed to verify anyone who accesses their network. This creates a problem for you if you don't have a SIM because if you can't access your email separately of the Wi-Fi, then you can't access the Wi-Fi at all. If you find this is the case in the country you're in, you'll need to get on data somehow before you can continue. Europe specifically is known for this.

Although "internet cafés" are slowly starting to disappear due to increased access to mobile data, they used to be the main method of using the internet while traveling. These "cafés" are really just a room with a bunch of computers. I do not recommend using internet cafés unless you absolutely have to, mainly because it's very easy for anyone to install software that captures everything you do on that computer. That makes it very easy to steal your account passwords and this could be catastrophic for you. Even if you do need to use an internet café, use your own device to connect to their internet. In some places, you may have to do this anyway because the keyboard layout may be foreign and all of the computer's text may appear in a foreign language. Meaning, it may be very difficult just to navigate to the option to temporarily change the computer settings to your language of choice. It's much easier to just use your own devices.

SET UP YOUR BANK ACCOUNTS PROPERLY

The bank accounts and credit cards you currently use are probably great for your daily needs, but unfortunately, most "regular" accounts are fairly inefficient for travel. This is because most bank accounts charge fees for using out-of-network ATMs and many credit card companies charge a foreign transaction fee.

Worse, the accounts you use while traveling have a higher chance of being compromised. This can happen through theft of your cards, devices that steal your card data, or malicious software at internet cafés that steal your account information when you log into your accounts.

For these reasons, I highly recommend getting a special set of accounts just for traveling. It's very easy to transfer money between banking accounts, and your bank can help you figure that out, but isolating your travel accounts makes it very easy to contain any issues that may occur.

What you'll want to do is find a credit card that has no foreign trans-action fee, and you'll want to find a bank that doesn't charge any out-of-network ATM fees. You'll have to do some research to find these, but resources like Nerd Wallet for the US will help you find this kind of information.

At the time of writing, for the US, I personally recommend a Schwab checking account and the Bank of America Travel Rewards credit card. Neither have any ATM fees or foreign transaction fees and there are no charges or minimum balances to keep your account open.

When you head out on your trip, only bring these cards with you and, if at all possible, only use your personal devices to log in to your accounts and manage your finances. Because it takes a few weeks to set up these sorts of accounts, you'll want to do this at least a couple of months before you leave for your trip to make sure your cards arrive in the mail and your money successfully transfers.

BOOKING YOUR TRIP

Usually, a good time to start purchasing your transportation and accommodations is about two to four months before your trip begins. If your trip is the type that needs to be completely planned, you will want to purchase everything before your trip. Not doing so can cause serious disruptions in your plan if trains aren't available or tours are full, etc. This is very much in contrast to a looser, more open-ended trip where you may only want to purchase tickets and tours for the first leg or maybe even only the first few days of your trip.

In general, going back to the archetypes, On Retreat folks, some Explorers, some Outdoorsman, Get Me Out of My Comfort Zone types, Culturists, and Foodies will likely need to book more of their plans upfront. This is because of specific travel desires, possible time restrictions, and you don't want to miss out on something you really want to do. Conversely, Gap Years, Hippies, Avoiders, Drifters, and *Eat Pray Love* types will likely need to book less up front. This is because they generally have more time and are more fluid in their plans.

The major things you need to purchase before you leave are generally airfare, train passes or tickets, accommodation, and rental (hire) cars. I recommend you book these items in that order since your transportation is going to dictate when and where you're staying, whereas rental cars are usually fairly easy to book. You will need to have your passport already for most of these purchases since your passport number is required to book most forms of long-haul transportation.

Important note: If you are on a loose trip, be aware that most countries will not let you inside their borders unless you can prove that you are planning on leaving their country eventually. This can include proof of a future airplane flight or some other form of transportation, even if it's departing from another country. This is super annoying when you're on a more loosely planned trip, but it's required by many countries, so you'll have to work around it. Any sort of proof will work, even if it's totally bogus. For example, if you're entering the UK, they may ask for proof that you are leaving. If you show them a booking for a plane flight leaving from Rome and explain that you're making your way to Rome by taking trains through Europe, you have sufficiently met proof that you intend to leave the UK. The idea here, from the border agent's perspective, is that you're not going to purchase a plane ticket and then intentionally not show up to use it, so you're almost certainly leaving their country by the time your visa expires. To get around this issue, using a bogus printout of a trip itinerary, or a real plane ticket purchase that allows for free refunds or changes is the way to go. Getting a plane flight with the option for free change of dates will run you slightly more money, but if you know for certain you are going to leave from somewhere but aren't sure when, these types of tickets are great options. A travel agent can provide you with a bogus trip printout option, but I don't recommend using travel agents.

Travel agents used to be big business back in the twentieth century and it's pretty easy to see why. Not only were computers rare or nonexistent, but trying to call tons of people on the phone and comparing individual airline prices and all that kind of stuff was very difficult and time consuming to accomplish manually. Your travel agent was someone who made a profession out of knowing all of this information. They knew who to contact for everything and they could do all the work for you for a nominal fee to square your trip away.

Now, however, the internet can pool so many resources together in intelligent ways that you don't need to worry about working with a travel agent anymore. One search on Matrix ITA, booking.com, Kayak, or any other number of sites will show you just about every flight option you can possibly consider and show them all to you in whatever order you care about. What is a travel agent going to offer you that's better than this? They have to get paid somehow, so you're going to be paying them money for doing exactly what a free web search can do. I say don't bother with the travel agents unless you are trying to save time and are willing to pay for it. You'll likely end up using travel agents while you're traveling in order to book more localized things and this will likely be unavoidable due to SIM cards, language barriers, etc., and that's fine, but the tour agents at home are the ones who might warrant more scrutiny.

For most people, because the cost of air travel is so high compared with the rest of the costs in a trip, cheap air travel usually factors in when putting together the plans of a trip. I won't cover the basics of air travel again here, but if you'd like to review them, please see the "Getting around during Your Trip" section.

If you are planning on staying in hostels, Hostelworld (hostelworld.com) is a great website for finding hostels all over the world. Be very careful when booking accommodations to read some of the reviews for any place you think you may stay. Because hostels are generally very social places, hostels can have distinct personalities to them, which means you could be booking a party hostel or a really quiet hostel. Figure out what type of place you're looking for and then book your accommodation knowing what you're getting into.

If you're staying in hotels, Kayak (kayak.com) and booking.com are similarly great resources. Just like Hostelworld, you can see reviews for hotels and compare options really easily. You can also get cancellation protection and deals on packages combined with airfare.

Couch surfing (couchsurfing.com), Airbnb (airbnb.com), and VRBO (vrbo.com) are also potential options to find places to stay. In each of these cases, you are staying in a person's private residence. If you are couch surfing, you are staying with that person in their home while they are also there. In the Airbnb and VRBO cases, you are typically renting the place to yourself. Couch surfing could be an interesting way of really getting immersed with the locals, but so far as I've seen, most couch-surfing options tend to be way outside of major cities. This makes getting into and out of the city very challenging. For Airbnb, I have had a lot of problems. Sometimes owners cancel at the last second. Sometimes codes to get the keys change and you aren't made aware. Sometimes you can't access the Wi-Fi. Worse, I have seen numerous checkout checklists that read like a legal contract which I don't have the time or care to interpret. Frankly, they're not worth my time and frustration unless I'm unable to find other accommodations. Your mileage may vary.

TRAVEL INSURANCE

I highly recommend getting travel insurance once you've booked your transportation, accommodations, and any major tours. If you're on a long trip and your plans are a little looser, then insurance can focus primarily on medical care in case there's a serious situation. If you're on a shorter trip that's planned out very precisely, then insurance should also handle any interruptions or cancellations. The important thing is, don't skip out on travel insurance because if everything goes sideways during a trip, traveler's insurance is what will save you.

I recently met a woman who broke her back parasailing in Costa Rica and her travel insurance saved her from being permanently crippled. Because she had insurance, she was able to medevac out of the jungle to her home in the US and be treated at a world-class hospital. If she hadn't been able to receive or afford this care, which was some $200,000 in the end, she might never have walked again. If you're in a place where there's poor medical care, it's likely that medical transportation to better care—probably in another country—may be very, very expensive.

Similarly, if your trip is completely interrupted, this can also be a very expensive loss. When I was trying to go to Antarctica, I had unusual-situation cancellations two years in a row (the ship engine broke in a freak repair accident). Were it not for trip cancellation insurance,

I would have been out nearly $10,000 overall *per cancellation*. The $500 insurance fee was beautiful in comparison.

I use travelinsurance.com to find my insurance for trips, but there are a number of sites and companies that offer travel insurance. Make sure your insurance meets your needs and don't skimp on the medical aspect. Remember, your at-home medical insurance doesn't work abroad.

PACKING

At this point, you have your trip planned out, you have your documents and medical requirements taken care of, and you have your trip plans and insurance purchased as needed. Now you just need to get ready for departure and a huge part of this is intelligently packing.

WHAT TO PACK

During the course of my own travels, I've seen people pack like they were getting ready for a one-way trip to Mars. They bring anything and everything and plan for every contingency. I've also seen people pack for a yearlong trip with the clothes on their back and only two T-shirts and flip-flips for their spare clothing. In the first case, folks have a heavy 90 L bag that they can barely close. In the latter case, I've seen some people pack more to go to the local park!

I'm going to argue that neither of these packing extremes is generally correct.

I'm further going to make the statement that no one can tell you exactly what you need to pack. Only you can figure out exactly what works for you.

Why is this? Well, some people want to dress trendy while traveling, and some people are more minimalist. Some people don't mind washing their clothes in the sink, and other people can't be bothered with this. Some people are into photography, and some people use their phones to take their pictures. These sorts of things are going to wildly affect the volume of stuff you take with you, and this is of course going to affect bag size. Also, some trips may require special gear, for example bulky winter gear, and that's going to affect your packing strategy as well.

Also, whatever you pack initially is going to be refined as you gain more experience. I've completely changed my travel gear three times now from what I packed when I initially started traveling. If you have some way of scheduling a stop at home a couple of months into a trip, it may be worth taking that stop just to repack your stuff. I guarantee that you'll want to repack at least something based on your travel experience so far.

One packing rule that is never going to change, no matter how much experience you have, is that you never want to take anything overly valuable with you while traveling. Don't travel with anything irreplaceable or of significant value like gold watches and diamond jewelry. These are simply a target for thieves while traveling. If you're afraid to lose something, it shouldn't come with you abroad.

In a lot of packing guides, you'll still see lots of mentions of laptops, guidebooks, reading books, all sorts of electronics, phone cards, etc. To me, one of the coolest things that has happened to travel is the creation of the smartphone which has changed just about everything apart from toiletries and clothing when it comes to packing.

When I first traveled in 2009, the iPhone had just come out in 2007 and was still a relatively new product. At the time, the price tag also scared a lot of people off, and for me, I was waiting until the technology was a little cheaper and more mature. This meant that during my first trip, I needed a physical guidebook and a compass in order to navigate around cities. Seriously. Due to necessity, I got really good at reading maps and figuring out directions to places.

Now, though, all of that is totally unnecessary. Your guidebooks, maps, music player, camera, and more are all potentially replaced with just your phone. This drastically reduces your packing needs (and pack weight!) and simplifies your life while on the road because all of your stuff is on one device.

With that said, you can find many guides that will tell you that you can fit all of your travel needs into a 40 L bag. Getting to 40 L in the past was pretty tricky but doable, but because smartphones now replace so many potential packing items, 40 L is totally doable unless you need specialized gear or winter gear for your trip.

Why target 40 L? Well, 40 L is roughly the maximum size of a carry-on bag for both airplanes and buses.

That said, I have personally traveled for a long time with a 70 L bag, although I have only packed 40 L worth of stuff. I do this because you inevitably end up picking things up along the road. Water bottles, snacks, souvenirs, a box of candy, additional clothing...Having this extra space can be nice. But as I've traveled more, I've also been trending towards picking up less stuff. With some practiced restraint, 40 L is very doable. However, when I went to Antarctica, I fully filled my 70 L pack *and* my 20 L daypack with cold-weather gear, for a total of 90 L, so the extra space was definitely useful for that trip.

For completeness, any bag larger than 40 L will need to be checked in to board a plane. The maximum size check-in for most airlines is around 120 L. Most daypacks are around 20 L, though the common Jansport pack seen in US schools is closer to 30 L. Most airlines will measure baggage requirements by "linear inches" (or "linear centimeters"), which is a fancy way of saying they expect your bag to be roughly shaped like a box, and the length of the sides added together, i.e., length + width + height, has to be under a certain total amount. This will vary slightly by airline, so double-check if you're just above 40 L.

I will assure you now, no matter what, that unless you are moving to another country, you can fit any travel needs you may have into a 70 L bag and a 20 L daypack. A 40 L pack is definitely doable, but each person's needs vary.

My intent in the following pages is to teach you the "why" and "how" of packing, and then you should be able to figure out how to pack for your individual needs. I would suggest reading this section and thoroughly doing your own research before you purchase anything. Before I traveled, I reread a few packing guides about twenty times each before I left. Packing is not easy, but I'll try to make it easier.

In the introduction, I mentioned the US Army Special Forces, otherwise known as the Green Berets, and I want to bring them up again here. Special Forces' methods are very relevant to traveling because their whole mission profile is packing up and wandering unassisted into foreign territory. These guys are extreme travel experts. Unfortunately for this section, there is something called the "Special Forces curse," which states something like:

You will fill up whatever pack you take with you.

Add to this the traveler packing adages:

You know what you should have packed after you come back from a trip.

And:

Your stuff never fits into your bag when you're coming back (because you don't have time to pack it as nicely).

When you put all three of these packing proverbs together, this paints a fairly grim picture. You're going to have a bag, fill it up to capacity, put the wrong stuff in it, then go on your trip, and not be able to fit everything in there again. That's a bad day.

Let's try to avoid these problems right from the get-go. You can and will adjust your packing as you gain experience, but after reading the following sections, hopefully you shouldn't run into this horrible bad day situation of a full bag filled with the wrong stuff.

Clothing

I would argue *the* major packing hurdle is your clothing. This is because your clothing is the bulkiest part of your packing. Your clothing choices will play a large part in determining if you need a 40 L, 70 L, or 120 L bag. For your travel clothing choices, I want you to forget everything you know about clothing at home and start from scratch.

Start by asking yourself this question: "Do you have to put on fresh clothes every day?" I argue the answer is no. With the exception of a few people, I have found almost anyone can wear a shirt for two days without feeling gross or smelling. Three days is possible but pushing it a little bit. If you don't believe me, try this as an experiment at home. Unless you're doing a workout, you probably won't even notice that you're wearing the same shirt for a second day.

That said, while this works with shirts and pants/skirts, it is different with socks and underwear. I know this sounds gross, but most guys can get away with wearing underwear for three to four days before things get funky. On the other hand, women can unfortunately get an infection if things are not kept clean. I would recommend that women change their underwear every day.

Socks need to be changed daily because your shoes can start to build up a stink if you don't change your socks daily. Once this stink gets really bad, there is no way to remove it from your shoes. If you ever have the misfortune of smelling shoes that have this odor, you'll know immediately because the smell is awful, strong, and unique. To prevent this from happening, change your socks daily. Even if you don't bathe daily, which can happen in MICs and LICs a lot, changing your socks will go a long way toward preventing your shoes from being irreparably damaged.

As for clothing materials and styles, a lot of new travelers get pulled into the rabbit hole of synthetic-fabric hiking clothing as being their main type of clothing. A lot of this stems from the hyped-up advertising that heavily promotes the fast-drying properties of synthetic clothing. To be honest, I fell into this trap also. What isn't mentioned in the advertising is that synthetic fabric is much more likely to stink than natural fibers and that the fast-drying aspect only works if the surrounding environment is dry.

When I first started traveling, I was wearing only synthetic clothing to try and save money by washing my clothes in the sink. I mean, it's quick-drying, right? What I ended up finding out almost immediately, like literally two weeks into my trip, was that if you're anywhere equatorial, such as Costa Rica, and if you hang your clothes up in your bunk to dry, they won't dry because it's so humid and wet. It doesn't take long for your continually damp clothing to start to stink like mildew and body odor, and this smell will burn itself into your clothes.

To avoid all this, I recommend you skip the misleading advertising hype and ignore blogs that tout how awesome sink washing and air drying your synthetic clothes is, and stick with your normal cotton clothing that you probably frequently wear at home. Wool is another great option because it dries faster than cotton and resists odors, but it can be expensive and irritates some people's skin, so be sure to try it out first. If you want to bring something that's not cotton or wool, that's okay, too, but you don't need to go out of your way to bring anything that's one fabric or another. Just bring your normal clothing.

Preparing for Different Climates

Another thing you will need to consider is "layering." The challenge during travel is that you don't know what the temperature is going to be where you're going. You may have some idea, but you never know when a cold snap or heat wave is going to come through. To avoid being unprepared, focus on thinner layers of clothing and bring multiple layers of clothing so that you can adapt to your environment easily by simply putting on more layers and thus you pack minimal amounts of clothing.

I don't know where the concept of layering originated, but if I had my guess, it was likely perfected because of hiking and mountain climbing. Limited pack space while doing serious physical activity, which could include things like ice climbing while you're in an environment well below freezing, necessitates being able to stay warm enough while not moving but also to be able to take off just enough clothing so that you're not burning up while you are physically active. This is why layering is helpful.

Typically, in hiking literature, you'll find the three main layers in layering referred to as "base," "mid," and "shell." The base layer for hikers is a thin, usually synthetic layer with the main job of wicking moisture away from the body up into the mid layers. The mid layer is the warmth layer and may be comprised of many sub-layers of warmth-providing clothing. Again, for hikers, these are usually synthetic layers. Thinner layers usually go nearer to the skin. The shell layer is a breathable but waterproof layer that is meant to allow your sweat to evaporate off from the inside but to not allow moisture and wind through from the outside. These shell layers come in varying thicknesses, but the outside material is similar to rain jackets and snowsuits.

For our traveling purposes, all this layering advice is spot-on, but we're going to modify this to be more traveler-friendly. Your base layer is going to be your regular cotton shirt.

As for the mid layers, you'll want a sweatshirt (jumper) or sweater and two top and bottom thermal layers—one thin and one mid-weight. Some people call these "long johns," and some people call them "thermal underwear." Leggings can be used for these; it's all the same thing. I personally use Patagonia Capilene lightweight and midweight, which Patagonia used to call layers "two" and "three" for this purpose.

Next, your shell layer is going to be a simple rain jacket. Don't buy a thick jacket for this because you may very well be in the rainforest where it's melt-your-face-off hot outside, and it's still pouring down rain. At this point, you're going to want the thinnest raincoat you can find, and you're going to be opening the under-arm vents so you don't steam to death inside the jacket. Also, if I know I'm going somewhere especially cold, I'll also include a fleece in my bag.

For the shell layer on the bottom, I just wear jeans, which admittedly isn't really a shell layer at all by traditional definitions. However, I'm not too worried about these getting a little wet, and if it's really raining hard, I figure that I'm probably not going outside for long periods of time in most locations anyway. The main exception to this so far in my travels has been my time in India, where it was exceedingly hot in the dry season equatorial weather, near 115°F (46°C), so wearing synthetic hiking pants worked really well since all my sweat was wicking and evaporating away, and the pants were very thin so they weren't insulating my body heat at all.

If I'm wearing everything mentioned so far at the same time because it's really cold, this looks like the following:

TOP LAYERS, FROM THE SKIN OUTWARD

1. T-shirt

2. Lightweight thermal layer

3. Midweight thermal layer

4. Fleece

5. Sweatshirt (jumper)/sweater: I wear this over the fleece since these tend to be roomier

6. Rain Jacket

And then:

BOTTOM LAYERS, FROM THE SKIN OUTWARD

1. Underwear

2. Lightweight thermal layer

3. Midweight thermal layer

4. Jeans or hiking pants in some hotter climates

With all these layers on at the same time, I have stood outside for hours in below-freezing temperatures and have been totally fine despite all these layers individually being fairly thin. In fact, this is essentially what I took to Antarctica and simply just replaced the rain jacket with a parka and put on actual shell pants over the top of all the bottom layers. Freezing temperatures? No problem.

If you're going on a longer trip that covers multiple geographic regions that might include colder climates, I'd recommend taking the entirety of these lists. However, if you're heading to mostly spring and summer climates, you can probably drop the fleece and maybe the midweight layers. Even if you're heading to only summer climates, the sweatshirt is useful on long, chilly flights and in museums and restaurants with the air conditioner cranked up high, and the lightweight thermals are helpful in the evenings if there's a breeze. I wouldn't remove more than this or you're likely to be cold on occasion.

Day-to-Day Clothing

So the previous section covered the extra clothing you should take with you, but what about the actual day-to-day clothing? How much should you bring? There's no exact answer for this, but I have personally found that ten days' worth of clothing is what I prefer to take on longer trips. The main reason for this is that doing your laundry can be tedious and time consuming, so doing laundry every eight to ten days or so means that I'm not doing laundry constantly, but I'm also not packing a ton of clothing. Ten days is a pretty good balance for me, and if you're just starting out, I would encourage you to give ten days a try. Your towel is probably going to stink anyway by the time your clothes need a wash with this setup. You may find a little more or a little less clothing works better for you. Keep in mind that I recommended wearing most things for two days, so ten days' worth of clothing is really five different sets of clothes: five shirts, five pairs of underwear for men and ten for women, and ten pairs of socks.

One thing I would keep in mind is to try and make your clothing interchangeable. That means no matter how many tops or bottoms you bring, everything should match regardless of what combination you wear them in. See Project 333 or look up "capsule wardrobes" to see more ideas about this. This is mainly to avoid a situation where you might put on a skirt and simply can't wear a certain top with it because it looks ridiculous combined. I see a lot of jean skirts and black or white cloth skirts because they match with almost anything and avoid this problem. I try to keep my hiking pants black or khaki and my shirts plain colors for this reason also.

Another aspect to keep in mind is that if you are in very hot sunny climates, wearing long loose clothing will keep the sun off of you and actually cool you down. Plus, you avoid sunburns. I try to wear somewhat loose jeans as much as possible and then T-shirts on top.

It can be tempting to wear less clothing in the form of shorter skirts, shorts, and tank tops when it's hot, but beware that this does expose you to the sun more, which will dehydrate you faster and potentially sunburn you more. Also, many cultures around the world are still very conservative. Exposed skin may cause offense and may bar you from entry to many of the places you want to go. Try to keep the exposed skin to HICs and beaches and tend toward more covering in other regions.

Depending on your destination, your final clothing checklist looks like this:

DAY-TO-DAY CLOTHING CHECKLIST

- 1 pair of jeans

- 1 skirt as desired

- 1 bathing suit (keep in mind a pair of board shorts for men doubles as shorts, but Speedos are legally required in some countries' public pools; research in advance)

- 5 shirts

- 5 pairs of underwear for men, 10 pairs underwear for women

- 10 pairs of socks

- 2–3 bras as needed

- 1 hat

- 1 set of sleeping clothes

ADDITIONAL CLOTHING FOR WEATHER CHECKLIST

- Lightweight thermal top and bottoms (may be leggings)

- Midweight thermal top and bottoms

- Hoodie (jumper)/sweater

- Fleece (if heading to freezing areas)

- Thin rain jacket

If you are planning a resort-style trip or something involving a cruise, you may want to also bring some sort of fancy dress clothes for the nice events that are put on during those kinds of trips. If you're planning on bringing fancy clothes, you may want to alter your baggage to make sure you can protect these clothes from damage.

Shoes

More than absolutely anything else you purchase, your shoes are going to be the most important thing you take on your trip. Think about it. You're going to be wearing your shoes all day long every day. They must be functional and comfortable because if you have sore feet, you're not going to want to walk much. Everything during travel requires some walking around, and if you're too sore to keep walking, you're going to miss out on sights and activities, and that's an easy way to ruin an entire trip.

I see a lot of Gap Year folks, who are typically pretty casual, wearing nothing but flip-flops every day. While I do bring flip-flops for the evenings, the beach, or when there's a dodgy shower, I don't recommend walking in these daily. If you look at hiking boots, they're designed to have an incredibly rigid sole. The reason for this is that the more your foot deforms (i.e., changes shape) during the day, the more tired your feet are going to become. In a flip-flip, your foot will deform if you even step on a pebble. Do that over the course of a day with rocks, steps, and pavement cracks, and you're going to have very sore feet very quickly. Some Hippie types say that minimal shoes are more natural and will build your foot strength up, and maybe they're right, but unless you've been doing this for years, experimenting with this philosophy to build up your feet during a trip is not a good idea. On the flip side, however, while great for the reasons mentioned, hiking boots look odd when you're not actually hiking.

Based on my experience, I try to shoot for a middle ground and instead travel around in "stability" running shoes. I shoot for darker neutral colors, and the stability aspect helps keep your heel straight. Plus, there's plenty of padding and a little give in the sole to keep you comfortable longer. This will take you a long way and it fits with most clothing. Darker colors don't show the inevitable dirt and wear and tear of use, which is also good.

Wearing running shoes doesn't exactly look trendy, but it's not particularly unusual to see locals in most places wearing running shoes, so this style still mostly fits in, except in Europe. Many European countries think it's funny to see people in running shoes walking around in regular clothes. That said, in a place that you really stick out anyway, you're going to look unusual to the locals no matter what you wear, so wear whatever feels comfortable.

Also, bring a shoe bag for your flip-flops to keep your main bag clean, but make sure the shoe bag is big enough to hold your daily shoes when you're wearing the flip-flops.

One last word of caution, heels can eat up an enormous amount of space in your bag. Don't forget that you can buy them while you're traveling if needed so you don't have to take them with you.

Toiletries

You're going to need to bring with you some way of washing yourself. This is one of the packing areas to carefully consider before you buy anything. Depending on the length of your trip, you may need to refill your toiletry items while you travel, and many parts of the world don't have Western toiletry items like shower gel and conditioner.

To really make your toiletry kit work for a longer trip, you'll want to pack your kit as if you were living a hundred years ago. That means bar soap and regular shampoo are your main shower items.

You're also probably going to want to clean your ears, brush your teeth, and put on deodorant. You also may need to shave parts of your body or trim your beard. Pay attention while you get ready in the morning and see how many products you put on and items you use. You may be surprised how many things you use at home.

Now you need to figure out how to travel with a big chunk of these things, since most of those self-care tasks are likely things you won't want to ignore for long periods. But you also don't want to take a bathroom full of stuff with you. Use refillable smaller bottles to take the place of the items you normally use and try not to skip anything significant. In my experience, cleaning yourself up to your standards makes a big difference in your comfort level. You don't want to skimp on this.

At home, I use ten products when I get ready in the morning, and that's not including gear like beard trimmers and loofahs. Although I use all of this at home, I don't really *need* a lot of those things, like exfoliating face soap and special face-specific moisturizer, so I don't bother with those while I'm traveling. Instead of the face scrub and special moisturizer, I just use bar soap while I'm traveling and use a general sunblock that also acts as a moisturizer.

Also, in my experience, a standard-size bar of soap lasts a good two or three weeks of showering daily. You'll want to get a "clamshell" case for your bar soap and make sure you drain it of any water before you store it again. For your hair, 1 oz (30 ml) of shampoo will last you roughly a week if you have short hair and don't overuse shampoo. Some people really like non-aerosol dry shampoo that resembles a bar of soap, so that is also an option. Aerosol dry shampoo is also a thing, but the cans are typically huge and you likely won't be able to find a replacement during a longer trip. If you decide to go the dry shampoo route, I recommend that you experiment with dry-bar or aerosol shampoo extensively before your trip since not everyone likes it. Dry shampoo is also great because it lasts much longer than liquid shampoo and doesn't use any plastic.

For any trips lasting less than two weeks, I've been able to micro-size my toiletry kit down to a 1 L airport-security-compliant see-through bag, but this has required finding "travel-size" versions of things and some specially bought small containers. Somewhat problematic for longer trips, it's hard to find travel-size versions of things like deodorant, toothpaste, and shampoo in many parts of the world. When all you can find is a full-sized deodorant stick somewhere, you won't be able to fit it into a 1 L bag.

For this reason, I recommend bringing a "full-size" toiletry kit with soft sides and packing it less than full for longer trips. This way, if you can only find full-size items, you may still have the ability to stick them in with the rest of your toiletries.

For liquid shampoo for longer trips, I recommend bringing a 3 oz (100 ml) container, refilling your container from grocery store-bought liquid shampoo during your trip, and then leaving whatever is left in the shampoo bottle for someone else in your accommodation when you depart. This reduces the weight and volume that you're carrying. Yes, you are wasting some money here, but it's not much and someone else will gladly use the remainder.

For anything else in your kit, I recommend bringing very small amounts to get you by, as needed. Nalgene and many travel stores will offer tons of container kits with containers of various small sizes. Use the smallest container you need for a given item and refill this during your trip.

Be careful to buy reputable containers, like Nalgene, because cheap containers may crack and/or leak in your bag. Many people take air travel and find their toiletry kit has leaked during the flight due to the reduced pressure in the plane causing the air bubbles in the bottles to push the liquids out. This can create havoc in your bag and could potentially ruin packed items.

Also notable is that many accommodations around the world do not provide you with a towel, so to dry off after showering, you'll want to bring a towel. That said, don't bring your normal fluffy bathroom towel with you since it's going to take up a huge amount of space and never dry out. Instead, you can buy a "pack towel" which is a highly absorbent, nearly flat towel. These are used better "patting yourself down" as opposed to the normal shower towel "rub down" but are still very effective. Unfortunately, these start to stink fairly quickly if they're not allowed to dry out fully, so your pack towel is likely going to dictate your laundry schedule if you're using it frequently. Many women like to bring a sarong, not only to wear but also to use as a hair towel because the pack towels are not super nice to the touch and will pull on your hair during drying.

I recommend a folding toothbrush. A regular toothbrush is huge and very awkward to pack and the little snap-shut covers that go onto your toothbrush always get lost or broken. Instead of fooling around with those covers, just get a brush that folds in half and puts the head of the toothbrush into the handle. Not only are these smaller and sturdier, but they're a built-in cover for the brush, too.

For shaving, there's an Australian product called "King of Shaves" that is a shaving oil. Rather than bringing bulky shaving foam, use a few drops of this and it works just like normal shaving cream but at a much-reduced size.

Similar to toothbrushes, don't bother with a cover for a razor. Get a small razor that has a case. Women's travel leg-shaving razors are great for this, and the razor works just the same as a men's face razor. The Gillette Venus Snap is a good example of this and you should be able to find replacement Gillette blades fairly easily. If you can't find replacement blades, disposable razors are usually easy to find even in places where the locals don't grow much body hair. For a more sustainable alternative, bring your own "safety razor," one of those old-school-style razors where you replace the razor blade only, and some extra razors.

Make sure you take sunscreen or moisturizer with an SPF rating, and wear a hat as much as possible outdoors. Don't be the person who looks like an aged piece of leather after your trip. I have rarely worn sunscreen during my two and a half years of travel, except when I knew I was going to be shirtless and hat off during the day. Because of this, my forearms and lower face were almost always exposed to the sun, and I can already see that my skin has taken significant damage in those areas. Also, you're going to get sunburned at some point, especially if you go to the tropics, so bringing a small bottle of aloe is wise especially since most aloe containers are usually monstrous in size and aloe/sunburn relief can be hard to find in some places.

For many of the products mentioned, there are some cool travel-inspired alternatives, like pill-based toothpaste, solid conditioner, ultra-concentrated body wash, etc. These things are interesting, but replacing them on the road is going to be nearly impossible, and what happens then? You're going to end up with the normal things people use daily anyway. If you're on a shorter trip, these alternatives may save space because you won't run out of them. But if you're on a long trip, I would instead plan on using easily acquirable stuff, and initially put those into appropriately sized travel containers to ensure that when you do need to refill an item, you'll already have a non-full-sized container ready.

Last, I also recommend bringing a universal sink stopper. It has come in handy for me before when I've needed to fill the sink to either wash myself or my clothes.

TOILETRIES CHECKLIST

- Pack towel

- Toiletry bag

- Bar soap and clamshell (don't lose your clamshell like I did once. These are hard to find in MICs and LICs!)

- Shampoo and conditioner in refillable containers

- Deodorant

- Toothpaste

- Folding toothbrush

- Q-tips

- Tweezers

- Nail clippers

- Razor

- King of Shaves shave oil if needed

- Universal sink stopper

- Chapstick or lip balm

- Collapsible funnel for refills

- Eyeshadow and eyeliner if desired (From my friends: they recommend getting waterproof make-up and please believe them when they say, "You likely don't need that entire makeup kit!")

- Sunscreen

- Small aloe bottle

- Other toiletry items, such as contact lens solution and cases, glasses, skin ointments, makeup remover pads, etc.

Medical

People have a tendency to go absolutely over-the-top crazy when it comes to their medical kits. I was also guilty of this when I first started traveling, having even brought things like an emergency blanket and a fire-starting kit. I laugh about this now, like what was I thinking? Am I going to end up sleeping in the cold somewhere where I have to build my own fire? Unless you are going to really remote spots, the answer is almost certainly no. Also, if you don't have medical training, you won't suddenly figure out how to use everything in a large medical kit if you don't already know.

So keep it simple.

Think about this: how often do you need to crack open a medical kit at home? Maybe a few Band-Aids (plasters) for a few cuts or scrapes? Or maybe some moleskin for a blister? Maybe some acetaminophen (paracetamol) for headaches? Some cold medication? Sometimes? Maybe?

Whatever you typically use at home is all you really need to take with you. The main thing you will definitely want to take with you is diarrhea treatment since traveler's diarrhea will be a primary concern. Keep in mind that pretty much everywhere in the world, except the most remote and uninhabited of places, will carry anything else you may need. You may pass through these remote areas but probably aren't going to be hanging around them for long periods of time, so take enough supplies to last you a few days and no more.

I also pair my medical kit together with some emergency repair items. A small tightly rolled 3 ft (1 m) length of duct tape is highly useful. I also carry a dental floss card (which looks like a credit card) and a fat sewing needle for the floss to repair any rips in my bags. I also carry a few small zip ties and a single-use tube of superglue. These few items can go a shockingly long way in fixing shoes that are falling apart, bags that tear open somehow, or clothes that malfunction. Don't bring your entire toolbox!

My medical kit now, which probably still has too much stuff, looks like this:

MEDICAL CHECKLIST

- Band-Aids (plasters)

- Diarrhea treatment—Pepto Bismol (bismuth) and Imodium (loperamide)

- Constipation treatment (highly personal choice here but probably won't happen often if you keep up on your hydration)

- A couple of days' worth of common cold treatment

- Motion sickness medication

- Minor aches and pains medication

- Moleskin (though Leukotape works much better!)

- A few safety pins

- A few zip ties

- Mini roll of duct tape

- Floss and sewing needle

- Superglue

For any prescription medication that you need to take with you, be aware that all medications have a "trade name" and a "generic name." The generic name is the name of the chemical, and the trade name is the advertising name. There may be many trade names for a given generic name. If you need to bring medication with you, make sure you know the generic name of the medication in case you need to get a refill on the road. Pharmacists or shopkeepers may not be aware of the trade name from your home country, but the generic name will get you the right medicine.

I have also run into the situation a couple of times where I don't immediately have access to clean water. Because of this, I am starting to think that bringing a LifeStraw or possibly chemical water treatment may be a wise idea. I have not done this to date and have not had any issues yet, but it's something to think about if you're going somewhere like India but won't be in large cities where bottled water is readily available. If you're going remote for a long time, bringing iodine tablets or an emergency water filter isn't a bad idea.

Electronics

I know I mentioned this before, but the technological advancements of the past twenty years have made the electronics category of packing much easier than it used to be.

Back in the late 1990s and early 2000s, people who used to travel with laptops were called "flash packers." This was a somewhat chic, somewhat derogatory term as it implied a new style of travel where people "had to have" their gadgets and were trying to remain connected to home. There was an attitude of "how needy these travelers are expecting internet!" To do this, they were bringing an expensive, bulky laptop with them. This was shocking and frowned upon at the time, but this attitude is comical now in retrospect.

Keep in mind that for the time period, this was new, and a lot of early electronics were unable to take the various different sources of power around the world. This meant carrying around power converters which were also heavy, bulky, and expensive.

Plus, because there weren't integrated devices like smartphones at that point, all of the individual device needs were separate. Separate cameras, separate video cameras, separate books, separate phones, etc. were necessary. Can you imagine having to carry around physical film rolls for your whole trip? Things were a lot different then, so you can imagine why bringing even more bulky, heavy stuff like a laptop was almost scandalous.

Thankfully for us, things have changed quite a bit over the last twenty years and handling our now-commonplace tech is super easy and, in my opinion, kind of awesome.

However, if you are traveling with any electronic items, there are a few things you should know related to global electronic use. The easiest way to say this briefly is that there are two voltages used in electricity around the world, 110–120 V electricity and 220–240 V electricity, *and* there are two frequencies used around the world, 50 Hz and 60 Hz, for a total of four combinations of voltage and frequency. In the past, if you plugged a device rated for one of those four electric ratings into another of those four ratings without a huge heavy power-converting device, you were risking electrocution or fire. With the invention of the "switched-mode power supply" twenty years ago, nowadays you'll see a label on your device that typically says "110–240 V 50/60 Hz." If your electronics say this, that means that as long as you can get this device into one of the world's four outlet (socket) shapes somehow, even if it's using paperclips, your device will work in that outlet without having any issues. These are essentially universal devices except for the plug shape. Anything you take with you will need to be checked for this universal label.

That said, anything with a USB plug is universal anyway, so you don't have to worry about those devices, and luckily, that seems to be most devices now. For these, only the USB charger needs to be universal.

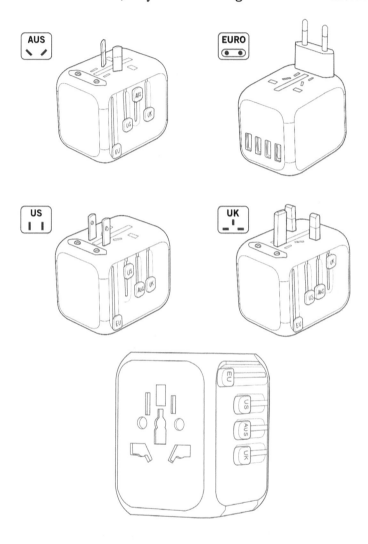

The four main outlet (socket) shapes around the world and a small plug adapter that allows you to select the correct plug configuration for your location. The front face of this adapter is a "universal recipient" plug and can take any of the four shapes' prongs in both two- or three-prong configurations. Note that many of these adapters now contain USB charging ports, as seen in the Euro plug picture.

My recommendation for electronics is to first get a universal plug adapter kit. These are not power converters but really just a way to change your current plug shape into the outlet shape you're looking at. Think about this as purely one metal shape to another metal shape; there's nothing else these adapters do.

Then get an extension cord with multiple outlets (sockets) on the end. In many older rooms and non-boutique hostels and hotels, there may only be one outlet for multiple people and their devices, so having a way to "pass through" someone else into your cord chain is invaluable. What I mean here is that everyone traveling will have a set of adapters, so if you can plug into the wall while also allowing someone else to plug into your cord while you charge, it's like you're not even there and they can charge, too. If someone else is already using the wall outlet, you can hop right in the middle and they won't even notice. Plus, if the wall outlet is far away from you, your extension cord allows you to move your valuable electronics closer to you during the night for security and still have them charge.

Most of your items are probably USB these days, so get a high amperage USB charger. USB devices generally all operate on the same 5 V USB voltage, but the devices can regulate their own maximum amperage. If you don't know exactly what that means, don't worry about it, but basically having a higher amperage value means your devices charge faster. Think about amperage like water flow. For electricity, more amperage means more electric "water" into your device. The maximum USB amperage you'll typically see is 2.4 A, "A" for Amps, and this will charge devices *much* faster than a 1.0 A charger.

Be aware that there are combo cords available that combine an extension cord with a USB charger, but these units tend to be *very* bulky compared to the individual items. Also, they tend to have three-prong plugs, whereas many devices and outlets you'll find traveling will only have two prongs. Many laptop chargers have three-prong plugs, so you may need an adapter to get those into your cord outlets. That third prong is only there to protect you from electrocution in the case your laptop is damaged, meaning it can usually be safely bypassed.

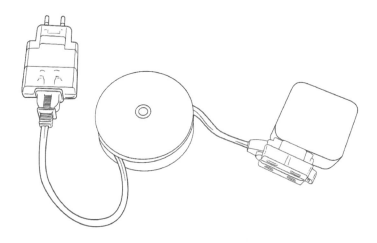

This is my actual electrical setup. Starting from the left: This is another type of plug adapter that folds into the different plug shapes like a Transformer from the movies/shows/comics and is super compact. Connected to that is a 6 ft (2 m) extension cord with three outlets at the end, two of which are visible here. The disc in the center is a "cable turtle." The sides of the turtle flip up so that you can wind the excess cable around the center of the disc. The thing at the end is a 4-port, 2.4 A USB charger rated for 110–240 V 50/60 Hz. Plug this into a wall and someone else can plug into one of your remaining outlets. You can also stretch this across a room as needed and coil it back up in your bag.

Next, get some cables for your devices, probably one long one for your phone or tablet so you can use it while charging, and then some shorter ones for other devices. As for actual devices, a phone and tablet may be all you need unless you want a dedicated camera or a laptop.

I strongly recommend against taking a Digital Single-Lens Reflex (DSLR) camera unless you are planning on selling your photography professionally or are really passionate about taking professional pictures. Not only are DSLRs and extra lenses really huge and annoying to carry around and pack compared to using a phone or a point-and-shoot camera, but they're also insanely valuable devices for their size, meaning they're prime targets for thieves. Worse, you can't really hide a DSLR out in public while you're using it, so it may make you a target for theft.

I also travel with AirPods now and those things are great. Not only are the headphones nice in general, but going completely cable-free with your headphones is *so* liberating.

Because smartphones have become critical to our existence, I recommend bringing a backup portable charger if there is even the slightest chance your phone could run out of power before you get back to an outlet (socket). Charging cases are also available now, which is just a larger case for your phone that acts as the backup battery.

I mentioned this previously, but really inspect the items you are taking with you and make sure they all say "110–240 V 50/60 Hz" somewhere on them, usually toward the power plug. If your device does not list those exact numbers, your device is not universal, and attempting to plug it in somewhere outside your home country can start a fire or get you electrocuted. Be very careful to check for this. The print may be *extremely* small on your devices. USB devices do not need to be checked.

ELECTRONICS CHECKLIST

- Universal plug adapter

- Extension cord with multiple outlets

- USB high-Amp charger

- USB cables for devices, 1 long cable and 2-3 short as needed

- Charging case or backup battery charger

- Small camera (optional)

- Headphones

Other

This section is some of the leftover bits that a lot of people tend to forget because they don't fall nicely into a broader general packing category. Don't forget this stuff. It's all just as critical as anything else you pack.

Books and Movies. You're going to need a guidebook, and you're going to have enough bus trips, plane flights, and evenings that you're going to want some entertainment. Books and movies/shows are great for these times. If you brought your phone and tablet with you, stick your books on your phone and tablet, and your movies/shows mainly on your tablet.

If you prefer the feel of real books, just be aware of the space and weight trade-off that you're making. If you're confident that you can maintain charge on your devices, you can skip bringing physical books really easily. Book trades at hostels are still a thing, but they're becoming less common.

Once I have all my books loaded up onto my devices, I like to use an app called "@Voice" to have my books read aloud to me by my phone through my headphones. Yes, it does sound all computerized, but I essentially just turned an e-book into an audiobook so I can listen to books with my AirPods while I walk around. Also, I really like being able to adjust the speed of the reader which allows me to "skim" sections of books as needed. You can also get an audiobook app like Audible or use the Amazon Kindle read-aloud function for the same purposes.

Copies of Documents. Make copies of your passport, vaccination records, and visas. I don't think this needs any explaining, but you should either scan or copy the important passport pages for your trip and email them to yourself. That way, if you *are* robbed for some reason, you have proof of who you are and documentation of your permission to be at your destination.

Passport Storage. I recommend getting a small pouch to hold your passport and documents, but I do not recommend the around-the-waist money belt that everybody swears by and recommends. Why? Because I constantly see people walking around with these literally hanging out for anybody to see. If you aren't going to use the money belt properly, you are actually decreasing the security of your valuables because you've now made it easier for someone to grab them. Plus, it's not like any thief doesn't know these money belts exist, so you're not really preventing anything except maybe pickpocketing. But if you secure your stuff away correctly and pay attention to your surroundings, you shouldn't be getting pickpocketed anyway. Don't bother with the money belt. If you want extra security, use the around-the-neck-type wallet and keep it in your shirt or use a leg pouch if you always wear pants (trousers). Also, I recommend keeping some lower-value money accessible in your pockets or bags at all times so you're not rooting around in your money pouch in public. Do this in a bath-room stall or other private area as needed. Then, if you are robbed, you have something to hand over immediately and may escape with-out giving away everything you have on you.

I see this so often and it pains me so much. You're not fooling anyone wearing your money belt like this, and the reality is, you're probably putting yourself more at risk.

Luggage and Locker Locks. Do not take locks that require a key. Keys are really easy to lose and if that happens, you won't have access to your pack, and you'll have to either pick the lock or cut the bag, both of which are less than ideal. Bring combination locks instead, including for your TSA-approved baggage locks. Purchase enough locks for each opening on your bag and then one larger lock for lockers. Do not use three-dial locks as those only take about five minutes to brute-force all the combinations and unlock. Use four-dial locks and no one is going to sit around clicking away for an hour trying to get into your stuff.

I also bring a short metal "looped security cable," something lightweight and around 18 in (≈50 cm) so that I can lash my bag to posts or shelves when I need to leave it somewhere that isn't completely secure, like baggage storage rooms at hostels where anyone can walk in.

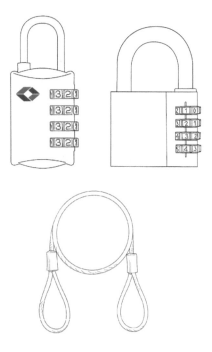

Top left: Small TSA bag locks with four dials. You'll also want to bring non-TSA locks of the same size for when you're not in airports. Top right: A heavier-duty lock meant for lockers. Bottom: A short "looped security cable."

Luggage Tags. I highly recommend that you find what look like little lamination kits and use those to make your own luggage tags. I have tried using all sorts of different baggage tags and all of them get ripped off by the airport conveyor belts. The laminated tags that I use look completely mutilated, which tells me how much force is being applied by the conveyer belts and hence why all my other tags have been ripped off.

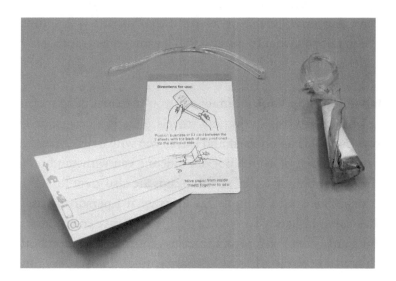

On the left: A new lamination-style tag kit. Just write your info on the card and then peel back the sticker and seal your info inside. You'll likely want to trim the lamination down a little. On the right: One of my actual bag tags from traveling around the world. I can't even imagine how many things this tag has gotten caught on to make it look like this. Since this tag is flexible and stretchy, it's managed to survive going through many airports without being ripped off of the bag.

Cameras. I did warn you against bringing a large DSLR camera, but I want to talk briefly about how to take good photos and use photography equipment. Unfortunately, photography is a huge subject in and of itself, so discussing it in depth would be going way off the rails from what this book is about. All I will say here is check out the "rule of thirds" and learn how to use "fill flash." You can easily find lots of internet pages and videos that explain both of those in depth. If you want to get more serious training in photography, there are opportunities for creative photography classes in most major cities. You can also find a lot of courses online where your work will be evaluated by someone, so you can still get real feedback on your photos. If you are serious about bringing a DSLR camera, I would highly recommend taking one of these classes. If you go down this route, your gear will be so specialized that no one will definitively be able to tell you what to do, and you'll want some training to make those decisions.

Collapsible Camp Cup. I cannot tell you the surprising number of times I have used this during my travels. This is a cup made out of silicone that folds up on itself and leaves you with a disk that's easy to throw into a pack or even a pocket. Silicone can withstand temperatures way over boiling water, so these cups are also great for hot liquid situations. The Sea to Summit X Cup is what I personally use. This cup has come in handy to pour drinks from larger containers, make instant soup, get tap water from sinks too short for my water bottle, or grab hot water on trains to make instant coffee. Almost every time I've pulled mine out in public, I get a lot of questions from other travelers who wish they had something similar with them so they could, at the very least, stir up some instant coffee.

Water Bottle. Rather than buying lots of small water bottles and throwing them away, bring a reusable water bottle and get large water quantities at the store and refill your bottle in MICs and LICs, or use tap water in HICs. If you travel for almost any amount of time, you'll sadly start to see discarded plastic water bottles all over the place and bringing your own reusable bottle can help that problem a lot.

"OTHER" CHECKLIST

- Travel guidebooks

- Other books

- Movies/shows

- Passport and visas (and copies sent to your email)

- Four-dial locks (enough for bag + 1 bigger lock)

- A very short metal cable loop (you already have the locks)

- Bag tag

- Collapsible cup

- Reusable water bottle

WHICH TYPE OF BAG SHOULD YOU USE?

What are you going to pack all of your stuff into? This is the second most important decision you need to make about your packing, the first being your footwear. There are a variety of options here including:

- Suitcases, typically roller bags

- Duffel bags

- Hiking backpacks

- Combination bags (these are both a backpack and a roller bag)

- Travel backpacks

- Daypacks (not really a full packing option but part of the packing equation)

While this may seem like a lot of options, I would argue there isn't even much of a discussion to be had here. Hands down the best options for travel are the travel backpack and the roller bag, both with an accompanying day pack. That said, even when there are clear winners for a category like this, it's not going to suit everyone or every situation. Even I still use other types of bags for specialized trips. That being said, let's go through each option and discuss the pros and cons, and then I'll come back to the general superiority of the travel pack and roller bag.

Overall, no matter what, at a minimum, you are going to need some sort of bag and a daypack for your trip.

Suitcases (aka Roller Bags)

The days of a regular suitcase with nothing but a handle have long gone and have instead been replaced by roller bags. I'm fairly certain that I haven't seen a suitcase that isn't a roller bag in the last decade. These bags almost always have rigid sides, some sort of wheels on the bottom, and a telescoping handle that allows you to drag the bag along behind you.

PROS	CONS
• Even if your bag is heavy, you won't be carrying most of the weight while walking on flat surfaces.	• Except in all but the most modern of HIC locations, most streets and walkways are uneven and in many travel destinations are cobblestone or dirt. I can't tell you how many times I've seen people dragging their bag, instead of rolling it, since the wheels were useless or had broken off the bag due to the uneven terrain.
• Easy and cheap to purchase since they're universally available everywhere.	• Walking with these is annoying for you and everyone else since you're essentially dragging a cart behind you. This gets caught on corners, trips other people, and it's easy to forget the bag is in other people's way.
• It can have a hard outer shell or rigid sides that may protect sensitive or fragile objects inside the bag.	• You can't avoid carrying your bag upstairs and jamming it into storage compartments and into overhead bins. Even though you may have a roller bag, you're going to be carrying it *a lot*.
	• The handle and wheels require extra structure and metal and therefore drastically increase the weight of your bag compared to if those items were not present, and now you have to lift that extra weight too when carrying the bag.
	• The rigid sides do not have any flexibility to them, so if you find a space for your bag that is a tiny bit too small, there's no possibility that your bag will compress to fit into that space, which can make finding an appropriate space for your bag much more challenging.

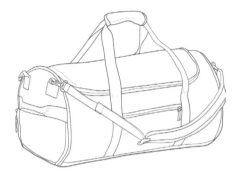

Duffel Bags

These are soft-sided bags with handles, sometimes a shoulder strap, and sometimes some very thin backpack straps.

PROS	CONS
• No internal structure so you can fit this bag into just about any space.	• Straps are almost always uncomfortable for any sort of longer carry, especially if the bag is heavy.
• Nothing but minimal cloth, very lightweight.	• Usually awkward to carry since the bag shape molds around you as you move.
	• Everything inside slides around due to a lack of internal structure, so it can be difficult to find things later. This same effect can also result in the internal contents constantly slamming into seams which can break the bag open over time.
	• Zippers frequently break or rip over time from overpacking and bag flexibility.

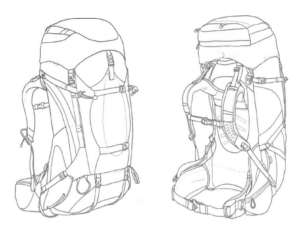

Hiking Backpacks

These bags are obviously designed to be used when hiking. Most modern packs have an internal frame and a top-entry opening like a giant drawstring sack. Many times, the bottom has a tent compartment that is isolated from the main compartment.

PROS	CONS
• Designed to carry potentially heavy loads. • Has an internal structure but is still soft-sided, so it can be somewhat compressed but things won't slide around everywhere inside the bag.	• Top loading makes finding your stuff excessively difficult and often requires you to dump your whole bag out to find anything. Using small internal bags (i.e., packing cubes) can help this to some extent but doesn't solve the problem of the opening being on the small dimension of the bag.

PROS	CONS
• Sits on your back and hips, which is the best and easiest place to carry things on your person. • Has shoulder straps, a hip belt, and a sternum strap designed to comfortably carry loads over long time periods and long distances.	• Opening is likely secured with a drawstring, so there's no way of locking your pack. Even if there's a zipper, there's usually no way to lock it. People don't typically get robbed while hiking so the extra weight incurred by security features is undesirable in a hiking backpack. • No way to hide shoulder straps, and these are not treated nicely by the conveyor belts in airports. Many people checking these in will later find buckles and straps torn off or missing. Many airlines will require hiking packs to be put into another duffle bag for this exact reason and that now adds another bag to your pack. • Must be carried all the time.

Combination Bags

These Frankenstein bags are both roller bag and backpack bag. Unfortunately, like anything that tries to do too many things at the same time, this means the bag is really poor at being a roller bag and it's really poor at being a backpack, too. I don't recommend these.

PROS	CONS
• One-stop shop for a bag that does it all, so arguably has the pros of all of the other bags.	• Added weight and space for the handle and added weight and space for straps. • Bag weighs more but with less space for your stuff due to the extra combo functionality. • Backpack straps are usually too thin and therefore uncomfortable. • Expensive. You're paying for all the engineering and materials.

Travel Backpacks

These are backpacks that are purpose-built for traveling. These packs are usually soft-sided bags with a large squarish compartment like a suitcase, and an internal frame with real shoulder straps like a hiking backpack. They also have locking zippers and usually have a flap that covers the shoulder straps when checking the bag.

PROS	CONS
• Meant for long-haul carrying and traveling. • Securely locks shut. • Compartment opens like a suitcase. • Straps zip away for checking on airlines, buses, or boats. • Internal structure and cinch straps keep things where they are. • Soft-sided so you can compress it a little bit. • Has shoulder straps, a hip belt, and a sternum strap designed to comfortably carry heavy loads over long time periods and long distances.	• Hard to find except at specialty stores and online. • Must be carried all the time.

Daypacks

Daypacks are your bag while you walk around during the day. This could potentially be a purse, a small duffel, a sling bag, a messenger bag, a waist pack, or a small backpack. There are all sorts of options here.

I personally recommend keeping it simple and sticking with a normal backpack that's about 20 L. While the other options are interesting, a small backpack is going to be the most comfortable to carry for long periods and doesn't require one hand to keep it secure like a purse or a sling bag. Also, a pack this size easily fits a water bottle and a jacket as well as anything you may decide to purchase during your day.

There are some fancy lightweight options for these, but I've found these aren't very practical. The lightweight items don't stand up well to the use, abuse, and abrasions that are the normal everyday part of life during travel. Lightweight items usually last one short trip and then need to be retired.

If you look at the bags carried around by the military, they are extraordinarily heavyweight compared to average consumer products because they're designed to carry very heavy and bulky things like ammo, rockets, explosives, etc. This type of gear has to last through a minimum of six months of combat deployments without being replaced. Lightweight gear would quickly be shredded in these conditions.

Any sort of travel will require something in the middle of lightweight one-trip needs and heavyweight military six-month abuse, so I recommend an ordinary, normal backpack for daypack use. And because of the technological advancements with smartphones (mentioned earlier), I've noticed I don't always need a daypack depending on the activities of a given day. If I go on a hike, or go on a day tour, or similar, I probably still want my pack because opportunities to buy water or snacks may be limited. In MICs and LICs, I also carry a medical kit and a bathroom kit, so I carry a daypack every day. In HIC cities, though, all that stuff you may need should be readily available, so you may find that a daypack is largely unnecessary.

The Right Bag for You

To quickly revisit the traveler archetypes, from what I've observed, most of the time, the archetypes seem comfortable with the following luggage:

- Gap Year: travel backpack

- Hippie: travel backpack

- Retreat: roller bag

- Outdoorsman: hiking backpack

- Avoider: travel backpack

- Drifter: travel backpack

- Explorer: travel backpack

- Out of Comfort Zone: travel backpack

- Pensioner: roller bag

- Culturist: roller bag

- *Eat Pray Love*: roller bag

- Foodie: roller bag

- Newb: travel backpack

I would argue that for any sort of travel that doesn't involve packing freshly pressed business clothes or being in a single accommodation most of the trip, a travel backpack is the preferable choice for luggage. That means that Pensioners, Culturists, *Eat Pray Loves*, and Foodies may want to reconsider the roller bag as their choice if it's a multi-city trip. If you'll be on a cruise or will be changing location infrequently, then a roller bag is probably fine. I tend to use roller bags for domestic trips and a travel backpack for anything international. Really, this choice is up to you for your comfort level, fitness level, destination, and *travel style*.

If you do go with the travel backpack, I would also recommend that you start with a 70 L bag. If you're more of a minimalist, a 40 L bag may work out for you just fine already, but as mentioned previously, 70 L is more versatile due to the extra space you have if you need to bring anything special or you intend to pick up additional items during your trip. If you are a smaller framed person, you might consider going down a few liters to a 65 L or 55 L bag because you may be drowning in a 70 L bag.

Be very careful about which travel pack you purchase, as not all companies create their bags at a similar functionality level. Some companies claim to make travel packs but then have top-loading holes or don't have any way to lock the bag, etc. Look for these features at a minimum:

- Three sides of the bag are on a single zipper so you can open the bag like a suitcase

- Lockable zipper slides/pulls

- Full internal frame and hiking-style shoulder straps, hip belt, and sternum strap

- A flap or bag to cover and contain the shoulder and hip straps to protect them on luggage conveyer belts

- Two handles like a suitcase for when you have the straps covered

- A pack that properly fits you. Some may have movable straps, and others may have sizes.

- Optional (nice to have and I recommend it): a rain cover

An example travel backpack with all the features you want to look for.
Top left: Hiking-style shoulder straps and hip belt and also handles to
carry the bag. Top right: Three sides of the bag unzip and this particular
bag opens like a clamshell with covers for the halves to keep your stuff
from moving around. Bottom left: Lockable zipper slides and this model
has a mounting point to keep the zipper slides in one spot. To use: Place
your lock through both zipper slides and the mounting point and then
close the shackle. Bottom right: A rain cover that doubles as a duffle bag
for the pack for when you need to stow the shoulder straps and hip belt for
checking in the bag at the airport.

Many of the travel bags that I've seen come with a daypack that you can attach to the outside of the main pack with a zipper or straps, but I would encourage you not to use the daypack in this manner. First, it moves the weight of your pack away from your back, which I'll talk about in the "How to Pack" section shortly. Second, it makes your daypack sit out in the open way behind you, which makes it easier for pickpockets to access and also increases the chances you're going to bump into something.

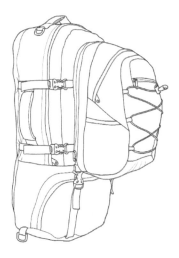

The ability to zip your daypack onto the outside of your main pack seems useful, but you'll find out quickly that it's not very practical. Just toss the daypack inside the main compartment instead.

Even without the daypack on the back, walking with a pack takes some getting used to, since you are now roughly as deep back as you are wide in the shoulders. Turning sideways will no longer make you narrower if you need to get through a crowded or a narrow walkway or similar. Getting onto trains and buses will be some of your most challenging moments in this regard. Adding a daypack that increases this distance only worsens the problem. My recommendation is to take the daypack and get used to packing it into your main backpack compartment or wearing it on your chest.

If you take a travel backpack on your trip, you're frequently going to end up in this configuration. A lot of people point to this and say that person has overpacked, which may be true if they have to do this every time they put on their pack, but in a lot of cases, this is just a useful transition position. If you're about to go through airport security, you're transferring buses, or just waiting to check in at a hotel, this can be a great way to have your daypack out and still comfortably wear your main pack.

One bag variant or attachment you may come across is a metal mesh security bag. This may be built into the bag itself, or it may be a cage that you can put around your bag. This is extreme overkill in my opinion. People who are overly security-conscious will point out that you can use a ballpoint pen to open zippers on bags even if they're locked. Search YouTube for "opening a zipper with a pen" and you'll see what I mean. The only really secure bag, then, is going to be a clamshell suitcase, which means that there is a lip that each side of the suitcase closes into and then one central locking point where you can put a strong lock. Even if you use one of these, though, there is nothing stopping someone from walking away with your entire bag. The metal mesh varieties are meant to give you clamshell bag security on non-suitcase-style bags. The only real thing this is protecting against, however, is someone slashing open the bag, which is extraordinarily rare. I wouldn't bother with these devices and packs because they're heavy and they're solving a problem that typically doesn't exist.

How to Adjust Your Backpack

First, you need to make sure you get the right size pack. The store where you purchase from should be able to help you with this, but what you are doing is measuring the length of your spine and then using that value to adjust the distance between the hip belt and the shoulder straps. There should be lots of diagrams in the user's manual to explain this process, or your bag should have a size chart. Once you have the correct distance set between the hip belt and shoulder strap locations, loosen all the adjustable straps all the way out. All of them! Then put it on your back. Take the hip belt and lock that in front of you and tighten it down almost so much that it hurts. Packs are meant to rest the weight on your hips, not on your shoulders. This is because your legs can carry weight better than your back can. Once your hip belt is as tight as comfortably possible, tighten your shoulder straps just enough that your pack is snug against your shoulders. Then tighten any remaining "load-lifter" straps, which will be connected to the main bag if you have them, in order to secure everything in place and keep the pack close to you. Finally, adjust the sternum strap. The sternum strap should just be tight but not too tight, and it's the one strap you may find yourself continually adjusting for in-the-moment comfort.

SPECIAL GEAR

Depending on your trip and lifestyle, you may need some specialized gear. The previous sections have mentioned gear that you're going to need regardless of where you go, but some destinations and lifestyles require more.

For example, on a trip through Europe, I was trying to train for a marathon that was going to take place six weeks after I returned, so I needed to do my training runs while I was traveling. Because of this, I needed to bring a GPS watch and some synthetic workout clothing. This was in addition to my regular items.

As another example, my trip to Antarctica was going to be much colder than I had ever needed to prepare for compared to any of my other trips. Because it was Antarctica, there was no avoiding freezing temperatures. So I needed a couple of extra layers, including a parka, gloves, a warm hat, waterproof pants for the shell layer, and more. This added an incredible amount of extra bulk to my pack, and I barely managed to fit everything I needed into the 90 L of space in my two bags. That said, I used every single item in my bag during my trip, so it was not a waste.

There are a lot of possibilities here depending on your trip. Your special gear items could include equipment for hiking, camping, scuba diving, rock climbing, snowboarding, video gaming, etc. All of this gear is great *if you're going to use all of it*. If there is even the slightest question in your mind that you're not going to regularly use something during your trip, don't take it.

Let me repeat that again because it's so important.

If there is even the slightest question in your mind that you're not going to regularly use something during your trip, don't take it.

Could you imagine how many bags you would need and how heavy they would be if you took that entire previous list of possible specialty gear with you on a single trip? I could imagine a really active person doing all of those things on a yearlong trip, but if you packed all that gear, you might as well be dragging your entire apartment (flat) along with you. So what is the solution to this if you are planning on doing a ton of specialized stuff? Well, you can usually rent (hire) things as needed. Anywhere known for camping, climbing, snowboarding, or scuba diving is going to have all the things you need, either for rent or purchase. Stay light and rent as much as possible unless you know you're going to be heavily using the special gear you bring. Don't weigh yourself down with what-ifs and maybes.

HOW TO PACK

You have all of your stuff for your trip. Now what? I can't tell you how many times I've seen people digging through their bag like it might as well have been someone else's bag. They don't know where anything is, everything is jumbled together in a huge mess, and their bag is so overpacked that it looks like they're trying to dig through concrete to find anything. They want to find something and they simply can't. That said, it's really easy for you to avoid being this person.

Before you start trying to pack your bag, I suggest sub-packing components of your gear into packing cubes and packing folders. Packing cubes are absolutely amazing and come in all sorts of shapes and sizes. I suggest using a company that designs their cubes to fit together so that things sit nicely in your bag.

In my pack, I use a packing folder for my shirts, a packing cube for my underwear, a packing cube for my socks, and a number of other bags and cubes for things like electronics, my beard trimmer, a miscellaneous odds-and-ends bag, etc.

For my socks and underwear, the cubes I use are double-sided. This allows me to keep clean clothes on one side and dirty clothes on the other. And because the overall contents of the cube aren't changing because a clean item comes out when a dirty item goes in, the cube itself remains the same size throughout my trip, so packing is easier.

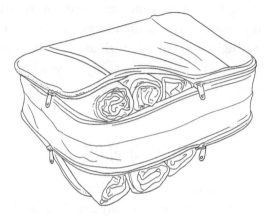

A two-sided packing cube. On one side, keep your clean clothes; on the other side, keep your dirty clothes.

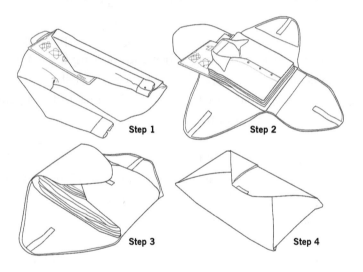

A packing folder. There's a plastic rectangle inside that you fold your clothes around so that your folded clothes match the dimensions of the folder. Then stack everything inside, including the rectangle, and close it up.

Whether you use packing folders or not, you can nicely fold your clothing articles like you normally would, or you can roll them up like a burrito. Both are good approaches, but I've found the burrito rolling is easier to maintain than folding when you're not using cubes. Without being held together by a cube, a stack of folded clothes easily pulls apart in your bag, which can cause your clothes to get wrinkled, or you end up pulling out more things than you wanted to, which leads to constant refolding and repacking.

If you decided on a backpack, you will want to arrange the weight in your bag so that the heaviest items are right behind your shoulder blades and things become less dense radiating outward in your pack. This keeps most of the weight close to your center of gravity, which makes it much easier to move around and walk for long periods of time. As a general rule, keep heavy stuff as close to your body as possible. This is another reason why you don't want your daypack, which is probably filled with water bottles and extra batteries, dangling around on the outside of your pack.

To keep items where they're at inside your bag, lay the bag down, and then make sure you evenly space things out in your pack, starting from the bottom. Once everything is laid out, close the back, and before picking it up, use the cinch straps, if available, on the sides to tighten everything down. This will keep everything in place by not allowing the internal space at the bottom to get bigger and thus cause everything in your pack to fall to the bottom when you pick it up. It's likely you'll have at least two compartments in your pack, so this will also help keep everything in place, but you will need to have items up against each other starting from the bottom of your bag to make sure heavy items don't slide down into the bottom of your pack when it is upright. I recommend putting your clothes in the bottom compartment since they are lightweight and this part of the pack is far away from your shoulder blades. The bulk of the clothes will hold everything else up and the lightest gear is away from your core.

If you decided on a roller bag, then stick the heaviest items closest to the wheels and lighter items near the top. This will move all the weight onto the wheels and out of your hand. It will also keep your bag from toppling over when you aren't holding on to the handle. Don't be that person whose bag flips over onto the ground every time they take their hand off the bag. I see that a lot in airports.

A very important thing to keep in mind is that your larger pack may not be with you at all times. Mainly, this is going to happen on plane flights and long bus rides where your pack will be under the bus. Anytime your luggage is out of your control, you need to be very careful to remove anything of value from your checked bag. I've already warned about not bringing anything you care about losing with you while you travel, but some of the items you bring are still going to be worth stealing. Think electronics, money, and IDs. These items should be placed in your daypack, which will stay with you in these situations. If you're going to sleep, make sure your daypack is secured against you somehow so that it doesn't disappear with all your valuables in it. By secure I mean, place your leg through the back straps and put the bag between your legs, or better yet, wear the bag with the pack facing forward and cross your arms. Essentially, do something that will prevent someone from walking away with your bag or digging around in it while you're asleep.

GEAR COSTS

Getting your pack together will be an up-front cost, but mostly this is an investment in your future life as a world traveler, and you won't regret it if you do it right the first time. With that in mind, realistically speaking, you are likely going to spend anywhere from $1,000 to $2,000 on your packing supplies. I know this sounds expensive if you're starting your first trip, but this up-front cost is hard to avoid. Once you have your gear, though, you never need to buy it again. You'll replace things over time as they wear out or your preferences change, but you won't have to buy everything at once again. Think about it this way: you're taking up a new hobby and need equipment in order to partake.

That being said, you'll need to factor this up-front cost into your trip if this is your first trip, because it will definitely affect your budgeting. Subsequent trips are likely to add another $100–$200 for gear from my experience.

I would also recommend getting your gear together a few months before your trip and then doing a few trial runs of living out of your bag for a couple of days and walking around the block a few times with everything packed. You're almost certainly going to find that you forgot something or need to modify something in your pack. You want to figure these things out before you leave and while you still have access to stores like REI and Amazon, and not when you're in MICs and LICs and can't find things as easily.

THE FORGOTTEN STEP: YOUR LIFE AT HOME WHILE YOU'RE AWAY

This is definitely one of the more annoying parts of preparing for a trip, especially if you're planning on being gone a long time. Banks, families, insurance; no one is really set up to handle someone who doesn't have a fixed address. Considering many people were more nomadic only a few hundred years ago, it's amazing how quickly we've become confused on how to handle travelers.

MAIL

For someone on a short trip, maintaining your at-home life may be as easy as unplugging some small appliances and putting a "mail hold" on your mail. This means the post office holds your mail for a few weeks and delivers the accumulation later at a specified date. Keep in mind that you usually can't do this for more than one month in the US.

For someone on a long trip, this can be much more complicated and may require enlisting the help of some friends or family. If you're keeping your current dwelling for the duration of your trip, they will need to open your mail to notify you of any important issues that arise. If you're not keeping this dwelling during your trip, you may have to use their address as your temporary address for the same purpose. Not having someone check your mail is a recipe for disaster if you miss bills, fraud notices, tax information, etc.

STORING YOUR STUFF

For a short trip, you probably aren't going to rearrange your life significantly, so everything in your life will stay at home. For longer trips, you may want to consider moving out of your residence to go travel. If you're in an apartment (flat), this would mean putting your valuables in a storage unit or someone's garage, or if you're in a house, this may mean renting your house as a furnished residence. If you're going to be gone a really long time, there's no reason to keep paying rent on something you're not using.

If you do plan on using a storage unit, I recommend getting rid of your furniture and downsizing your stuff if you aren't overly attached to these possessions. Storage units are surprisingly expensive, and most books and sentimental items can be converted into a digital format. Replacing furniture can be super cheap if buying used, going to Ikea, or purchasing from discount furniture stores upon your return.

PETS

If you have pets, you'll need someone to take care of them, and for a long trip, this may mean finding temporary new owners. If possible, I highly recommend leaving your animal with someone they are already comfortable with to reduce the stress on everyone. The most important thing here is to be sure to leave them with someone you really trust to take care of them to your standards.

CARS

Cars can be tricky if you're going to be gone a long time. If your car isn't in great condition, maybe selling it is the best course of action. But if your car is running fine and you're not paying an arm and a leg to have it sitting there, holding on to it is probably in your best interest if you plan on coming home eventually. You'll also want to find a friend who doesn't mind staring at your car every day and is located somewhere where your car won't get towed for sitting in the same spot for a long time.

Make sure to add fuel stabilizers to your gas (petrol) tank and follow the directions on the bottle because gas does in fact go bad after one to three months, and it's impossible to fix gas once it's gone bad. Furthermore, trying to remove the gas once it's gone bad becomes a huge hassle.

Note that the battery in your car can also die over time if the car is not started often enough. The solution to all of these car issues is to request a friend drive your car to work once every couple of weeks or so, and that should keep your car in good working order.

SAFE DEPOSIT BOXES

I would also recommend getting a safe deposit box to use while on a longer trip. Put your valuable documents and a backup of your computer in there just in case something happens while you're away. If you are willing to trust the cloud, a cloud backup of your computer can also do nicely and may even be cheaper than a safe deposit box.

INSURANCE, PHONES, ANYTHING THAT IS A MONTHLY ACCOUNT

This is mainly for long trips, but you should consider any recurring accounts you have and how those will be affected by your trip. Anything you don't cancel or pause, you may be paying for unnecessarily. Gym memberships are a prime example of this and many offer "hold" options on their contracts for up to two years.

Medical and car insurance are two major cost items. If your car is going to be parked somewhere and not moving at all, call your insurance company and see if you can get a nonoperational vehicle plan that basically protects your car from someone else causing damage but doesn't cover driving. This will be much cheaper. If you're gone for a long time outside the country, you also probably don't need medical coverage at home in the meantime because you'll be covered by travel insurance while you're gone. Be careful if you are limited by "open enrollment" periods that you don't trap yourself into not having medical insurance upon returning home.

If you aren't going to use your normal mobile phone plan while on the road, you may want to cancel your plan if you aren't locked into a contract. Keeping it could get very expensive because of roaming fees.

Assuming you got your phone unlocked, you should now contact your mobile provider and let them know you do indeed intend on putting a foreign SIM card in your phone. It is especially important to notify them of this in advance because they may flag and lock your account otherwise. Typically, the only people who switch SIM cards out a lot are drug dealers and terrorists, so to avoid the hassle of appearing suspicious, let them know what you're planning. You aren't required to use a foreign SIM card at any point, but you should definitely give warning that it might happen.

Again, gyms, magazines, and similar memberships can be paused or canceled, even for short trips.

If you're keeping a house you own and not renting it out, you'll probably want to turn off your utilities. Don't forget to throw out all of your perishable food items and defrost your fridge and freezer before leaving.

Make sure to also notify your banks around this time that you're about to leave for a trip. You don't want to surprise them and have them think your trip activity on your account is fraudulent and lock your accounts. This can usually be done online and takes only a few minutes.

It's also not a bad idea to check what the maximum withdrawal is per day on your bank card. If the amount is less than $500, I would recommend asking to up the value to $1,000 or $2,000 because you may have to make larger withdrawals if you know you will be going into areas for a while that may not have abundant access to regular resources like ATMs.

RIGHT BEFORE YOU LEAVE

In the week before you leave, there are a few things you should do to prepare for your trip. First, double-check everything about preparing for your trip, and make sure you didn't forget anything.

While you're doing this, start to transition to using your pack to get ready every day. Clothes can be taken from your closet to keep your travel stuff fresh, but check that anything you're picking out of your closet is also present in your packing. You'll find out really quickly if you forgot to pack anything.

You should also double-check all of your internet-connected devices and make sure you are logged into all of the accounts you plan to use on these devices. You may not have internet connectivity for a while after you leave, and if you can't verify some of your credentials online, you may not be able to open and use certain apps properly. If you have accounts that use two-factor text authentication and you know you may be planning to use another SIM card, you may want to turn off two-factor for the duration of your trip.

This is also a good time to set up any security at home if you feel like you need it. Alarms are the obvious security method, but many motion-sensing cameras are available now, and timed electronics are an old trick. Usually, just timing a light is enough to ward any burglar off, but on really long trips, I've also used a FakeTV "burglar deterrent," which is a light that mimics a TV. Setting this kind of device on a timer makes it look like someone really is home.

If you live in a cold-weather area, you may need to worry about pipes freezing, so factor that in as well. If you're going on a really long trip, you may also want to see your friends and family one last time before you go. Don't underestimate how much you can miss home while on the road. These last visits can mean a lot to you later.

PART 4

DURING YOUR TRIP

While so far, this book has been about planning your trip and preparing to get on the road, there are also things that you'll need to know *during* your trip, some of which may be obvious and some of which are not so obvious. Most guidebooks, videos, and travel agents forget to explain how to conduct your trip once you're actually traveling. What now? What are you *actually* supposed to do to get by now that you're traveling?

Most people figure it out eventually but not before having a whole bunch of issues, like food poisoning, having trouble finding medications, or running out of money in a spot with no ATMs, etc.

This part is meant to address the more common concerns that you'll encounter during your travels. Starting out with the knowledge of the things in this section will put you on solid footing right from the beginning of your trip.

For almost the entirety of this section, I will not be referencing the travel archetypes much, and nearly all of the information in this section is written from the perspective of a budgeting backpacker. Why is that? If everyone has different *travel styles* and levels of luxury, why would the viewpoint of a backpacker be the perspective to talk about? The reason is surprisingly simple. Backpackers are working on a shoestring budget, so they tend to do all of their own planning as they go, and they usually stay in cheaper hostel accommodations, which is more involved than staying in hotels. This overall increased "difficulty" means that backpackers are going to have the most concerns to worry about and the most issues to work through compared to any other types of travelers. If you can understand how to get by as a back-packer, any other style of travel will seem easy and streamlined.

If you find something that simply isn't going to apply to you, I would suggest that you read it anyway. It's not that you must travel like a backpacker, but rather, it's important to understand the backpacker's rationale in order to help you know how to handle a particular situation. You never know when this information will come in handy or what situation may happen, so this knowledge is worth knowing.

DAY-TO-DAY LIVING

There are so many things to consider on a day-to-day level while you're actually taking your trip that covering them all is nearly impossible. Plus, each country and every city is going to be slightly different. This section will cover a wide range of common things you may encounter. The following are the key principles, challenges, and concerns that will apply to most day-to-day travel. I will discuss actual safety tips and personal security later, but the challenges that follow next are typically going to be your main concerns during travel. The main thing to remember is that if you do come across something outside of your comfort zone, relax, take a deep breath, and don't worry. Think through the problem and work it out.

LANGUAGE ISSUES

If there's one thing I've consistently seen people get nervous about before their first trip, it's the fear of not being able to communicate with the local people. Even some more experienced travelers who know more than one language feel this when traveling to areas with more difficult languages like China and Russia, where it's hard for most people to even read the language. But in my own experience, even after having been on all seven continents and in many areas where the language isn't even remotely like English, I can assure you, not being able to communicate is mostly a non-concern. Beyond the fact that American English is probably the most common language in the world and is spoken in most places, even in the places where no English is spoken, human beings aren't really so different from each other. Eating is eating, drinking is drinking, buses are buses, trains are trains, and a bed is a bed. We all have the same needs and wants pretty much everywhere on the planet.

Hand waving, or maybe I should say "gesturing," and body language goes a really long way. Ninety percent of your communication isn't what you say but rather your body language and your vocal tone.

There have been many times when I couldn't say or understand something in a country, but either it didn't really matter, or I was able to figure out how to communicate some other way. The only country that has proved exceptionally difficult was China, but that's mainly because their written language consists of 40,000+ characters, and English there is rare. Almost everything needs to be communicated in gestures. That said, you can still get by just fine. I intentionally took a tour in China to ease the difficulties of trying to get between cities by ground travel when I knew I couldn't communicate. By the end of five weeks, I realized I probably would have been just fine utilizing the locals at the front desk of my hostels to help write out what transportation I needed and then could have used book-ing counters like anywhere else in the world. Everything inside the cities, with the use of my guidebook, was easy to get through, under-stand, and navigate. Also in China, most tourist-heavy areas tended to have restaurant menus with pictures, so no problem there either. Even if a restaurant didn't have a picture menu, I would look around a bit and point at something I was interested in and then gesture to my server. Easy.

Russia and India were the same way, and I thought those countries were going to be problematic as well. That said, I did appreciate having a guide in all three of these places initially to help me figure out what was going on around me. But in the end, gesturing and body language were all that I needed. I only speak English, some German, and a little Japanese, and using a translator has never really been necessary for more than fifty countries of travel. You're going to be fine if you don't speak the language at one of your destinations, I promise.

Even if you can't speak the local language at all, everyone will understand what you mean by saying in English "thank you" with an appreciative gesture and it shows you care about the people there. Don't be afraid to do this. Remember, most of your communication is not what you're saying, so smiling, nodding, waving, or saying an English "thank you" will be understood even if they don't speak English, just because of the body language involved.

That said, when you arrive in an area with an unfamiliar language, learning the words for "hello," "thank you," "yes," and "no" will go a long way in feeling more accepted by the locals.

Even if everything breaks down while you're trying to communicate with someone, relax, stay calm, and don't worry if you can't entirely understand. Just try a different method to explain something. For example, in my early travels, I often took notebooks around with me to jot notes on. If I needed to, I could draw a picture as a last resort. Your phone can also be used for this purpose.

If you are trying to speak English and it's not working, do not raise your voice and speak really slowly. People aren't stupid, and speaking really loudly isn't likely to make them understand you any better. They will understand that you're being rude, even if they can't understand what you're saying. If communication isn't working, speak a bit slower and remove any slang from your speech. Use simple language and common words and don't be condescending in any way.

I was talking with some Americans during my travels and as a response to something in the story being told, someone said, "They let the cat out of the bag!" then the next person said, "They spilled the beans!" and the last person said, "Oh wow, they showed their hand!" This is a really good example of what makes English so hard to understand for non-native speakers. So much of what we say is colloquial slang and not really proper English. If you don't speak English very well, what do those phrases even mean? If you speak like this, it's going to make communicating much more difficult while traveling. What you should say instead is something more like, "They told a secret." That is not slang and is much easier to understand by everyone. Avoiding contractions can also help.

Also, don't assume everyone speaks English. It just isn't the case. If I need to talk to someone and think they may speak English, I will usually walk up and look at them questioningly and say, "English?" If they say "okay" or "yes," go ahead. You may find out really quickly that English isn't going to work, and if you had just spoken English to begin with, you seem rather rude. You're in another country, so their language prevails. Be respectful of this.

One last thing, Google Translate is an excellent app for traveling. You can use this offline by downloading the language through the "offline translation" menu. Not only is it good for looking up single words and really simple sentences, but it can also be held up to written language like signs or packaging to give you a live translation using your phone's camera. It should be noted, however, that longer sentences typically do not translate very well. Sometimes a single word is all that's necessary to ask for something or make something clear, and Google Translate can help with that quite a bit.

CULTURAL ISSUES (MISUNDERSTANDINGS)

Cultural issues are situations like being in Japan and upon meeting someone, you throw out a hand for a handshake, and the Japanese person bows. Culture is so ingrained in your daily behavior that you may not realize where the culture is within yourself until you're in another culture and there's a mix-up. Much of human behavior is pretty similar across the world, so this further complicates trying to identify where the culture starts and human behavior ends. You will experience things like different gestures, variations on personal space, and different bathing habits. When you notice someone is doing something different than you would expect, take a mental note. There is a really good chance that what they are doing is what is normal for that part of the world. And if you do something and notice some startled reactions, take note of what you just did. Watch what others are doing in the same situation or ask a local what happened when you get a chance.

It will be very obvious in the majority of the world that you are a foreigner, so even if you do something weird, most people will be fairly understanding, even if you accidentally do something that's offensive. If people are consistently doing something that you find offensive, chances are, there's something you aren't aware of in that culture and it would be a good idea to ask someone about it.

Cultural differences can be some of the most interesting, mind-expanding, beautiful things you come across while traveling. Not all the culture norms you come across will be very different from your own, but some of them definitely are, and that's arguably the main reason most people travel abroad at all. They want to explore and see different ways of doing things than what they know at home.

Some things you come across may actually annoy you, but remember, this is why you're traveling, to see and experience these things. You don't have to like everything you come across, but don't get caught in the trap of thinking someone's culture should be more like yours if you find something personally distasteful.

The following are some examples of cultural differences I've experienced.

Awesome things:

- The vast amount of respect for all the gods of the world (India)

- The respect for the finite lifetime of things and trying to make the most of that time (Japan)

- The desire for everyone to have a fair chance in life (Australia)

- The extreme environmental respect of explorers (Antarctica)

- The love of life that seems to be second nature to everyone (Barcelona, Spain)

Examples of misunderstandings from my German/American perspective as I've come across during my travels:

- People swooping in front of you in lines (queues) (India)

- The dislike of tattoos and banning people with tattoos from spas (Japan)

- The stone-cold interactions of the older population (Russia)

- Babies and toddlers openly pooping on sidewalks (China)

- Spending ten minutes each buying tickets to a museum (Italy)

I travel to see all these kinds of things, and I'm thankful to have seen all of them, because it opens my eyes as to the possibilities around the world. Even if you realize you have made a cultural error, don't worry about it too much. People will read into your body language and verbal tone much more so than what you actually did. So if you were well-meaning and trying to be tactful but still made a mistake anyway, people will forgive you and it won't be a big deal. Just be apologetic and make corrections the next time.

TOURS

The tours discussed in this section are not the larger organized trips across a country or region. If you're looking to take a tour that organizes a large chunk of your trip, this should have been coordinated before you arrived at your travel destination. It's likely you won't be able to join those types of tours while you're already on your trip. Check out the planning sections again for more multi-week tour descriptions and discussions. The tours covered in this section are a few days or less, or even a few hours or less, and will pop up frequently during your travels. These types of tours are usually only bookable while you're at your destination.

For anything wilderness or mountain related, I highly recommend going on a guided tour. You don't want to get lost, and a lot of times, the guides will be so good at noticing plant and animal life that they will greatly enrich your experience. Some places, like climbing an active volcano, which I did in Antigua, Guatemala, should only be done with a guide and should not be attempted alone because of the obvious dangers.

On the other hand, tours of museums may or may not be in your interest. There is usually a lot of information in the museum and online, so paying for a guide may be redundant. I would recommend this kind of tour be reserved for something you're really interested in or about which you would like to ask lots of questions. That being said, audio tours are a good option in museums and at other cultural sights if you're very interested in detailed information, and they can be done at your own pace.

Booking any kind of tour can be somewhat of a challenge because there are a lot of scammers out there who are just waiting to take advantage of unknowing travelers. You can avoid nearly any issue with tours by not booking any tour from an individual who approaches you on the street. Yes, they may be offering you a huge discount on your tour, but it might be because your tour is going to be substandard and may not even be what you want. I suggest that you try to book tours through your accommodation because they'll know who runs reputable tours. If they don't book directly, they'll know someone reputable to help you.

If you're booking a tour at a museum, ask the museum employees for a tour guide, and don't trust the people standing around the entrance who offer you tours. Many times, these "guides" hanging around, especially in India, are just regular people effectively begging by telling you something they made up and then they expect money for their time. Pretty much universally in India, you are not required to have a guide to tour anything, so don't believe the friendly face that suddenly appears trying to usher you through everything. Very firmly say you don't need a guide and walk away.

Also, although they are sometimes reputable, I would caution you to also be careful of so-called "tour organizers" in small shops. Again, I recommend booking through your accommodation. If your specific accommodation can't help you with booking, go to another hostel or hotel and book your tour there.

MONEY/ATMS

It goes without saying that traveling around with a bunch of cash money on you is a bad idea. In the unlikely event you were to become a victim of theft or robbery, you could stand to potentially lose a lot of money. Thankfully, pretty much the entire world now operates on the same type of ATM system. You should have already contacted your bank before your trip to let them know you're planning on traveling and using your ATM card abroad, and now all you need to do is find an ATM to access your money.

Using an ATM abroad is pretty much the same as using an ATM at home, and usually, there will be an English option when you first stick your card in the machine. If there is no English option, it's usually pretty easy to figure out what to do because there aren't too many options on an ATM. One thing to note is that foreign ATMs will always show your account balances in the local currency, so beware of this in order to monitor your finances appropriately. If you notice that you can't withdraw your money, look around at the ATM signage. In many parts of the world, they have "withdrawal only" and "deposit only" ATMs. Some ATMs want a six-digit PIN, and if this happens to you and you have a four-digit PIN, add two zeros to the beginning of your PIN.

The only weird problem I've had finding ATMs has been in Japan, where, up until recently, only the post office ATMs were connected to the international network, meaning you could only make withdrawals at the post office. But more recently, convenience stores have started allowing this as well. Be aware that convenience stores will charge enormous fees for using their ATMs. This isn't a problem if your travel account waives non-network ATM fees but can add up quickly otherwise.

I usually pull out around $400–$500 USD worth of the local currency at a time and then live off of this for roughly one to two weeks during my travels. This way, I'm never loaded down with too much money, but I also don't need to constantly keep going to the ATM.

Do not keep all of the money you withdraw on you. When you go to an ATM, try to do it when you are able to immediately go back to your room. Drop off the bulk of the money with your passport into your locked bag or locker, and then take two to three days' worth of money out and put it into your pocket. Split the money you carry on you into more than one pocket, just in case something falls out of your pocket, you get pickpocketed, or you get robbed. You don't want to be stuck somewhere without any cash. It also hides how much money you have on you because you're not pulling it all out at once.

If you're about to head into a remote area or an area with very small villages, take out a little extra money before going. These places may not have an ATM and you don't want to find this out when you run out of money.

Be aware also that your bank account has a maximum withdrawal amount per day. This is usually $500 or $1,000 (or pounds or euros), but it's not a bad idea to be aware of the maximum so that you'll be aware if you try to withdraw too much.

When I drop off my ATM money in my room, which means either putting money in my locker or my main pack, I also drop off my ATM card. That said, I do carry around a credit card with me during the day. It's much easier to dispute fraudulent charges on a credit card than it is on an ATM card in the unlikely event your card and PIN are taken from you.

Credit cards are accepted very commonly in some countries like Australia and the UK, but in most countries, they are not the norm, so don't expect to pay for small things with credit cards. That said, most major hotels will take credit cards, and some hostels will do the same. I try to never count on credit cards and operate mostly on cash. You never know when your card may be rejected.

One thing to note when paying for things with cards is if you are presented with an option of paying in the local currency or your home currency, always choose to pay in the local currency. What happens in the background if you choose to pay in your home currency is that a third party does the currency exchange into the local currency and then charges you a significant fee to do so. Either way, you're paying in the local currency, but if you choose to pay with a local currency option, your bank is the party doing the conversion, and this is going to be much more favorable to you than any third-party conversion rate will be.

You may wonder how to deal with remaining extra currency when leaving a country, or first getting currency when arriving in a country. My typical practice is to have about $100 extra in my bag just in case I need to do an emergency conversion or payment. Once I get into the airport or other point of entry, I try to find an ATM to access my money. I will likely need local currency to even get transportation to my accommodation. If I can't find an ATM, I can convert some of my $100 to get to my destination. If I have any leftover currency from my previous country, I will convert that to local currency in my new country since it is no longer useful to me. Most currency conversion places have high fees, especially in airports, and they almost never take coins. I recommend you try and get rid of your coins before you leave a country. Currency traders don't want to deal with a bunch of heavy, low-value coins.

Note: Conversion rates are usually not as favorable from ATMs as they are directly from your home bank, so it is usually cheaper to get foreign currency from your bank before leaving for your trip. Many people in the US do not realize this is a service available to them, so be sure to use it when you can. That said, carrying around money for ten different countries is a bad idea for many reasons already mentioned. If you do get money in advance of your trip, only do it for a reasonable quantity for the first country and then ATM as necessary throughout your trip. Be sure to check the details of how your bank's fees and conversions work to ensure you're getting the best deal. A fraction of a percent or a single-digit ATM fee may not seem like a lot on paper, but over the course of a long trip, it can add up to thousands of dollars.

Also be aware, some countries like Mongolia, Albania, and Zambia have currencies that are not internationally traded. This is going to be fairly uncommon during your travels, but if you leave a country that doesn't have a traded currency and still have their currency, you will not be able to exchange it anywhere at that point. Check on this by talking to the currency traders in airports before you arrive in any less-common tourist destinations, especially in Eastern European and African nations. Many Eastern European countries now use the euro as the European Union continues to grow, but the further east you travel, the more likely you are to run into non-traded currencies.

Another thing to be aware of with your money is that in many countries, ATMs will give you currency in denominations that are much larger than what most people typically use going about their day-to-day life. This creates issues for local vendors when they attempt to give you change. Many times, you will be refused a purchase because the shop owner simply doesn't have enough money on hand to break your bill. This is incredibly annoying because the ATM forced those bills onto you, and there's no way around it. My strategy for this is to always use my bigger bills at places handling more money, like hotels, hostels, museums, big grocery stores, etc. This will give you smaller bills to use at other places. Be prepared for looks, even in more frequented locations, where the teller will ask if you have smaller bills. The best way to try and work around this is just to say, "No, sorry, that's the smallest bill I have." Or just say "Sorry" in the local language if the bill size seems to be a problem. If they can't accept your currency, you can always use smaller notes at that time.

On an interesting side note, Europe had a 500 euro bill for many years, but it was so absurdly large compared to any daily transaction of money that almost no one could ever break it. Because of this, the only people who ever used these notes were tourists and terrorists. Tourists would be incredibly frustrated trying to deal with these notes, and terrorists loved them because they were compact. As such, this bill ended up getting the nickname the "bin Laden" and has been slated for discontinuation because of these issues.

Also, if you are paying for something that was quoted in dollars, usually rooms or a tour, but you pay in the local currency because that's what you have available, make sure you check the currency conversion. If it's less than 10 percent off from the official conversion rate, I would just accept it, but I have caught situations where the conversion rate was off by 200 percent or more! One example was trying to pay for a room in South America. My bill was listed as about $100 through Hostel World and the local conversion rate was about seven pesos to one USD. The bill I got was more than 1,500 pesos, which is clearly wildly off. Had the math not been fairly easy on this conversion, I might not have caught this. Make sure to double-check any conversions.

EATING

Food is fairly easy to find almost everywhere in the world. Yelp is good for finding restaurants, but it is not very popular with locals in most of the world. Depending on where you are, there may be fewer reviews and mostly they will be from other travelers. Surprisingly, Google Maps is an excellent tool for finding good places to eat; however, you need to be online to get restaurant reviews and information, even if you have the local map downloaded offline.

If you don't have internet access and are looking for food, I highly recommend going a few blocks away from touristy areas. The food that is right next to or in touristy areas tends to be very low quality and very expensive. This is because tourists are constantly flocking in as they walk by, so the restaurants have very little incentive to offer quality food because these locations are in demand. A few blocks away, however, you will likely find higher quality food for a better cost. You are also much more likely to be supporting the locals by eating at these locations.

My personal pro tip for choosing where to eat is to always look for places with a lot of locals in them because they know what's good and what isn't. Street food can also be some of the most amazing food you try while traveling, but again, always eat at places where many locals appear. Street food stalls are notorious for being the places where people get food poisoning while traveling, also known as "traveler's diarrhea." More about that in the "Medical Issues and General Hygiene" section.

In some countries, people really like to take their time while eating meals, and if you're trying to see many things during the day, a two-hour meal can really impact your plans. Be aware of this and look around before you sit down to see if people at your restaurant of choice look like they're settled in for a while. If they do, you may be there a while, too. Street food tends to be fairly quick. I personally try to choose faster options during the day to maximize my available time during the core nine-to-five business hours, but that means I tend to grab fast food or street food for lunch and eat breakfast at my hostel. There's no wrong answer with food. Just be aware of your choices.

If you're trying to minimize your trip costs, cooking your own meals can go a long way because it's one of your main expenses after transportation and accommodation. Hostels usually have kitchens that you can use, but double-check that during booking. Using cooking gear designed for camping is also possible but probably only usable at actual campsites. Many hostels or hotels aren't going to want you firing up an open flame on a balcony or sidewalk. As for the actual food to cook, grocery stores and markets exist everywhere in the world but may have differing hours of operation and may have wildly different options than what you're used to at home. I do not cook my own meals almost ever during travel, and I'll talk about why shortly in the "Hostel Basic Procedures and Etiquette" section.

TIPPING

Some countries tip, some don't, some tip sometimes, and sometimes there are different rules depending on who you're tipping. Tipping is inconsistent, depending on where you go. The best way to deal with this is to ask your accommodation what the normal tipping policies are. I would ask about bartenders, waitstaff at restaurants, and taxis since all of these could be different.

You can also download apps, one called Global Tip Pro, on your smartphone that provides global tipping calculations, and this will at least give you a rough guess on what is appropriate. In general, the numbers in Global Tip Pro only apply to restaurants.

Many countries "round up" for tips, but this is imprecise and can be nerve-racking for someone used to percentage-based tips. The idea here is that if your meal is forty-six, just give them a fifty. Or if it's thirty-seven, give a forty. It's when the tip is a thirty-four and you give thirty-five that it seems weird, but this is normal. A lot of places that round up suggest to "leave the coins" that come with your change, which is pretty self-explanatory. Don't worry if leaving the coins doesn't seem like a lot. You have to keep in mind that in many countries, the coins are full dollar amounts, too.

Most tour guides, even if you paid for a tour through someone else, will be hoping for a tip at the end of the tour, but this is not required. If you choose, 10 percent of the tour cost is usually a good amount.

Ship crews traditionally also get tips, but usually the ship officers will recommend what they think is normal, and the officers usually do not partake in any of the tips.

Be aware that anyone who helps you move your bags around will be expecting a tip as well. This is particularly true for resort travelers and in MICs and LICs.

For cabs and private drivers, it's usually customary to leave some small tip to the driver, but this is not always required. Look for more local info on this.

HAGGLING

In many parts of the world, there is no such thing as a fixed price for something. Everything is bought through price negotiation, bartering, or haggling. Frankly, I can't stand haggling. Trying to go through this dance of arguing about a price is just a waste of my time and I'd rather be doing something else. But if you see something you want and you're in a haggling system, you will have to haggle or you'll end up paying a ridiculous price.

A big trick with haggling is to never say yes to the first price. You should also be aware that most vendors who are haggling will see you as a big fat bank account that's ripe for them to take advantage of, so their prices are going to be three to five times what they should be to start. But severely undercutting them is generally seen as rude. I personally like to keep saying "too much" and start walking away after a while to see how far down they'll go. Be aware that if you say a price and they agree to this price, you have essentially committed to buying the item, and walking away at this point will be seen as extremely hostile and rude. Try really hard not to get caught in this situation, and never say a price that you aren't ready to pay.

Also be aware that you should inspect any item you're interested in buying. Sometimes people will refuse to take it back and act like you've already agreed to purchase the item at this point. If you end up in this situation, lay the item down on the ground and walk away from it.

I wanted to buy some elephant keychains in India and the kid I was trying to buy them from kept insisting they were high-quality metal. Well, it turned out they were chrome-plated plastic. Once I figured this out after inspecting them, he didn't want to take them back, so I laid them down and walked away. He kept insisting on a price of around ten dollars, and I kept insisting on a price of around three dollars. After twenty minutes of him following me around and me continually quoting my three-dollar price in rupees, he finally agreed to a deal. The whole time, however, he kept insisting these were high-quality metal keychains, which they certainly were not. Be prepared for these kinds of shenanigans.

Most smaller items will fall under these rules, but sometimes expensive items can get almost silly with price negotiation. In many countries, it almost seems like it's required that if you take a tour that requires transportation, they're going to take a side trip to some "luxury" factory of tourist trinkets marked up to eye-popping sticker prices. One such place that I ended up in while in China had many paintings for $10,000+. One painting was marked for $15,000, and a guy in my group was trying to be cute and offered $1,000. The staff immediately went "OK." The "oh crap" look on his face at this instant price acceptance was priceless. He remained cool, though, and said, "Let me discuss this with my family to make sure they are okay with this," and then proceeded to call his family in Germany. None of the staff knew what he was saying in German, so he got off the phone a few minutes later and said, "Sorry, the family has already purchased another piece to fill where this would have gone." Since I speak some German, I could hear his phone conversation that he was just asking his parents how they were doing as a distraction. I was laughing listening to all of this. At this point, I offered $100 for a photocopy of the painting and the staff was mortally offended at this, saying, "Our clients like things to be original." I laughed and said "Well, I don't care if everyone here has a copy of it. I just think it's pretty. I don't need the original." That response got more offended looks.

The point remains, though, be careful. Make sure things are authentic. Make sure they are priced properly and negotiate thoroughly.

TOILETS

This is one aspect of travel that most people dread but probably shouldn't. Trying to handle your business while you're on the road can seriously fray some nerves. Imagine needing to poop really, really badly, then having to hold it for a long time until you get to a toilet, and then discovering this toilet is essentially a hole in the ground with wooden slats on each side. What are you going to do? Wait for another three to four hours for the next "toilet"? Probably not.

If this thought has never occurred to you, maybe you're rethinking your travel plans right now. Hold on, though. It's not a big deal. Read this section and physically practice what I'm going to describe here. The techniques aren't difficult, but you don't want to be standing there trying to figure this out for the first time when you actually need to do it for real.

There are three types of toilets in the world. The first is the "Western" toilet, which is the porcelain throne that most of you reading this book are probably familiar with. The second is the "squat" toilet which can have a bunch of variations ranging from a porcelain pill kind of shape embedded into a tile floor, to literally a dirt hole with a piece of wood on each side of the hole. The third is a camping toilet, i.e., doing your business out in open nature.

Western Toilet Variations

I think you probably understand how to use a Western toilet. What maybe isn't as obvious while traveling is that you may not be given toilet paper or soap. You should always have toilet paper and soap on you while traveling in MICs and LICs for this exact reason. Usually, you will not have to worry about this in HICs, but anywhere else is a different story.

Also note, in some HIC Asian countries, you may see people handing out flyers next to metro stations. Take a really close look to see if these are actually packets of toilet paper. This was an interesting system that I saw in Japan, where the toilets in the stations don't have any toilet paper, so companies hand out "flyers" to advertise their wares, but these are really packets of toilet paper. By doing this, they're guaranteeing that people will take the flyers and probably read them. Pretty smart, but still, don't end up without toilet paper in these countries. Take a flyer or two just in case if you're not already carrying around some toilet paper.

Be aware, there are some variants of the Western toilet. I have seen one of those variations only in parts of Germany, and I call this the "German shelf toilet." Rather than being a bowl shape, the toilet has a flat ledge and there is a hole with standing water toward the front. Upon seeing this the first time, most people assume that despite the odd shape that this toilet works identically to a regular Western toilet. They're correct, but as they soon find out, if you don't place some toilet paper down on the shelf before taking a poop, all the flushing water that runs over the shelf just runs around the poop. Then they have to awkwardly flush about twenty times to finally clean up their mess. It's easy to avoid this problem if you run across one of these toilets, though. Just lay down a couple of strips of toilet paper first and you're good to go.

For another variant, toilets in Japan typically have an electronic panel, kind of like an arm on an armchair that contains all sorts of options for using the toilet. They've made going to the bathroom a luxury experience with heated seats, the ability to play audio of flushing water sounds, a bidet attachment, and some other stuff. The main concern you will have is that the button to flush is typically on this panel and not on the toilet itself. Usually, this is going to be the biggest button.

Another Japanese variant is to have a sink on top of the toilet. When you flush, clean water is pumped up through the faucet on top of the toilet, and the water falls into the tank through the drain for use in the next flush. This means you have about thirty seconds to wash your hands while the tank refills. This may seem a little odd, but in my opinion, it's an ingenious way of conserving water.

An extra last thing I should mention is the bidet. I have only once seen a separate bidet fixture in a European bathroom, but sometimes you see a bidet option on the Japanese electronic toilets. Basically, this is a water jet to clean your butt after using the bathroom. By no means are you required to use this, but if you're curious, experiment around. There are some funny YouTube videos about this, and it seems like about half of the people who try a bidet love it. Your mileage may vary.

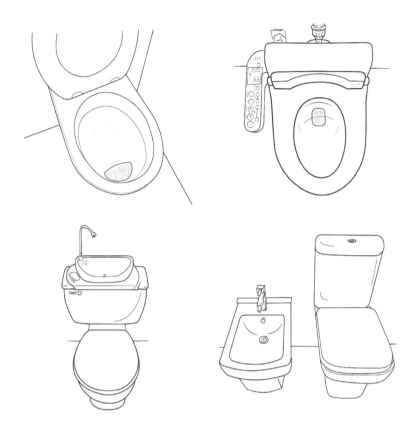

Top left: The German shelf toilet. Top right: The Japanese control console.
Bottom left: A sink for washing your hands on the top when you flush.
That is indeed clean water for washing your hands. Bottom right: A bidet.

Squat Toilets

As for the squat toilet, it amuses me still, even after all of my travels, how much fear, confusion, and dread the squat toilet inspires. I have also heard a number of stories of inexperienced squat toilet use "accidents." But I'll be honest, when faced with my first unavoidable squat toilet experience, it took me a few minutes to figure out what to do, and I found out later, when talking to a Chinese local, that I hadn't been using the toilet correctly. I found even more confusion later in India regarding their squat toilet "utensils" and then had a local Indian clear up even more about squat toilets and their procedures.

So let me clear up everything right here—it's really not so bad.

Here is the procedure for using a squat toilet:

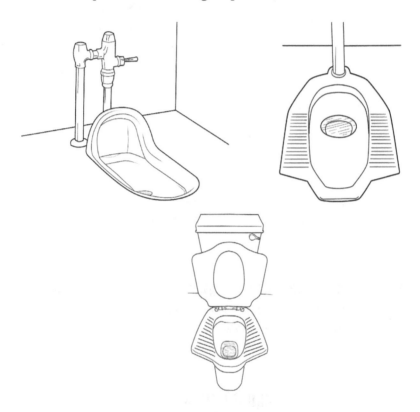

Top left and top right: These are the two most common kinds of squat toilets you'll see. For the one on the left, you'll face towards the raised part by the flushing hardware, and for the one on the right, you'll face the other way, outward away from the flushing hardware. Bottom: This is a hybrid toilet. You can put the seat down and use it like a Western toilet or you can leave the seat up and use it like a squat toilet. You'll face the same direction, away from the water tank either way on this toilet.

1. Premise: You have some sort of hole in the ground that is not a Western toilet.

2. If there is any sort of protrusion from the ground at one end of the toilet "depression," this is going to be the direction you face and is the direction where any flushing water will drain towards. If there's not a protrusion, look for the drain and face your rear toward that end. Any business you do will be toward the drain end already if you're facing this way. If there's no flushing system, you can face either direction and that's fine.

3. Don't do anything with your clothes yet, but stand over the hole, one foot on one side, one foot on the other. Any business you do is going to come out right behind the line that connects the back of your feet, so plant your feet accordingly.

4. Unzip your pants (trousers) or shorts, or hike up your skirt/dress.

5. With the exception of the skirt/dress getting hiked up, lower any pants (trousers) or underwear (pants) type garments down past your knees. No need to push them all the way down and you don't want to since your clothes will be almost in the hole, but just past the knees is fine.

6. Now squat. And I don't mean hover. Sit your butt down all the way as far as you can. If you weightlift, bottom out in what's known as an "ass-to-grass squat." Be careful not to fall backwards, especially if you are still wearing any sort of backpack as this will affect your center of gravity.

7. If any muscle is engaged from the waist down, you're not squatting, you're hovering. You should be totally relaxed and in a full squat.

8. Do your business.

9. Clean up (mentioned in detail later).

After cleaning up, all you do is stand up and put your clothes back on. This process should help you stay comfortable the whole time you're using the toilet. There's no risk of getting poo on yourself or anything else because of how you're aligned in the full squat position, and nothing should fall out of your front or back pockets either because they're below your knees, which means all you did was push them down, not turn them upside down during the squatting motion.

Note: This is why pushing your clothes past your knees is important. If your pockets are above your knees and then you fully squat, you are turning your pockets upside down, and the contents are now going straight into the toilet/hole.

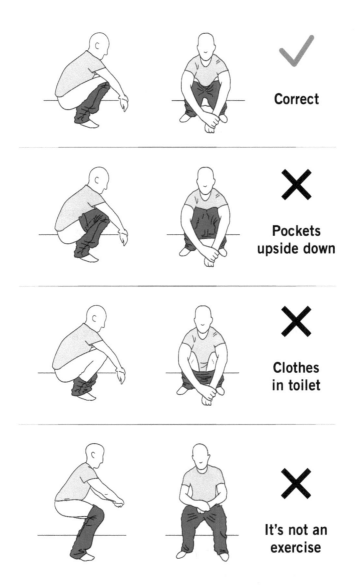

		✓ **Correct**
		✕ **Pockets upside down**
		✕ **Clothes in toilet**
		✕ **It's not an exercise**

The correct squat toilet position and the common squat toilet positioning mistakes.

Advanced Squat Toilet Technique

Now, before I talk about cleaning up, there's actually an advanced technique for this process that I learned in China.

If you know you're going to be spending some time using a squat toilet, there's an inherent problem in our human anatomy that for most people, your knees are going to bend so much while squatting that you're going to pinch off the arteries behind your knees that are allowing blood to flow to your legs. After a couple of minutes, your legs are going to start going numb and this can get uncomfortable really quickly. Hovering only works for maybe another minute while your thighs set on fire, and then you're left with the only option of standing up with a soiled butt, and no one should attempt that. That's a really good way to end up with poop on your pants.

So instead, keep the arteries in your legs open. Follow this procedure when you're about to squat down and know you're going to be there a while:

1. Lean forward a bit so that you're sort of looking at your legs.

2. Put your hands behind the back of your legs and grab one wrist with your other hand.

3. Now squat down slowly, and keep your forearms behind your calves. Your body weight at the bottom should now be resting on your forearms. Your arms should be smashed between your thighs and calves just a little back from the back of your kneecaps.

4. Now relax your whole body; it's really easy to tense up in this position.

You can stay in this position for quite some time to do your business. You've essentially left a space behind your knees for your blood to keep flowing.

The advanced squat toilet position. Look at your feet and grab a wrist behind your knees like on the left, then squat down and end up in the position in the right two images.

Cleanup

Cleanup in squat toilets can be a bit more challenging. Sometimes there's a hose, sometimes there's a bucket with water, sometimes there's toilet paper, sometimes there's nothing. Sometimes the toilet flushes, sometimes it doesn't. Generally, this is the order you should think about this:

1. If there's a flushing handle, you will be using that to flush the toilet.

2. If there's toilet paper, use it.

3. If there's no toilet paper, there's probably something that produces water, so you'll be using that. This may also be your flushing method.

4. If none of the above are true, you're probably over a hole dug in the ground, and hopefully, you brought toilet paper with you because there aren't many options left at this point.

You may have noticed I mentioned a water source that isn't for flushing. This took me a long time and some extraordinarily awkward Q&A sessions to figure out. I have just used my on-hand toilet paper in that situation, but the method the locals use is not something you're going to want to hear.

The water-only procedure is this:

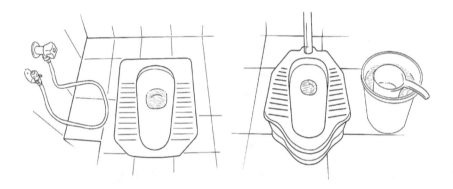

Left: A hose with a little holder on the wall. Right: A bucket with a scooper floating inside. In either case, the water does not go directly on your backside; it goes on your hands and into the toilet while you're cleaning yourself.

1. From the squat position, get some water started and pouring into the toilet with the hose, OR get water ready with whatever water scooper is present in the bucket.

2. ***DO NOT attempt to spray or pour water directly onto your butt. All you are going to do is get your clothes and shoes really wet and you're going to get poop everywhere.***

3. Instead, pour some water onto your hand.

4. Reach back and use a finger or two to wipe the poop off your butt.

5. Rinse hand as necessary and repeat step 3.

6. Rinse your hand at the end and clear the remaining visible poop.

7. Turn off water or replace water scooper.

8. Stand up. Put clothes on.

9. Grab water again and rinse waste into the drain as needed.

10. Then wash your hands very, very, very thoroughly afterward!

This is where that "don't use the left hand" for anything legend comes from. Without soap, this method is an excellent way to spread disease, and even with soap, this method is generally pretty crappy in my opinion (see what I did there?). Keep in mind, this is how most of the locals are cleaning up if that's what you see around town, which is why it's important to make sure that you eat only at reputable food establishments.

I mostly add this for comedic value, but there's one last way to clean yourself up if you're desperate, and you can find many sites and videos on this method if you search the internet for "how to wipe your ass with one sheet of toilet paper." Basically:

1. Fold the square in half, and then in half the other way, and rip off a tiny bit of the corner that is the center of the square. Hold on to this removed bit.

2. Unfold the square. You should now have a single square with a little hole in the middle.

3. Stick one finger through the hole.

4. Remove all poop from your butt using this finger.

5. When done, grab the square and fold it up around over your finger, and drag this off your finger in order to remove all poop from your finger.

6. Dispose of this square immediately.

7. Use the removed little bit of tissue from the center to clean under your fingernail.

8. Dispose of this little bit immediately.

Hopefully, you will never have to use this method.

If you are in a place that uses toilet paper but you're not supposed to flush it, you will see a trash can or other receptacle next to the toilet that contains soiled toilet paper. There will usually also be a sign saying, "Don't flush the toilet paper." If this is the case, please respect the locals so they don't have to call a plumber. After you wipe, throw your soiled toilet paper in the provided trash bin.

It's worth noting also that many places that require toilet paper trash cans, usually in Latin America, also do not have toilet seats. This seems revolting at first, but it's totally a mental thing. As long as the toilet is clean, a seat versus bare porcelain is the same thing. The porcelain hole is typically larger than a seat hole, though, so you'll have to lean on one butt cheek instead of just sitting, but you're just as clean as you would normally be. Don't freak out when you come across this; you'll be okay just like all the locals.

Camp Style

One last thing to mention is toilet use when camping. This is the same procedure as the squat toilet. You just have to make your own hole. To do this, dig a hole about one palm-width deep, and at least thirty feet (ten meters) away from any water source, and then use the squat toilet procedure. In this case, however, you likely have all the twigs and/or rocks in the world to wipe. After, toss everything in your hole, and when done, cover it back up with the material you dug out. It's usually camp etiquette to take two even-sized twigs and cross them over your covered hole so that someone else doesn't accidentally dig the hole up while it's still fresh.

Handwashing

For handwashing, make sure you check out what the situation in your bathroom is before you use the toilet. If you're at an outhouse, which has happened to me, there's not going to be any place to wash your hands, but this is no problem. You should have liquid soap in your daypack and water to drink if you're in a locale where this might happen. Bring both of those items with you for after you finish in the outhouse.

Hand sanitizer is potentially an option, but this is just something else you need to lug around. Hand sanitizer will not eliminate things off your hands. It just kills any bacteria and spreads around whatever is left. If you actually want to get your hands clean, use soap and water and skip the hand sanitizer.

Also, you should definitely always wash your hands. This is the single, number one best thing you can do to prevent sickness and disease. More on that in the "Medical Issues and General Hygiene" section.

Here's what to do to wash your hands without any sink or running water:

1. Use only one hand to clean yourself at the toilet.

2. Get out of the toilet and either go to open ground, away from water sources if you're camping, or to a sink even if it doesn't have running water.

3. Take the lid off your water with your clean hand and get a good mouthful of water, but don't swallow it.

4. Close up your water with your clean hand.

5. Use your clean hand now to open your soap bottle and put soap on the dirty hand.

6. Close up your soap with the clean hand.

7. Now, at the same time, wash your hands with the soap while very slowly spitting the water out of your mouth and onto your hands. One mouthful of water should be plenty to completely wash and clear any soap off of your hands.

8. Dry your hands by air, clothes, or something else.

9. Hand sanitizer at this point is good for killing off any mouth bacteria on your hands.

These are the common bathroom procedures. You won't really find any other bathroom situations than this, and it shouldn't feel scary if you follow the described steps. Again, please practice first. You'll be fine. After all of my travels so far, I don't really have a preference for either Western or squat toilets anymore. They're all just toilets to me now.

In terms of finding toilets, you shouldn't have too much of an issue. People live everywhere and people need toilets, so you should almost always be surrounded by toilets. You just need to find them. Usually, the universal male and female bathroom symbols, and the universal triangle and circle symbols, are just about everywhere. The other common but less obvious sign for toilets is "WC," which is short for "water closet," and in Hispanic areas, baño.

HOSTEL BASIC PROCEDURES AND ETIQUETTE

The first time in a hostel can be a confusing experience. Let's walk through a typical experience from check-in to check-out.

Let's say you arrive on your shuttle, train, or taxi at your hostel of choice. Head on in and talk to the person at the front desk.

Check-in and Payment

In order to check in, you're going to need to show them your passport and then pay for your room. If for some reason you don't have enough local currency, most hostels will take what you have and then you can pay the rest later after visiting an ATM. If you don't have any local currency at all, they'll usually check you in but expect payment shortly after with the expectation that you are heading straight to an ATM.

Whenever you check in to your accommodation, I highly, highly recommend that you take their business card during your check-in process, and keep this on your person throughout your stay at that accommodation. Especially in countries where few people speak English or the written language is very hard for you to read, it can be very easy to get lost and not have a clear way of finding your way back.

Having their business card will save you in these cases, especially if you don't have mobile data on your phone to look up directions.

Early Check-in and Using Bag Storage

If you arrive earlier than three in the afternoon, most hostels will check you in, but you'll have to store your bag since the room hasn't been cleaned up yet. Yes, the room always has people in it due to the nature of the different schedules of the people staying in a dorm-like room, but the cleaning staff will be cleaning bathrooms, removing sheets, etc. for your specific bed, so it's like a regular hotel in that regard. You'll be assigned a room and may also be assigned a bed number or letter. This is to figure out who to charge for any damages and to make sure the correct beds are cleared by the cleaning staff, but most hostels will just allow you to choose any unoccupied bed.

If you can't check in immediately, you can use the hostel's bag storage. Bag storage in hostels can be used before, during, and after your stay for any baggage you don't immediately need. Some hostels are really good about making sure your bag has a numbered card that matches a numbered card you take with you, but most hostels will just have a big closet that you can toss your bag into. Do not, I repeat, do not leave anything of any value whatsoever in the baggage storage room. It's usually better to walk around on the street with all of your valuables on you than to leave them unattended in an area that anyone can access. If you have big clunky valuables with you, this may become an issue. That said, you're almost never going to see any problems with the bag storage area, but I have seen it happen before where someone walked out with another person's bag. My guess is someone else knew what was in the bag or they would never have taken it. Who wants someone else's dirty clothes?

Getting Your Bed and Locker Together

Once it's okay to go to your room, you may be issued sheets, but sometimes they're already on the bed. Look for your bed number or letter once you're in the room if your bed is assigned.

If you were given sheets, put your sheets on your bed before you leave the room again. You don't want to make your bed in the dark when you return later in the evening. Also, getting your bed together upon check-in indicates to others that the bed is taken. Also, set aside any chargers you will need for your stuff during the night and get those ready as well but don't plug them in yet. A lot of older hostels have one to two outlets (sockets) per room, which is seemingly ridiculous in our current technological age when you have eight people in a room, but it still happens sometimes. Most newer and up-to-date hostels have an outlet near every bed.

Once your bed and your chargers are all together, put your stuff in your locker and be sure to lock it. Also be sure to guard your combination against prying eyes if you're using a dial lock. Ninety-nine percent of hostels have lockers that can usually accommodate your whole pack, but that other 1 percent presents a challenge because you either get a really small locker or no locker at all, meaning everything valuable will need to come with you during the day. When I say valuables, I mean anything that would be worth stealing: passports, bank cards, electronics, and anything else of value to you. If the locker is very small, put your key valuables in there and then take what you can't fit with you. No matter the locker situation, never leave your valuables out in the room, especially in an unlocked bag. Leaving your bag out with your non-valuables is fine because bag theft is exceedingly rare, but you should still lock your bag anyway, even if it's just dirty clothes in there.

Some newer hostels issue you an RFID card that acts as both your room key and your locker lock. This is fine, but keep a close eye on your card at all times and definitely don't lose it in public somewhere.

Bathrooms

Usually, showering is the most difficult time to keep all your valuables secure.

Bathrooms are different in each hostel. Sometimes you'll have bathrooms and showers in your hostel room, called "en suite," and sometimes they're shared and will be in the hallway elsewhere. Sometimes the bathroom is coed, sometimes it's gender-specific. Sometimes showers and toilets are separated and sometimes they're in the same room.

For toilets, be sure to check and see if there is soap at the sinks. I've always had toilet paper in every hostel around the world, but sometimes there's no soap, so I bring my own. Remember this is how you prevent sickness, so don't skip your soap when washing your hands.

For the showers, this is a little different than home. Sometimes you have a little area to stage taking off your clothes and have your new clothes ready. Sometimes there's just a bench outside of a bunch of stalls with little more than shower curtains. Either way, you're going to head to the shower covered in something and head out of the shower covered in something, and you'll need a towel and your toiletries in the middle. Since hostels are inherently mostly common areas, you will likely want to avoid stripping naked in front of a bunch of people in your room. This means your current clothes and the clothes you're changing into after your shower come with you to the shower. Take this stuff and your room key and leave everything else locked in your locker. If you don't have a locker, your daypack of valuables should go with you to the shower, but this can be hard to watch if you only have a common bench to store your stuff while showering. Be vigilant in this case and check your bag frequently.

Few hostels provide soap, shampoo, or towels in the shower area, so remember to pack these with you.

Once you're done in the shower and dressed again, head back to your room and be sure to hang up your towel somehow. Make sure this will dry where you hang it, or at least is able to attempt to dry properly, because pack towels become full of mildew really quickly if they remain wet. This drying process can be very tricky if you need to leave or check out shortly after showering.

Wi-Fi

A note on hostel Wi-Fi: Wi-Fi might not be available in your room but should be available in the hostel somewhere.

During the Night

At night, I like to have my phone charging close by so that I can hear the alarm and because a phone is a big theft target since it's small and worth a lot of money. I recommend using your extension cord or pre-charging so that you can sleep with your phone, and any other valuables that are out during the night, slightly under your pillow. This way, no one is going to take it in the night without somehow disturbing you in the process.

Also at night, try to wear shorts or pants (trousers) that have pockets of some sort. If you have to get up in the middle of the night to use the restroom or for some other reason, bottoms with pockets are helpful to hold your room key and phone. I sleep with my room key in my shorts pocket to ensure that I don't accidentally get up in the middle of the night to go to the restroom and lock myself out of my room. You don't need a key at home, so it's easy to forget in the middle of the night when you're sleepy.

Kitchens

Many hostels allow you to use a kitchen for cooking your own meals. Many people try to save money by doing this and it typically means that mealtime in the kitchen is complete anarchy. Tons of people are moving around with hot pots and knives and it's almost always shoulder-to-shoulder in the kitchen. I prefer to avoid this chaos, but if you do decide to cook your own meals, be prepared that the kitchen utensils and cookware will have extreme wear and tear, and you will likely only be able to use one heating element while you cook. Base your meals around this. Also, be sure to wash and rack the stuff you used immediately after you're done. Prewashing when you grab something isn't a bad idea either since you never know how thoroughly the person before you cleaned. Be aware that if you need to store groceries in the hostel, you are opening yourself up to easy theft and this can be a hassle all by itself.

Checkout

When checking out, you may be asked to remove your sheets, and if this is the case, you will be told upon check-in. As you're leaving the room the last time, make sure to double-check that you have all of your stuff. When you're ready and confident you have everything, head to the front desk and drop off your room key. If you know you're leaving very early or late, ask beforehand about how to check out in case no staff are available at that time.

General Tips

The hostel procedure shouldn't be too weird or confusing, hopefully. Etiquette can be a little trickier, though. The biggest thing to remember is that you're not the only one in the room. Following these general rules will help make things better for everyone:

- Don't walk around naked. This will get you kicked out of a hostel very quickly.

- Don't play music at even remotely loud volumes, and in general, use headphones.

- Don't watch movies without headphones.

- Don't set an alarm and then keep hitting snooze all morning.

- Don't masturbate or have sex in your bunk. Use the bathroom.

- Don't turn on the room light at night. This is incredibly rude and wakes everyone up instantly.

- Don't be a drunkard (being loud, knocking things over, or puking everywhere).

- Don't leave your filth in the bathroom or shower. Flush the toilet and rinse the bottom of the shower stall after you're done.

- Don't use a bunch of plastic bags in your pack and then go digging around in the middle of the night. Plastic bags are shockingly loud and this will wake everyone up.

- If you're planning to leave really early, try to mostly pack up the day beforehand so that you're not making a huge commotion in the middle of the night. If you still need to do some packing as you're leaving, which almost always happens, take all of your stuff into the hallway first, and then start digging around and packing up. It also helps to get your next day's clothing out and leave it sitting on top of your stuff so that you can easily change into these clothes without more digging around and noise.

- If you know you snore, consider getting corrective surgery before your trip, or get some device, like nose strips, that help stop or reduce your snoring.

- If you do puke somewhere by accident, tell the staff so they can immediately clean it up, and be aware you may be charged for this.

- Don't smoke anything, including marijuana, in the room. While the marijuana itself may not bother anyone, the smoke does, so take it outside.

- Don't put your wet stuff, towels, or whatever it is directly onto anyone's mattress for drying.

- If your shoes stink really badly, get new ones.

- Don't make a complete mess of your stuff. Other people are in this room and you don't have the right to take up the floor with all your stuff strewn everywhere. Plus, this is a great way to end up with stolen and misplaced stuff. I recommend keeping your bag as packed as possible at all times so that things don't wander off.

- Don't steal other people's stuff. I hope that goes without saying.

I would think most of this would be pretty obvious, but you would be surprised how many of these I've come across frequently. Sometimes just politely mentioning to someone, "Hey, can you use headphones?" or "Can you take your wet bathing suit off my bed please?" can fix the issue, but sometimes people are just jerks and you're either going to have to move rooms or deal with it. You will drastically cut down on experiencing these things if you avoid party hostels.

A lot of these things seem to have become issues more so in the last ten years, maybe because more people are traveling now than ever before, but there's been a lag in handling some of the worse problems. The good news is that a lot of places are catching up now and in areas known for partying, I've been starting to see hostel-specific security guards, and I've also seen people get asked to leave hostels for generally being rude and disrespectful toward others. I've also seen many more security cameras installed and police being immediately involved in any sort of theft.

All in all, hostels are not so bad and I still stay in them frequently to this day.

LAUNDRY

Laundry is pretty simple, but don't expect the machine signage to be in English. The staff at your accommodation should be able to help you out here. At most budget accommodations, you can do your laundry yourself, and the front desk will have soap you can purchase. Make sure you schedule in time to handle laundry while traveling since a load is going to usually take about two hours to wash and dry, and you want to clear out the machines for others to use. I like to do my laundry in the evenings or during a day off for this reason. If you need to do more than one load of laundry at a time to get your travel clothes clean, you probably packed too much clothing. Your travel towel is also probably going to get smelly every ten days or so, which you aren't going to want to rub all over yourself after showering, so this is usually a pretty good indicator that a laundry session is due.

If your accommodation doesn't allow you to do your own laundry, which happens a lot in really poor areas and parts of Asia, it's okay. Usually, you can drop off your clothing and have it returned to you either the next morning or late that evening. Make sure to ask when you drop off your clothing how long it takes to return. You don't want to drop things off in the morning, have a departure at night, and then find out your clothing isn't ready when you need to leave.

Every now and then, your accommodation won't do laundry at all. But I guarantee the staff will know a nearby location to handle your washing needs. One of the times this happened to me was in Krakow, Poland, and I ended up in some awesome bar/coffee-shop/laundromat (launderette) thing. It was actually pretty cool. Imagine literally doing your laundry while you sit in a bar!

Even more rarely, and I think this has only happened to me once in Costa Rica, was that I had to go to a laundromat and it wasn't a self-service laundromat. Still not a problem. Use the same drop-off principles as before. You don't have to worry about theft in this case, unless you have a lot of designer clothes, because no one wants to steal your used clothes.

Some folks on a tight budget recommend washing everything in the sink in order to save money. I've had to do this a couple of times just for special wash needs. For these situations, you should have a tiny bottle of detergent with you, but doing your washing this way comes with some cautions. Some issues that arise trying to wash your stuff in the sink:

- You can't really control temperature and agitation very well since sinks are generally small. So your clothes don't wash very well and, therefore, are not very clean.

- You'll also have to do many rounds of individually washing things because the sink will be small.

- You'll likely make a wet sopping mess of the room.

- You will have problems drying your clothes. If you have a clothesline and dry sunny weather, great, but when you're in the rainforest, it's 100 percent humidity, and you have a bungie line over your bed, your clothes aren't going to dry, and they're going to start to smell like mold.

I do not recommend sink washing unless you have to, but if you are serious about budgeting, nothing can beat the cost savings there.

BAG STORAGE

Many people during their trip are going to run into a situation where they aren't checked into a room but need to drop their bags off somewhere while they do other things. This could be because you checked out of your room in the morning and are leaving at night. It could also be that you arrived somewhere really early and can't check into your room yet. However, it gets more complicated if you are making a stop while in transit between cities.

If you were or are about to stay in a room somewhere, almost certainly the hotel or hostel will let you leave your bags in their storage. Unfortunately, many hotels and hostels won't let you leave your bags there if you aren't staying with them. Terrorists and drug dealers messed this up for everyone. Because you check into a room with your ID, they know who you are and thus you can leave your bag. A random passerby doesn't get their ID logged and as such, can't store their bags. This is for everyone's safety and security.

Fortunately, train stations, tourist info centers, and some museums will allow you to leave your bag with them. Many museums will insist you leave even your daypack in their lockers before you wander about, so they're expecting to store small bags at least.

As an example from my own travels, mentioned in detail during the planning phase, I discovered the trains in Switzerland from Zurich to Geneva took most of the day. If I'm going to be on a train all day, I might as well see something on the way. So my girlfriend and I decided to visit the HR Geiger museum in Gruyères, which was just about in the middle of the train trip. If you aren't familiar with that name, he's the guy who created the artwork that became the alien, or Xenomorph, that the *Alien* movie franchise was built on.

When my girlfriend and I took this trip and arrived in Gruyères, the train station was basically a restaurant. There weren't any lockers and there weren't any station officials around, let alone a bag storage desk. No problem. We decided to carry our bags into the village center. While this turned out to be an uphill climb, it wasn't that bad. This is also an example of when a travel backpack is useful as opposed to a roller bag. When we got onto the main street, we noticed a small tourist info shop. We popped in there and asked if we could leave our bags for a few hours. They were happy to help us and off we went. No problem.

COMMUNICATING WITH THOSE BACK HOME

Your family and friends are probably really important to you, and you should give some thought as to how you want to handle keeping in touch with them while you're away.

Talk to the people you are specifically going to keep in contact with and figure out how you're going to communicate and when. Will you email first? Will you use Google Meet, Zoom, FaceTime, or WhatsApp? Maybe Skype to call a physical phone? What about emergencies? Can they send a text to you? Can you receive a text where you're going? It is generally free to receive texts internationally, but it can be very costly to send texts. If you're on a local SIM card, you won't be on your regular mobile number anyway, so this could also be an issue.

Make sure to figure out how your important contacts can reach you before you leave. I find email is the easiest way to keep in contact, even for emergencies, but it does require that you are serious and consistent about making sure you regularly—if not daily—keep up with your email. Also, because of time zones, an important email may not be read by the other party until the next day.

Most people have a very consistent day-to-day, week-to-week pattern of going about their lives. You, on the other hand, while traveling, are going to have a different day every single day. This day-to-day change means everything is unique and memorable, and you'll hold on to these memories for a long time. I can remember almost every single day of my travels with only a slight memory jog, but when I'm at home, I can't tell you what I did last week and certainly not what I did a month ago.

This blurring of memory makes time fly by for people at home and slows your time down to a crawl in comparison. So when you come back feeling like it's been centuries since you've seen your family and friends, and for all you know people are living in mansions, had kids, and are using flying cars now, from their perspective you've basically just left on your trip and you're immediately already back. I can't tell you how many times it's been months since I've been home and seen someone, and the first thing they say is, "Didn't you just leave?" or "I thought you said your trip would last for months. How are you back already?"

I can pretty much guarantee that your friends won't disappear, your life won't drastically change, and nothing that happens while you're away will be earth shattering. But you'll have had a life-changing, mind-expanding, incredibly awesome time in the meantime.

For the purposes of communication, people may wonder why you want to talk so much while you're traveling, but it's this time-dilating effect creating that confusion. Just roll with it. Things are carrying on as usual back home while you're away.

I should also mention that gifts are a great way to say thank you and let people know you were thinking about them during your travels. In my experience, though, the gifts that you buy while traveling can seriously lack context when you come back and give them to someone. What might have been the coolest experience of your life may just be clutter to them because they didn't see and experience what you did.

If you are planning on giving someone a heartfelt gift to say thank you, it's a great idea to ask them before your trip if they're interested in anything you may be able to bring back. If they aren't sure and you don't find something to give them that immediately seems like the perfect gift, I'd advise that you wait until you get home to get something more locally familiar and meaningful to them.

PHONE CALLS

I recommend using Skype if you need to make an actual phone call while traveling. The way Skype works for this purpose is that your phone sends internet data over to the country you're trying to reach and then uses a local phone to actually dial the number you're calling. There is a per-minute fee for this, but it's usually really cheap. The main benefit here is you aren't technically making an international phone call; you're using the internet. Using a regular phone call could potentially cost you dollars per minute. Calling cards are usually not very cost-effective either, and using them can be very difficult to figure out.

If for some reason you do need to make a regular phone call, know your country's telephone code. Many international numbers contain a "+" at the beginning and this is shorthand for two zeros. So to dial the UK, which starts with +44, you would dial 0044 first and then the rest of the number.

To complicate things, the US writes all its phone numbers in a 1-xxx-xxx-xxxx format. We never see a "+" here usually. The US telephone prefix is "+1." Don't get confused here. That means a full number in the US is +1-1-xxx-xxx-xxxx or 0011-xxx-xxx-xxxx. Notice there are two ones leading the number now.

Many countries will write their numbers like +61 (03) 8598 6200, which is an Australian number. The parentheses are confusing for many people because the phone number when dialed within Australia is really 03 8598 6200, but if you were dialing this from outside Australia, the 0 is dropped, an international prefix is added, and the number dialed becomes +61 3 8598 6200 (or 0061385986200).

To make things even more confusing, some countries like Australia have an international access code that isn't just the "+." In Australia, you need to dial 0011 to even get out of the country with a number, so then +44 really becomes 001144 and the rest of the number. Dialing a US number from Australia would start with 001111 and then the area code and the rest of the number. It can be challenging to figure all that out if you need to make a normal call wherever you are, which is what makes Skype so great for calling phone numbers.

Also, keep in mind that if you're contacting someone on a device, then video chat and messaging also become an option. Zoom, Google Meet, Skype-to-Skype, FaceTime, Hangouts, WhatsApp, iMessage, and Facebook are all great options. Because of COVID-19, I think we all have pretty good practice with this, so use whatever works for you. In the future, keep an eye on metaverse technology because it will make people appear like they're in the room with you which will almost certainly help remove the feeling of distance between you.

LOCAL LAWS

One of the most confusing and annoying things in the US is the weird system of federal laws versus state laws and how those laws can be different from state to state. You can be driving along the road and be totally in compliance with the law, and then cross a state line on the same road and suddenly be violating a law. For example, front driver-side and front passenger-side window tint is legal in some states and illegal in others. This is a huge source of confusion for people outside the US because almost no other country on earth functions like this. Usually, an entire country follows the same set of laws. For what it's worth if you're outside the US, this is very confusing and annoying for Americans, too.

Unfortunately, you're going to be going through the same state line experience while traveling except that you're likely going to be crossing country borders when this happens. Every time you enter a new country, a different set of laws is now applicable. And it's not like you get a rundown, inspection, or legal pamphlet when you cross a border to let you know that something unexpected is against the law. Thankfully, unless you plan on importing vehicles or bringing commercial goods to sell, you're probably not going to have any issue with violating any local laws.

People are people everywhere, so you're not really going to find any extremely exotic laws anywhere. Pretty much everywhere has the same set of laws: don't kill anyone, don't steal, don't be drunk in public, don't have drugs, don't rape anyone, etc. It's pretty easy to stay in line with this. A few places like Singapore have very strict laws against things like littering, so be respectful and put trash (rubbish) in trash cans (bins) like you should be doing anyway, and you won't have any problems.

The two big ones that can get people in trouble are alcohol and drugs, since both of those are always present at parties, and who doesn't like to party every now and then, especially while traveling? The biggest concern with alcohol is making sure it's legal in the first place. In countries where the majority populace is Muslim, alcohol is usually completely illegal altogether. If you're in a country like this, respect the rules and don't import alcohol accidentally. Definitely don't go looking for it.

Beyond that, you shouldn't do stupid stuff while drunk. I think this is self-explanatory.

As for drugs, anything illicit, which usually includes marijuana, will carry serious penalties in the vast majority of the world. A few countries go as far as the death penalty. The death penalty seems incredibly harsh, and it is, but most of these countries rarely carry out executions for drugs. More likely, if you get caught, you'll end up in a nightmarish prison for years and years and finally get released after great expense to both lawyers and your overall well-being. All I can say here is, don't mess around with drugs in countries in which you're not sure what the law states. Know what the local laws are and be prepared to face those consequences if you decide to do drugs anyway. In some places, even though certain drugs may be illegal, they may be intentionally "overlooked" by the police, meaning "decriminalized possession." Examples are Amsterdam in the Netherlands and Nimbin in Australia. In places like these, it's usually illegal to sell marijuana, but buying and personal-use possession are generally not pursued as crimes.

As for medical drugs, the laws are usually pretty similar across countries in regard to possession, meaning that it's illegal for you to have prescription medications unless you were prescribed these medications by a doctor. That said, when you're in Zambia, they have no idea who Dr. So-and-So is from the US who prescribed you your Xanax. Make sure you take a written prescription note from your doctor with you during your travels, and keep anything that could be recreationally abused in an original pharmacy container with your name on it. These two things will ensure that if you are inspected by border officials or police, that you can actually verify that these medications are really for you and you were legally issued them from a pharmacy. Also, don't take more than a reasonable personal amount of such drugs. You can refill common prescriptions while on the road if necessary. In general, officials aren't going to care about things like migraine medication and antibiotics because people don't take these types of drugs for fun. Again, it comes down to the recreational use of certain substances that becomes the issue.

If for some reason you do end up in trouble with the law, things can get really horrible and confusing. Every country is going to be a little different, and MICs and LICs are notoriously corrupt in terms of proper legal representation and due process. Insist on contacting your embassy and on having a lawyer present at all times. The best way to avoid the scary realities that arise here is to not get in trouble in the first place. Use your common sense and act like you would at home and you shouldn't have any problems.

Also, be aware that some countries and regions aren't as socially accepting as we might like. Being a woman in public without a head-scarf or being openly LGTBQ+ could potentially also land you in jail for violating the law. Be aware of this before entering any country.

Also keep in mind that protected speech is not recognized everywhere in the world. In places where that's true, this mainly involves insulting a deity or political figure. Depending on where you are, deities can be different entities, but some places will convict you and throw you in prison for any perceived insult against their god. Similarly, some places will convict you and throw you in prison for insulting the monarchy. This is easy to avoid by simply not insulting the country you're in while you're there, and be careful about other forms of communication, too. Examples of this include insulting the king in Thailand, insulting Allah in many Muslim countries, insulting Buddha in Sri Lanka, and having tattoos of Buddha in Sri Lanka.

Again, be smart, don't speak aggressively toward anyone, and be respectful. If you follow these basic social rules, you shouldn't have any problems with the law.

DRESSING APPROPRIATELY

First, I hope you adhered to my advice and did not pack expensive designer clothes and tons of jewelry. Even if you are planning on taking a really fancy or luxurious trip, you should leave that stuff behind in your room when you are walking around and interacting with local people and other random tourists. Don't walk around with solid gold jewelry and incredibly flashy clothing because it's only going to draw unwanted attention onto yourself and potentially get you robbed.

Beyond that, if you know you're going to be doing a lot of walking or hiking, be smart and wear appropriate footwear. Wear good sturdy shoes that can stand up to some abuse and have some cushioning so that your feet will be able to walk all day and then still function the next day, too.

One thing that maybe isn't so obvious is that different cultures may have wildly different opinions on what is appropriate clothing in public and at beaches. Unfortunately, this mostly applies to women. If a female were to walk down a street in San Francisco wearing a bikini and flip-flops, she might get some looks, but no one is going to think it's really *that* weird. If a female were to do the same thing in Iran, she might end up in prison for a really long time.

In most HICs and some MICs, women don't need to worry about their clothing, even at the beach, but in LICs and the other MICs, the situation is not as simple. Many MICs and LICs are fairly conservative, so tank tops and miniskirts are not recommended for daily wear, but a wide shoulder strap tank top and a knee-length skirt are probably fine. Countries that are majority Muslim will be much more conservative than other countries, and you may need to wear full-length pants (trousers), a T-shirt to cover your shoulders at a minimum, and possibly a head scarf as well.

Before any woman reading this goes on a trip, it's not a bad idea to go onto Google Maps and drop into street view for the city and country you're planning on visiting and see what the women there are wearing. Try to match what you see as best as possible. You can also find a lot of resources online that discuss cultural fashions. I recommend doing this search before you pack your bags.

For the beach, many local women in MICs and LICs will still wear bikinis to the beach, but they will significantly cover up as soon as they leave the beach. In other places, being in a bikini anywhere is going to attract unwanted attention. Be careful with this and look at what other women are doing at your destination. Try to blend in as much as possible and don't stick out unnecessarily as this will attract unwanted attention.

The biggest attire concern for most travelers, both male and female, is entering temples and holy places. In some countries, no one will care what you're wearing inside. Some places won't even care if you're wearing a hat inside. In other places, men can only enter a holy site while wearing a "sarong," which is a large piece of lightweight fabric that you will need to wear like a skirt by tying it around your waist. If you're visiting sites in a place that requires sarongs, it is often possible to rent them at the entry of each location. But if you know you are planning on going to a few sites, it's much easier and you'll likely save money if you go to the local market and just buy yourself a cheap sarong.

Some places will refuse shorts, while other places will refuse flip-flops. For women, sometimes any exposed shoulder skin will bar entry. In some places, if a woman is on her period, she's not supposed to enter.

Every country and site will be slightly different. Unless you are visiting religious sites that are part of a religion you are familiar with or are visiting HIC countries, I would ask the locals working at your accommodation in advance what the dress requirements are for entering holy sites in those areas.

RESPONSIBLE TRAVEL ON THE ROAD

The usual things you hear about responsible travel are avoiding prostitutes and not doing drugs. I don't think I need to get into why doing these things while traveling isn't exactly supporting the local community, but there are some other things to consider.

A big one is begging. Even though on the surface, giving a few spare coins to someone who looks like they are in need seems like a good karma booster, especially if they're a child, what you're not seeing is that every single person coming by day after day is doing the same thing as you. With kids, what this is actually causing is more kids shun school and also start begging. Rather than helping someone in need, you're encouraging more begging. Many of the locations I've been to have actively encouraged me not to give money to beggars.

In some cases, parents will prevent their children from going to school in order to send them out to beg to make more money for the family. When the kids get old enough, the parents kick them out. Is anyone winning in that situation?

Beyond begging, trying to avoid making unnecessary waste is another thing to be careful of. When you walk around India, many areas are completely blanketed in plastic garbage that will never break down. While you can't avoid purchasing clean water there, you can avoid contributing to the mess. Make sure that your bottles, cans, and other recyclables actually end up going to recycling. If you can buy something with less plastic packaging, try to do so. Additionally, filling your water bottle on a plane saves a plastic cup. These little things add up.

When you are in nature during your travels, be careful not to disturb anything and definitely do not take souvenirs out of any park or site. I went to a cave in China where for decades people were coming in and breaking off little pieces of the stalactites and stalagmites, and when you go in the cave now, it looks completely demolished. That cave will effectively never repair itself, and in my opinion, it's fairly pointless to visit there now because it's been destroyed. Don't be one of these people.

The main thing to keep in mind with this is that whatever you're doing while you travel, ten thousand other travelers are going to do the same thing. If all of you did the same thing at the same time, what would happen to that place? Try to make as little of an impact as possible. If you want to help a particular community, ask your accommodation who is running civic projects or community programs and donate your money to them.

SCAMS

I'm going to cover all sorts of scams and travel safety issues in the "Safety and Security" section, but I put this mention of scams here because you need to develop a continuous daily mindset that you won't be able to hide the fact that you're a tourist. Further, simply because you're traveling as a tourist, you are better off financially than the majority of the world's population. This makes you a target for scams. Be sure to always remain vigilant. Anything that seems suspicious probably is. We'll talk about scams in depth later.

TRAVEL PSYCHOLOGY

In this section, I want to talk about your mental approach to your trip, including the approach you take to planning each day, your approach toward taking care of yourself, and your view of other people, all of which are going to impact how you enjoy your trip.

ON-THE-ROAD DAILY TIME MANAGEMENT

One thing I would highly recommend here is to structure your day around what you want to do and then fit in other necessities around that. For example, let's say I'm a Gap Year type on my trip, and before I go to bed that day, I have laundry to do, I need to plan out what I'm doing the next day, and I just arrived in that city by bus in the late afternoon. The rest of that day may be spent trying to get to my hostel, dropping everything off and getting settled there, and then heading out to find dinner since it's probably early evening by this point. After grabbing dinner, I would inquire how laundry works at the hostel, and let's say I can do it on my own, but it's full currently. I might take this time to research the next few days, and let's say I find out getting to the next city requires a pretty early bus, and I know I'm probably only going to stay where I am for two nights. That already tells me that my next night probably isn't going to be a big night out on the town where I'm drinking and hanging out late. So what I'm going to do instead is probably take a shower first and then maybe go out on this first night and have a couple of beers and maybe talk to some new people.

The next morning, I'm going to wake up, I'm not going to shower because I showered the night before, and I'm going to do all the stuff I want to do in this city during the core nine-to-five hours. During this time, I'm going to be eating at places, tipping, bartering, buying stuff, maybe using ATMs, navigating, etc. After this, I'm going to grab some dinner and then head back and start doing laundry because I didn't do it the night before. I'm going to book all the things I need to book for the next place I'm headed. I'm also probably going to shower tonight again since I have to wake up early. Then, the next morning, I'll wake up early and catch my bus to the next place.

Try to maximize your time around what you want to do somewhere in a similar fashion. Sometimes you need a break day, which I'll talk about in the next section, but in general, try not to waste your core nine-to-five business hours doing things like laundry and cruising the internet. I really doubt that's why most people want to travel. Doing daily maintenance during the late evenings will help fit more local activities into your schedule.

Unfortunately, your overall schedule may dictate what you *need* to do over what you *want* to do. You may see a really cute person at the hostel bar on the second night when you come in from your daily activities, but you know you have to get ready to leave early and still need to do laundry, so you may not get to talk to that person. It's happened to me before that as I'm wrapping up booking things for my next stop that a cute girl has sat down next to me and we hit it off. Unfortunately, I was already committed to heading out. My options were to either cancel my plans, not all of which may have been refundable, or I had to keep going. If this is happening to you a lot during your trip, and it's starting to bother you, you need to slow down a little and adjust how you're spending your time.

TAKING TIME FOR YOURSELF, BURNOUT, AND MOVING AT A NORMAL PACE

This is maybe one of the harder concepts to explain to someone who hasn't been on the road for a while previously, but it's really easy to find yourself rushing through cities and locations, and that can lead to some serious travel burnout. This is even truer for anyone who is on a tight budget, because a tight budget can potentially cause you to rush through things to save money. Similarly, people on a short timeline for their trip may try to pack in everything that they possibly can. Even if you have followed every piece of advice in this book and didn't overcommit yourself in your planning, after pushing hard for a while, your hygiene, your emails, or something else in your life can start to get behind.

The point is, going hard day after day on the road can very quickly start to feel like work.

During my first long trip, I didn't know travel burnout was possible while being on a "dream trip." However, after about four months of moving on the road, I was totally demolished. I wasn't interested in meeting people, and every day felt like I was slogging through things that I had previously been really excited about. It was still very enjoyable, but it just felt...exhausting. During my travels, I've met a solid number of people who have traveled for about a year, but I have only met a handful of people who have traveled much longer than a year. What's the secret to these multiyear folks not burning out during such a long trip? They move much slower than someone who is traveling only for a few weeks.

I've realized since my early travels that being on the road is sort of like running. If you're running a hundred meters, you can easily sprint. If you're running a 10k, you're going at a moderate pace, and if you're running a marathon, you're likely going to be running an even slower clip that allows for multiple hours of push. Push harder than that on any of these races and you're either not going to finish, or your finishing time will be terrible and you'll be miserable at the end. Imagine running a hundred-mile race and what that would do to your speed. You should apply the same concept to your traveling. The longer you plan on being on the road, the slower your pace probably needs to be.

From my own experience, a big part of what starts to drag on you if you move too fast is the inconsistency of your day-to-day. Having to check out, transport, check in, do new stuff, find your way back, meet new people, catch up on those things you have to do...if every day is an entirely new set of stuff, it becomes sensory and psychological overload after a while, so be careful about this.

From my own and others' experiences on half-year or shorter trips, you can mitigate this burnout feeling by moving slower and/or you can take breaks often. I personally like breaks better and try to schedule a day off for myself every two to three weeks. By this I mean scheduling time in which you have nothing planned except naps, lying in bed watching movies, and eating. Take a rest. Go sit at the beach all day. Just don't do anything substantive. If you're out for a really long time, maybe take a week somewhere and do nothing every two to three months. Or between travel legs in different areas, stop at home for a week or two and then keep going. These breaks in your day-to-day travel, even if you're moving fast, will do quite a good job at letting your mind and body relax enough to keep plugging on after you feel recharged.

Someone asked me during the writing of this book if switching your trip emphasis around periodically would alleviate this problem. They asked if doing outdoor stuff for a bit, then focusing on food a bit, then focusing on museums a bit would alleviate this burnout feeling, and my answer is that sadly no, it does not. Unfortunately, the frequent changing of everything in your day doesn't go away with changing your activities, so a total rest period is still likely the only way to recover from this problem.

Once you start to feel this burnout feeling, don't ignore it. Either take days off more frequently or cut your trip short a little. There's no reason to travel and not enjoy yourself while you're doing it. Once you start feeling this burnout, it's going to keep building up until it's really affecting you, so don't ignore it.

YOUR ATTITUDE TOWARD DIFFERENCES

This section is a caution for some of the feelings that can stir up while traveling. I've seen it happen in others and I've felt it in myself before. It's hard to avoid, and it's ugly when it happens.

The feeling that can come up is bigotry.

Now, before you say, "I'm not a bigot. How dare you!" please let me explain.

Bigotry is any feeling or thought where you see another person doing something and think, *I'm not okay with that.* Certain things you may not be okay with get into morality. I doubt most people anywhere are going to say that theft, rape, or murder are okay. Those aren't the things I'm talking about.

What I'm talking about is more like religion, customs, and social inter-actions that make up a society. This is what makes up a culture. Maybe you've never thought about this before and aren't sure what culture really means. It's hard to identify it if you haven't seen other cultures to compare yourself against yet. Culture is something that grows within a group of people without them sitting down and writing out some-thing like a constitution for a government. I doubt anyone ever sat down formally and discussed the procedure for how they were going to nod heads at each other. It's just something that happened and has now become tradition. But imagine that every country, all over the world, has developed its own methods with little outside influence.

Every group has its own culture. And you can even see new cultures arising in workplaces, even though they're within another culture. It's just how we, as a species, evolve together in groups. We naturally make a culture when others are around us in a closed group.

That group element is a big part of what culture is. It's a social contract between individuals to make a group function. But if we go back to caveman times, your group is your survival. So not adhering to the group's ways could be life-threatening. We don't want to live our lives without being part of a group. That's why countries, companies, gangs, sports teams, and militaries become such powerful forms of self-identification. Our bodies even release feel-good chemicals like dopamine and oxytocin in our brain when we feel this sense of belonging. Culture is powerful stuff for us, all the way down into our DNA.

But here's the thing: different countries have a more pronounced set of cultural differences than say, a company within a country. A lot of this is likely due to geographically isolated cultural development in the past, whereas a company was created within an existing country culture, so the company culture won't be shockingly different than the country's culture.

Why am I mentioning this here? Well, you may see things happen while you're traveling that really, really bother you. But you may be looking at their activities through your sense of belonging to your group, and that doesn't apply to them. They're belonging to their group. In reality, *you're* the one who isn't doing things properly in that country because you're in *their* culture.

Let me try to illustrate this point.

For me, and I would think for a lot of Western people, China is very shocking culturally. Many things that are totally normal in China are simply not day-to-day things in Western cultures. Because of this, I'm going to use China to illustrate my thoughts about bigotry.

A good basic example of something that is very different culturally is that everyone spits in China. There's actually some interesting history related to theories on the spread of disease as to why the Chinese spit, and Europeans use tissues to hack and blow their noses (which you can look up yourself), but the concept of clearing mucus out of your body remains the same. The thing that shocks most Westerners, though, is that the Chinese spit everywhere constantly. So imagine walking down the street and seeing a professional in nice business attire hacking a big green chunk of mucus right into your footpath as you're walking along right next to them.

Are feelings of disgust popping up in you? Thoughts like "What the...?" or "Ew, that's gross!"

Well, this is that bigotry feeling I'm talking about.

It's totally normal in China to spit like this and totally normal to spit it out on the ground. In some areas, you may even see people spitting on the floors in restaurants and museums. While that's not exactly polite behavior even in China to spit indoors, it's not exactly impolite either.

So where are your feelings coming from?

In my opinion, those feelings are your feelings of belonging to a group, your culture, telling you this behavior could get you kicked out of your culture or group.

If you blow your nose in China, meaning the Western mucus solution, you're going to get some weird looks. That's because you're doing the right thing from your cultural perspective and the wrong thing from theirs.

Furthering the spitting example, I actually saw someone from China forget where they were and spit on the floor in the middle of the Palace of Versailles in France. A number of people saw this, and I thought for a second that this woman was going to be physically confronted, but everyone just stared at her *very* disapprovingly, shaking their heads. This is the same feeling I was talking about, but in this case, the Chinese woman was wrong. It's not okay in France to spit on the ground, especially inside a historical palace, so this is an example in which she should have kept her "normal" behavior in check. You should also be modifying your out-of-place behaviors to fit into the local culture.

Another example of this attitude concept is a conversation I overheard in a hostel in China. A woman from England was really pissed off that when she went into a clothing store in a shopping mall, someone was following her around the whole time.

"Oh my god, I'm trying to look at things in this shop, and this man will not stop following me around and hovering over me. I finally got so creeped out that I had to turn around and shout at him to go away, and he did for a couple of minutes, but then I saw him staring at me down the aisle and he was still watching my every move. I finally had to leave. Like, seriously, just piss off, mate!"

What happened here?

I had the same internal reaction when a similar thing happened to me the first time only a couple of weeks beforehand. I was lucky, though, in two ways. First, I'm a big, tall male, so I wasn't threatened by having someone hover around me. Second, I had a local guide who I could ask questions. When I got back to my guide after my first incident like this, I immediately asked what was going on with this hovering behavior in stores because once I noticed it, it seemed to be happening to everyone. I then learned that this is a deeply ingrained part of Chinese shopping.

As far as I understand now, the Chinese shopping experience is about being catered to and having expert salespeople guide you to the perfect items for your needs. So, for example, if you're shopping for a suit jacket, male or female, it's expected that when you go into a store that a salesperson will ask what color and cut you'd like. They may bring a few things out and watch as you try them on but then suggest that a certain shade or cut modification may improve the jacket's appearance on you. They will go get these, too. They may also suggest something in both higher and lower price bands and explain the pros and cons of each jacket. I think you get the idea here where this is going, but imagine all you wanted to do was try on a single suit jacket, and now you're swimming in options that might fit your needs, and you're being seriously fussed over.

If you're Western and just wanted to try on that one jacket, you're going to feel uncomfortable with all of this attention. You never asked for help. You just wanted to try on the jacket. But that's exactly what I'm trying to get across in this section. The shop workers here are behaving within their culture correctly. In fact, they're confused why you don't want any help and suggestions. It's so far out of their norm that when you ask them to back off that they only sort of back off and hover nearby just in case you change your mind.

Thus, getting angry or shouting at someone hovering over you, or any actions of that sort, are not going to do you any good and will only result in you becoming more frustrated. Potentially worse, it could cause you problems when you make the local populace angry because you may appear to be rude.

It's completely understandable to have these negative feelings sometimes, especially when it's something far out of your comfort zone, but remember, you traveled to see the world and its peoples, and this is truly seeing it and experiencing it. You don't have to like everything you come across, but trying to understand differences can go a long way in improving your trip experience and your empathy toward others.

Remember if this comes up that you may be the one doing strange things from their perspective, and you're in their country. Be respectful, be polite, and try not to let these feelings that may come up get in the way of you experiencing and enjoying a new culture. This may be hard in places that are extremely misogynistic or don't let women in public without being completely covered and with an escort, but again, you're in their culture. Try to understand their perspective and realize that you are not going to change their culture while you're there.

ROMANCE ON THE ROAD

You may find while you're traveling that you end up having strong feelings toward someone. This is totally normal. Unfortunately, you're not in a normal life situation at that point when that happens. If the other person is a traveler also, then neither of you are currently in normal life situations. This may seem like an obvious thing to point out, but what it can cause is somewhat of a "Disneyland effect." Because you're both having the time of your lives and are probably carefree and relaxed in your travels, the connection you form on the road can seem stronger and more genuine than other relationships you've previously had. This can then cause a strong attachment.

If you were at home getting attached with strong feelings so quickly, after some introspection, you'd probably tell yourself to calm down. But during travel, it can be hard to convince yourself of the reality of the situation. Also, both of you will have lives to return to at some point, so the relationship is likely transitory, even if you're able to share each other's company for more than a few days. Mix all of this together and what you end up with can be a very short, very intense relationship, followed by a sudden heartbreak. If you're on a longer trip, this may even happen multiple times.

Try and remind yourself that this kind of relationship is temporary. If you were at home, maybe this person wouldn't even be someone who catches your eye, but during travel, they may be the three-day love of your life. I know this sounds callous and may be impossible, but try not to get hurt by this.

Some people may read this and try to convince themselves not to get into these romances at all, but I would encourage you not to take this route. The connections that you form while traveling are just as real as those in your normal life; they just don't usually last due to distance. That doesn't mean the connection is any less significant or meaning-ful. If you found out someone you were dating at home was going to die in a week, would you walk away from them? Probably not. You'd probably enjoy the time you had left. I would encourage you to look at these types of connections in the same manner. The short time frame doesn't mean the connection isn't worthwhile.

MEDICAL ISSUES AND GENERAL HYGIENE

One of the things most new travelers find out the hard way is how to take care of their bodies. Water, food, and your environment all contain perils when you're away from home. It's important to practice cleanliness and good hygiene to avoid illness. Let's talk about some of these issues.

TRAVELER'S DIARRHEA

By far, the most common medical issue while traveling is getting food poisoning, which can happen due to water or food. This food poisoning is a little different than your at-home food poisoning, though, which is why it's usually referred to as "traveler's diarrhea." This also goes by names like "Montezuma's revenge," "Bali belly," and "Delhi belly."

A big part of why this affects so many new travelers is because there are no warnings about the dangers of the food and water they're being exposed to. In the case of water, almost all HIC water is sent through a purification plant before it goes to city water pipes, and these plants filter out all sorts of toxins, chemicals, and particulates. In MICs and LICs, however, there may be no purification plant in the system at all, and this may mean that your water source is coming straight out of a body of water that could be contaminated by factory chemical runoff or local sewage.

India, for example, has some of the most toxic water on the planet as it can contain certain bacteria and chemical levels one hundred times over what is considered safe in HICs. They generally do not filter for viruses either. Taking just a small sip of water in India could be enough to make you very ill.

You may wonder, though, where are the locals getting their water, then? Well, they're drinking this water and they're fine, but that's because they've been drinking it their entire lives, so their bodies are acclimated to it. You, on the other hand, aren't used to it, and this chemical-laced, viral, bacteria sample is going to be a bomb to your gut.

Unfortunately, it's almost impossible to completely avoid the water getting into your system. If you order coffee, where did the water come from? If you order food that's even slightly moist, where did that water come from? When the dishes were cleaned, what water was used? When you shower, is the water getting in your eyes and mouth? Did you brush your teeth by wetting your toothbrush in the sink? All of these things are putting that water in your system. And while boiling and cooking will kill most viruses and bacteria, it doesn't do anything to remove any chemicals that may be in the water.

So what do you do? Well, you do what you can and you have to hope for the best beyond that. If you are not in HICs, drink only bottled water. For those with really sensitive gastric systems, you may consider only drinking bottled water everywhere. Also, use bottled water to brush your teeth. It's annoying, but it reduces exposure to ingesting tap water. Don't order cold beverages with ice because you don't know how the ice was made. And when you shower, avoid getting the water in your eyes, up your nose, and in your mouth. Beyond this, there's not much more you can do.

Be very aware also that it's a common scam for non-shop-based street vendors to take empty water bottles, refill them with tap water, reseal them, and resell these used bottles back to tourists. The spots you're going to find this shady bottled water are usually in major tourist areas, where you're not near to any kind of shop, like the top of the Great Wall of China or right by the Colosseum in Rome. Generally, these vendors only sell water and maybe a few other things out of a cooler. The easy way to avoid buying refilled water bottles is to not buy from these vendors, and make sure you bring water with you every-where. Only buy water from actual shops.

As for food, quality and freshness can be highly variable. Plus, you don't know what the kitchen looks like. For all you know, you just had old unrefrigerated meat that just got cooked in a sauce made from tap water.

It would be nice if you could avoid eating, but that's not really an option, so what to do?

After I'd been to some forty-five countries already, one traveler told me something ingenious that made me have a real "You've got to be kidding! How did I not realize this before?!" moment, and I'll share it with you. His food strategy while traveling is to only eat from places that have a lot of other people, preferably locals, eating at them. This is incredibly smart, and as I thought back to the few times I've gotten really sick, I didn't follow this rule. Basically, the idea here is that locals aren't immune to food poisoning either, so they're not going to eat at places that serve shady food that makes them sick. This doesn't mean your stomach isn't going to get upset anyway because of the foreign water and bacteria in the food, but you're vastly mitigating potential problems this way.

It should be noted that street food, while super delicious, tends to be a notorious source of food poisoning for many people. If you're braving the street food, especially make sure you follow the "only eat at places with other people" rule.

Even following these strategies, though, you may still get sick.

When I was in university, I heard this riddle: "What's more powerful than god, more evil than the devil, poor people have it, rich people need it, and it will kill you if you eat it?" Turns out, most adults can't answer this question without some serious thought, but kids usually get it right away. The answer is "nothing." One of my university buddies (mates), however, heard this riddle and immediately answered "traveler's diarrhea."

Having had traveler's diarrhea three times now, I can tell you that my buddy's answer was probably more correct. I was so ill those times I got sick that I seriously started questioning if I was going to die. I'm not joking. It's an absolutely terrible experience.

So what is traveler's diarrhea? Well, if you read medical sites or Wikipedia, there's not really a clear definition as to what causes traveler's diarrhea, let alone the symptoms. The real common thread in the various descriptions is that it occurs to travelers who are typically from HICs and are traveling in MICs and LICs.

In fact, the symptoms and causes are so broad that you might start having issues immediately or you may have them days later after exposure. Chemicals, bacteria, and viruses are all sources of problems and treat you differently. And because of the broad range of sources, you may experience anything from serious bloating and feeling bad, all the way to crippling, explosive, bloody diarrhea.

You should have packed a broad-spectrum antibiotic before you left, and now is the time to pop one of them. To tell you how seriously this can affect you, before I traveled the first time, I asked my doctor when I originally got the antibiotics prescription, "How will I know when to take this?" and my doctor's response was, "You'll know." That sounded incredibly ominous and as I found out firsthand, you will, in fact, *know*.

When you feel so ill that you can barely function, it's time to pop your antibiotic. Also, you should try to take your antibiotic right after you finish a round in the bathroom so that you don't immediately flush the pill out of your system. Even if you take your antibiotic when you get really sick, it may not necessarily alleviate your problems. Not all the possible issues are caused by bacteria, and that's all the antibiotic can alleviate. If you still have problems, which you probably will, try to remain calm, stay in a safe place with access to a toilet, and let your body pass everything out. If you're having gastric issues but aren't feeling near dead from them, don't take your antibiotic. Instead, take Pepto Bismol (bismuth) or something similar.

Be aware, having lots of repeat bouts of diarrhea can kill you. It's not the diarrhea that's the problem so much but rather that you're dumping liquid every time you excrete waste. You will become dangerously dehydrated if you have too many bouts of diarrhea. Seven to eight bouts is when it becomes a concern. This is where rehydration salts and chugging water are critical. A good time to start taking Pepto Bismol (bismuth) or Imodium (loperamide) to attempt to stop diarrhea is after the fifth bout or so. Be aggressive in your water and medications and you'll lessen your discomfort.

The reason I suggest that you wait until after a few bouts is because your body is trying to get rid of something. If you start medications immediately, you've now made it impossible for your body to get rid of whatever is causing the problem. Let your body do its job first, then start medicating as you're entering risky dehydration territory. If you brought an antibiotic, taking the antibiotic a couple of bouts in is the appropriate time to do so.

Also, be prepared, as getting sick like this can strike at any time. Have your medications on you at all times when in MICs and LICs.

If really bad symptoms last longer than one day, or you have more than eight bouts of diarrhea in a day, or if you have blood in your stool, seek professional medical attention *immediately*. Any hotel or hostel you are near should be able to help you with this. Let whoever is taking you to the hospital or clinic know what has happened to you in case you pass out on the way to the doctor.

While recovering from traveler's diarrhea, use the BRAT principle to keep eating. It will seem awful at first, but you absolutely must do this to keep your energy levels up and allow your body to fight off whatever it's fighting. BRAT stands for bananas, rice, applesauce, and toast. These are four very neutral foods that should be well tolerated even if your stomach and abdomen are in serious pain. Keep eating BRAT foods until you are feeling significantly better and then slowly start reintroducing other foods. After that, eating at familiar fast-food chains may not be touristy, but the food is familiar to you and can help you readjust to eating normally again.

All this said, don't worry too much, though. After years of traveling, I've only gotten sick enough to warrant these instructions three times. And even though all of those times have been terrible, it didn't hamper or ruin my trips by any means.

HYDRATION

Water intake is something that gets a lot of people into trouble. Even if you aren't moving at all, you should be drinking 1.5 liters of water a day. If you're doing just about any activity at all, you should be drinking about 3.0 liters of water a day. And if you're in a hot area, your body can't cool off well just by sweating, so it compensates by sweating even more, meaning you should be drinking around 4.0 liters of water a day. That equates to a full gallon of water a day!

If you aren't peeing clearly and frequently, you are not drinking enough water and are risking health problems if you don't catch up on your water. If you're in a hot climate and don't drink enough water, you could very well give yourself heat stroke, which can be fatal. If you notice that you're cramping or feeling clammy and faint, you need to start drinking much more water.

Even knowing this, when I was in India during their hot season, I once woke up and peed like I normally do, then chugged almost a full liter of water. Over the next three hours, I drank another liter of water. But three hours later, now six hours after waking up and almost halfway through the day, I hadn't peed again. I wasn't drinking enough water, despite starting my day with two liters down the hatch. Sure enough, I started feeling lightheaded and weak later that afternoon. By the end of the day, I had drunk six liters of water and was still thirsty. Listen to your body and watch your pee.

Be aware you need to be eating salt with this much water. Unless you have high blood pressure, it's hard to overdo salt. Everyone has heard that it's healthy to eat less salt and that's simply not true. Eat whatever tastes right to you or use electrolyte mixes in your water. You don't need to go crazy with your salt, just have a reasonable amount, and if you start cramping, eat a little more.

Before we continue, I should also mention a thankfully less frequent traveler problem—constipation. Changing time zones, being on airplanes, not drinking enough water as you hop from airport to airport—all these things can make you constipated when you get to a destination. So far as I've seen, this is typically when most people get constipated. Your timing and diet are thrown off while you're hopping around the world and this can tie your system into a knot. This is not really a problem and most people normalize within a couple of days. That said, if you can't go to the bathroom for more than five days, you are starting to risk some potential medical issues. If you haven't gone to the bathroom after five days, seek over-the-counter medication to try and loosen your system up. If that doesn't resolve things by day seven, seek out a doctor.

JET LAG

I should mention jet lag, which occurs when taking most long-distance flights. If you've never flown long distance (i.e., greater than five hours on a plane or so), you've probably never really experienced jet lag. Jet lag is an odd phenomenon caused by crossing a bunch of time zones rapidly. Your body effectively experiences a "lag" where it remains used to sleeping on your original time zone's schedule, despite not being in that time zone anymore. The only way you can really induce this effect is by flying, since no other transport moves fast enough to cause jet lag. Also, if you're only crossing four or fewer time zones, your jet lag will probably not be significant enough to be a problem.

I've read about jet lag a bit, and as far as I've read and experienced, it takes about one day for every one time zone you cross in order to fully adjust your sleeping habits to the new destination time zone. However, most of the adjustment occurs in the first two to three days. Some of the weird symptoms that jet lag causes are diarrhea, constipation, headaches (though my guess is this is from dehydration while on the plane), being hungry at strange times, not wanting to eat at meals, inability to sleep, feeling so incredibly tired that you can't safely function, and waking up at unusual times of night and then being extremely wide awake.

That's a weird symptom list of opposites, right? Well, the reason all these things are happening is that your body is really stressed out while trying to fight being sleepy, and then the lag your body is experiencing is throwing your schedule off, which is then further affecting your nutrition and energy levels. You may normally eat dinner at 6:00 p.m., but that's at 3:00 a.m. in your new time zone. What's going to happen is, you probably won't be super hungry for dinner in the new time zone, and then you'll wake up in the middle of the night wide awake and starving. This is all pretty typical and why your symptoms can vary.

In my own experience, and many other people have echoed similar experiences, going seven to nine hours, or seven to nine time zones, east on a plane is the hardest to adjust to. Going west is significantly easier to recover from, and for whatever reason, shifting close to twelve hours is a pretty rapid one- to two-day recovery.

To make things easier on yourself, make sure you stay hydrated, which means always getting water in addition to your desired beverage whenever drinks are offered on the plane. Then drink at least a liter of water before taking a nap on arrival at your destination. Make sure to bring a couple of snack bars with you as well so that there's something on hand to eat in case you wake up starving. You may wake up in the middle of the night and be in a very unfamiliar area, so trying to find food right away in your new locale can be tricky or impossible, so prepare ahead. Other than that, expect the first day upon arrival in a totally new faraway time zone to be mostly a jet lag recovery day. Expect to take it a little easier than normal on the second day as well, but you probably won't be floored at any time on day two. By the third day, you should hopefully be able to power through any jet lag symptoms, but you probably won't be feeling normal yet.

MALARIA

Malaria deserves its own section. Malaria is a major annoyance that most equatorial travelers are going to have to worry about. Malaria is a disease caused by a single-celled parasite that is spread through mosquito bites. Because mosquitos thrive in hot, wet areas that have a lot of standing water, pretty much anywhere along the equator is a malaria risk zone.

Malaria symptoms are characterized by fever, headaches, vomiting, and general muscle and joint pain. Basically, it sounds like a really bad flu—except that getting rid of malaria is much harder than getting rid of the flu. Since malaria is a parasite and not a virus, no amount of sitting around in bed is likely to cure the malarial infection. You're going to need to see a doctor and get some antibiotics, and if the malarial infection has progressed significantly, you may be spending some significant time in the hospital. If left untreated, you can die.

Unfortunately, the best way to avoid dealing with malaria is to not get it in the first place, which really means don't get bit by mosquitos. Mosquitos are generally much more active at night than they are during the day, so using a mosquito net over your bed at night in areas with known malaria issues will greatly reduce the amount of exposure to bites. But be careful. If the net is directly resting on any part of your skin, then it's easy for the mosquito to just land on you and bite you right through the net.

While this seems like a great general solution, how many of us go to bed immediately upon sundown? This means you have a good bit of exposure to the mosquitos anyways, and you should avoid wearing dark clothing, which attracts mosquitos. Also make sure you're wearing some sort of spray or lotion with DEET or picaridin in it.

Another option is to pretreat your clothing with a chemical called permethrin. This turns your clothing into a mosquito repellent, but the chemical itself is not meant to be applied directly to your skin. However, permethrin only lasts through six clothes washes or six weeks, whichever happens first. Be very careful applying this chemical since permethrin is very toxic to some animals, particularly cats.

It's not well understood at the moment, but some people, like me, are mosquito magnets. This may have to do with your genetics and the way your blood smells to these little critters. If you're like me, opt for something that is 100 percent DEET and make sure your ankles, wrists, and neck are covered with some of the repellent or clothing. Also be careful to wash your hands after applying DEET or picaridin. It should go without saying that if something is repelling a wide range of insects, you probably don't want to eat it yourself.

I have been seeing more ads in the last few years regarding essential oil wristbands to deter mosquitos, and these are usually cloth bands soaked with citronella and other oils. Mosquitos don't like citronella, but these bands alone are not enough to stop mosquitos completely. I personally found they helped, since even 100 percent DEET doesn't completely save me as a mosquito magnet, but they are definitely less effective than DEET. DEET remains the gold standard mosquito repellent, but I'll keep doubling up with these bands since I still get bit anyway.

If for some reason you forget your mosquito repellent and end up in a mosquito-infested area, keep in mind that the locals don't like mosquitos either, so they're going to have some sort of repellent available that you can purchase. The options available may not be lotions or sprays, but they'll have something that will help you out.

Beyond taking these simple precautions, some people choose to take prophylactics. The prophylactics for malaria are small doses of the same antibiotic medication that would be used to treat malaria, with the idea being that your body becomes somewhat inhospitable to the parasite and so you're less likely to contract malaria with an infected bite. Notice I didn't say the prophylactic actually stops malaria. It just makes it less likely that you'll catch malaria. For this reason, a lot of people choose not to take the prophylactic because they all have nasty side effects and can be expensive. If you're in very large urban areas, your likelihood of infection is much smaller than if you're in rural areas, but this is not guaranteed.

If you develop a fever and joint pain during your trip and they won't go away, go see a doctor. You may have malaria.

METHANOL POISONING

When we drink beer or spirits and talk about alcohol content, what we're actually talking about is the content by volume of a chemical called ethanol. However, as part of the fermentation process that causes the production of ethanol, another chemical, methanol, is also produced. Unfortunately, methanol is incredibly toxic and can easily kill you, even in small quantities. In beer, the concentration of methanol is so low that the methanol is typically not removed. Beer is safe to drink.

The production of spirits, however, requires an extra step called distillation. Once a vat of liquid has been fermented, in order to concentrate the ethanol and be left with a spirit, the liquid is heated and the steam that comes off of this heated liquid is collected. Because ethanol is a small molecule, it steams off the liquid first and you end up with concentrated alcohol, which is your spirit.

There's a problem here, though, because there's also methanol in that liquid and methanol is actually a smaller molecule than ethanol. When the distillation process starts to take place, the first part of the spirit collected has a very high concentration of methanol and must literally be thrown away to prevent the creation of a poisonous batch of spirits.

People brewing their own local alcohols may not realize this methanol process or they may not be testing their spirits to make sure that they have removed the vast majority of the methanol. I have heard a few stories of people liking the way a local spirit tastes, then drinking a few cocktails with that spirit, only to die due to methanol poisoning.

So what happens if you get a drink with methanol? Well, you'll never know it's happening at the time. Methanol and ethanol smell and taste nearly identical and actually have a fairly similar list of effects on the body. Both cause loss of consciousness, loss of coordination, vomiting, and stomach pain. The main difference in symptoms is that a common complaint after ingestion of methanol is blurred vision. This is where the notion about drinking strong spirits, usually home-made illicit moonshine, led to the idea that "you'll go blind drinking that!" It's not the strong spirit that's the problem. It's that the person may have been drinking methanol.

I'm sure you can understand why this is so dangerous from the symptoms list. If you drink something with methanol in it, you have almost no way of knowing until you realize you aren't recovering normally from your night out. By this point, it is likely already way too late to do much for you. To drive this point home further, and I said it doesn't take much, only one-third of a shot glass of methanol is enough to make you go blind, and anymore than this amount is enough to kill more petite people.

My suggestions are:

- Avoid 100 percent of local spirits in MICs and LICs. These are going to be things you can't buy in professional-looking bottles.

- Be very wary of local alcohol that is in bottles that don't have state inspection stamps. If it's opened already or the vendor seems dodgy, don't risk your life.

- If you must drink hard liquor at a bar or club, make sure it's a recognized brand and looks correct in the bottle.

- If you are willing and able, drink beer instead of spirits, especially in less frequently visited, cheap, remote areas.

Places like Cancún are likely to not have problems with methanol, but the Gili Islands, which is an easy day trip from Bali, are going to be more suspect. Be careful. Don't take risks.

FEMININE HYGIENE

For ladies, your primary medical concern while traveling is going to be keeping your lady parts clean. There are three main issues that can arise if things are not kept generally clean: urinary tract infections known as UTIs, bacterial infections, and yeast infections.

A UTI is caused by bacteria that travels up the urinary canal and causes an internal bacterial infection. This infection usually starts in the bladder and causes burning urination and a strong desire to urinate even when the bladder is empty. Left untreated, this infection can spread up into the kidneys and this can be potentially life-threatening. The infection itself is usually caused by the bacteria *E. coli*, which lives in the intestines and is present in our environment as well. *E. coli* is usually harmless, but some variants can make you seriously ill.

The other two issues are hard to differentiate because of their similarities. Both cause the general symptoms of having a white or gray discharge from the vagina combined with possible redness and irritation. Itching is also a common complaint. If the infection is caused by bacteria, this is known as bacterial vaginosis, or BV. Yeast infections, also known as "thrush," are an overgrowth of the yeast strain known as candida. Both infection types have very similar symptom sets, but BV discharge may smell slightly fishy.

Be aware, highly perfumed sanitary items and changes in the acidity of water and food can throw off your system and cause these infections. If you are a person who is prone to infections at home, you will need to be vigilant while traveling to stop these infections before they get too bad.

Keeping your body clean is the main key to help prevent all three of these issues. Obviously, introducing dirt and grime into the vagina is not going to help prevent any infections. Unfortunately, one of the main treatments for UTIs is antibiotics, and taking these antibiotics can actually trigger a BV or thrush infection in response. Overall, sweat and sex are going to be the biggest contributing factors to getting bacteria into places they shouldn't be.

Sweat naturally contains a ton of bacteria and the fact that sweat rolls off of you also moves these bacteria around over your body. Any sort of tight clothing that creates rubbing is going to help rub sweat, and the bacteria it contains, up into the urinary tract and vagina. Cotton underwear is thought to help prevent this bacterial rubbing because cotton can absorb sweat, whereas synthetic fabrics cannot. Because underwear and rubbing are such an issue, it would seem on first thought that wearing no underwear and loose bottoms would arguably alleviate many of these issues. The open air would allow the sweat to dry and there wouldn't be any clothing to cause rubbing. That said, going around commando (no panties) is far from practical. If you do decide to go commando to avoid rubbing, make sure you aren't wearing an outer clothing article that has a seam right under your bits. That situation will actually make things worse than panty rubbing since clothing seams tend to be much coarser, which will harbor more bacteria.

Be sure to change your underwear every day as bacteria will build up in the underwear which will further worsen these issues. This is why I recommend women take twice the amount of underwear as men. Men can get away with wearing underwear for days or months, but most women likely cannot do the same without seriously risking infection.

There are some other underwear options besides just traditional panties. Athletic clothes meant for running, yoga, and weightlifting are usually made of synthetic materials, but check to make sure they have no seam under the crotch and are meant to allow sweat to evaporate.

Another option is to wear silver-infused panties. The metal silver is a natural antibacterial, and you can buy all sorts of athletic clothing with silver sewn into the fabric to avoid getting smelly from sweating. But you can also buy underwear made from the same silver-infused fabric. This will help reduce bacteria presence and is especially helpful if you are on a trek and are limited on how much clothing you can bring. For longer treks, if you don't go with the silver fabric, wool panties will also absorb sweat better than cotton or synthetic panties. Plus, wool naturally absorbs odors, which can be nice after days of hiking.

Sex also moves around these same skin bacteria. Many people have romantic encounters while traveling, so a potentially increased frequency of sexual encounters compared to being at home can cause more issues. Also, bacteria survive in water very well, so having sex in water will increase the chances of an infection.

Another thing that will help prevent infections is using wipes after the bathroom and sex. The products that you would likely prefer to use for wiping are unlikely to be available where you're traveling, so bring them with you. Baby wipes are usually fairly easy to find almost anywhere, but anything specific may be hard to come by, especially in MICs and LICs. Be sure to bring appropriate products with you if there is something specific you prefer at home.

As for treatments for these infections, UTIs and BVs are going to require antibiotics. Thrush can usually be treated with over-the-counter medication. But differentiating BV and thrush may not be easy and may require a trip to the doctor's office. If you are prone to one of these issues, I would recommend talking to your doctor at home and taking a supply of treatment with you when you leave.

If you are unable to immediately seek treatment, cutting down on alcohol and simple sugars in your diet and adding lots of veggies can potentially lessen the effects of these infections. Cranberry juice can also help, but finding cranberry juice in a large portion of the world may be difficult. Making these changes is unlikely to stop the infection, however, so make these changes as soon as you realize you're starting to have a problem and you may be able to prevent the infection from getting worse.

Another major feminine concern is going to be handling menstruation. In many very conservative countries, tampons are completely absent as a product choice because preserving the hymen is of utmost importance to "maintain purity." Many people in HICs would roll their eyes at this since strenuous physical exercise, such as running, can potentially break a hymen. But be aware, many cultures still think this way and may even forbid menstruating women from entering temples and holy places because they are "dirty" during this time. Also note that many tampons in Europe and other parts of the world do not come with applicators, so they must be inserted manually. Be sure to have clean hands first if you use these. Menstrual pads are generally available everywhere but are not a preferred option for many women. If pads work for you, you might look into reusable menstrual pads as another option, but consider the fact that doing laundry may be a very public operation during your trip. If you are considering using a "menstrual cup," I recommend paying close attention to the care instructions as you may find it very difficult or impossible to adequately clean them in MICs and LICs, particularly if the water in your location isn't drinkable for you. If inadequately washed or inserted under unsanitary conditions, you may suffer from infections even beyond those mentioned in this section. Overall, if you have a specific brand of products you use, bring enough to last your trip duration if there is any question that you might not be able to get a hold of your usual products. You might also consider coordinating with someone at home to send you a resupply during your trip.

Another thing that you may want to consider is to look into purchasing a female urination device (FUD). This is useful for women while traveling in LICs, while camping, or when visiting generally remote places. It's also useful in areas that may require outdoor relief in very cold temperatures. This device takes a little practice to use but allows women to urinate while standing up and without having to remove a lot of clothing.

Last, be very careful when buying any feminine product, including makeup, anywhere in the world. Many products contain skin whiteners because pale skin is considered to be "more attractive" and "purer" in many parts of the world. These products can permanently affect your skin and may cause a blotchy appearance to be stained into your skin. Look at the label and make sure that nothing you buy contains these whitening ingredients. These could be in the treatments mentioned in this section but could also be in lotions, cosmetics, and soaps.

MINOR SICKNESSES AND PHARMACIES

Another thing you should be concerned about is religiously washing your hands. People who do not wash their hands thoroughly or frequently enough are thought to be one of the significant sources of traveler's diarrhea. This is where having a water bottle and a small bottle of soap on you at all times in MICs and LICs is incredibly important because you may not have a sink, but you should still wash your hands anyway. See the "Toilets" section for how to wash your hands without a sink. Another reason for washing your hands is to avoid getting the common cold and the flu.

If you get a common cold or the flu, which can be hard to distinguish between, you may need medication to treat your symptoms and these can sometimes be hard to find. Make sure to bring at least a few day's worth of your regular cold medication to hold you over until you can get to a larger city and find a pharmacy. Many developed countries will require your passport if you need to buy a decongestant because one of the ingredients common to many decongestants can be used to make methamphetamine, a powerful and illegal drug.

When I was in China, I got a sinus infection after a couple of weeks of being sick with a cold. I didn't need to see a doctor because I'd had enough sinus infections to know what was happening. Lucky for me, many pharmacies outside of the Western HICs will just sell anything you ask for to you over the counter. That said, no one in the pharmacy spoke English and none of them knew what drug I had written down on paper. They kept taking me to cough drops and such, but I needed antibiotics. I started looking around, and sure enough, what I had written down on paper, which was "6 x 250 mg Azithromycin" was sitting on the shelf just behind their counter. When I pointed behind the counter and made a questioning "Can I?" look, they let me behind the counter and I showed them that what I wrote down matched the box. They sold it to me without question, and I was feeling great a few days later.

Because of this experience, I highly recommend knowing the chemical name of the medications you commonly take at home, and this will go a long way toward self-treatment during your trip.

SCUBA DIVING SAFETY

This is super brief but important. Getting decompression sickness or "the bends" is a real thing and can be life-threatening. You can also severely injure yourself if you hold your breath while ascending. These things will be covered in depth in any scuba certification class you may take, but be really careful while traveling to avoid these issues. You may be significantly far away from treatment, so even a mild dive injury could prove life-threatening if you're hours away from a knowledgeable doctor who has a hyperbaric chamber and can treat you.

If you plan on scuba diving a lot during your trip, I highly recommend getting Divers Alert Network insurance, commonly called DAN. This insurance will connect you with dive injury treatment centers around the world in the case of an accident and will help you get to one of these centers quickly in an emergency. Don't mess around with your life. Insurance for medical emergencies is always justified.

KNOWING IS HALF THE BATTLE

Beyond what I've mentioned so far in this section, I highly recommend taking at least a first-aid class before your trip. The American Red Cross offers good basic courses within the US. They're relatively cheap and will teach you about basic medical emergencies and how to handle them. Chances are, you won't come across most emergencies while you travel, but if you do see something, it will probably be cuts and broken bones. Just knowing what to look for can make a huge difference in an emergency.

For cuts, apply pressure until it stops bleeding and be vigilant about keeping it clean. If the cut is even remotely long or deep, get to a medical professional as soon as you can and get the cut cleaned out and stitched up. Not properly taking care of cuts can result in infections, and infections can easily kill you if left untreated.

For broken bones, splinting a break is an art form, but the basics are that you need to immobilize what's broken *and* the joint at either end of the break. So if someone breaks their forearm, the wrist and elbow need to be secured so they can't move, and the forearm also needs to be held still. The easiest way to do this is to wrap up the person's arm against their chest, with their hand on the opposite shoulder. This will keep their elbow from moving as well and secure their forearm. Just from this description, it should be pretty clear that splinting is not something that is obvious or easy to do. If you do not understand how to properly splint a bone break, do not attempt to do so. You will cause more damage to the injury, which will obviously make the injury worse.

Regardless of your medical training, if you see any bone breaks, get medical treatment immediately. Smaller broken bones are not usually a big deal but do need to be treated in a timely manner. Large broken bones like the legs and pelvis can be immediately life-threatening. For anything more serious, like head trauma or stroke, you will need to seek immediate professional medical help. In LICs and rural MIC areas, this could be very hard to find and you're at the mercy of their medical system. My general medical advice to you is to avoid taking risks that could cause you physical harm to begin with. Analyze your environment and your remoteness, and don't take chances.

SAFETY AND SECURITY

The question I probably get most frequently when it comes to traveling for the first time is, "Is it safe there?" I even see experienced travelers get really nervous about this when traveling to new places, too. For the most part, unless you are traveling to a war zone or a country with very serious social issues (i.e., revolution, famine, or lawlessness), the answer to the question "Is it safe?" is "Yes, the country you're going to is safe."

One thing that newer travelers greatly overestimate is the differences between groups of people around the world, and this is exactly what leads to the concerns about safety. Cultural differences do exist, but I would argue that they're mostly matters of etiquette and civility. However, nearly every single person on this planet wants the same basic things: safety, a home, education, a job, a family, and the freedom to go about their daily business. Because you're already part of a group of people like this in your own country, you already understand how everyone around the planet is thinking about life.

The area where this becomes confusing for some people is when there is extreme poverty in the country they're visiting. You have to keep in mind that just by the fact that you're physically in that country and on "a vacation" (holiday) in whatever sense means that you could be financially worth literally thousands of times more than the local people around you. This can be true even if you're on a tight budget. Because of this, to some of the locals in those places, you are literally a walking ATM of potential financial relief for their situation. Spending one dollar on a bottle of water may not even faze you, but it could be worth days of food to the person you're giving that dollar to.

The people you may be interacting with may be desperate for money in order to sustain themselves, and you may represent the solution. This desperation, especially if someone is hungry, can lead them to commit acts that more financially well-off people would never consider. But these are still people, just like you, who just happen to be in a different, more desperate life situation.

It is possible that you could be robbed, but it's more likely you may have people very aggressively begging or trying to get you to buy something from them. It is very, very uncommon, though, that people will resort to actual violence. The vast majority of people around the world do not want to harm someone, but that doesn't mean they won't threaten you with violence to potentially shed you of your valuables. The more likely scenario is pickpocketing and petty scams, both of which are theft in different ways.

Not everyone in a poverty-ridden country is going to be looking at you like a hungry lion looks at a zebra. Furthermore, not everyone is going to try and rob you. Both of these things are rare, even in poverty-stricken countries. It's simply that by comparison, you are fabulously wealthy compared to some of the locals who you may be interacting with, and this can make you a target for desperate people.

Also, even in wealthy areas like Europe, you as a tourist are walking around with all sorts of goodies—passports, cameras, phones, etc. Anyone who has chosen theft as a way of life will be attracted to tourists because tourists are fixated on seeing things and aren't paying attention to their surroundings, which makes them an easy target.

Although these issues are rare, it's still important to learn to deal with anything that arises. Just like you avoid bad areas and strange people on the street in your hometown right now, you need to do the same while traveling. This is where a lot of travelers leave their brains at home when they go on a trip. Just because you're away from home and are expecting to have fun on your trip doesn't mean the day-to-day rules have somehow changed.

Let's talk about the common things that might happen to you and how to avoid them.

SCAMS, PICKPOCKETS, AND SOCIAL TRICKS

The first and foremost rule of safety and security to remember is be very cautious of anyone who approaches you in public. This is so important that I'm going to repeat it.

Be very cautious of anyone who approaches you in public.

Think about it for a second. How often does a stranger come up and talk to you randomly while you're at home? Beggars maybe? Once a year maybe someone asking you for directions? If you're a female, maybe some guy trying to hit on you? However, when you travel, you will be approached constantly by beggars and scammers. Every now and then, someone will ask me to take of picture of them, but be aware that this can be a scam, too.

Being cautious of people does not mean you should avoid talking to locals and interacting with people. The other travelers you meet will be a huge part of your trip because you are all having the shared experience of being away from home, not knowing where things are, and are experiencing a culture likely for the first time. Other travelers are usually pretty easy to pick out.

As for locals, there are many countries where you may be a curiosity because they don't frequently get visitors. The locals in these places will genuinely want to know about you and talk to you if they can. This is an excellent way for you to learn about the culture and the people, and if you are able to effectively communicate with a friendly local, I highly recommend you take that opportunity. There is simply no better way to see a culture than through the eyes of someone who lives there.

If you're in a shop or at a market and the person you're buying from starts chatting with you, this is fairly normal. If you're on a train and someone in your aisle or compartment says "Hello" and talks to you, this is also normal. If you're at a restaurant and the family at the table next to you keeps looking at you and asks to take a picture with you or buy a dessert for you, this is, believe it or not, fairly normal because they're curious about you.

But if you're standing in the street looking at a map and someone walks up and tries to tell you to follow them, this is not normal; do not go with them. If someone walks up to you and says they know a good place to book tours, you do not know who they are, so do not give them your money and do not follow them. If you're in a bar and suddenly locals start buying you rounds of drinks, this is not normal because no one would just start throwing money at someone else like this. You may be a robbery target and they may be trying to drug you.

That said, you'd be weird if you started running away from anyone who gets near you. That means you are going to have moments of interaction no matter what. Stay cautious when you're approached. Be aware of what they are trying to do and know they may have other motives. Once you understand what the common scams look like, you'll be much better prepared to determine what's happening when you're experiencing it firsthand. Let's go through some common scams.

People Asking You for Directions

Let's analyze this. How often do you visit tourist sights in your home city? Not often probably. Once you've seen something, you've seen it and don't frequently go back. Most people don't repeatedly go to the tourist sights in their hometown. That means, in general, that almost every person at a tourist site is not from the city where that site is located.

Next, how often do you travel around with a daypack? Some people, like me, carry a laptop bag to work every day, but most people don't carry around a pack when they're just out on the town. The reason why is because you know the area really well and you're probably not too far from home, work, or school. You know where there are bathrooms, water, and food readily available and nearby, so you don't need to carry your own supplies.

However, when you travel, you're almost certainly going to carry around a daypack. You need a guidebook (or a digital copy which is easy for anyone to see that you're looking at on your phone or tablet), water, cameras, chargers, etc. You're likely out all day and in a location where you don't have your normal goods readily available, so you have to carry your own supply.

So when you go to a tourist site and see people wearing backpacks, chances are, you're looking at someone who is from out of town and is almost certainly not familiar with the area they're in.

Which brings up the question, "Why would anyone be asking you for directions if you look like a tourist and therefore almost certainly don't know the area?" Chances are, you're being targeted by a pickpocket. What's happening here is someone is distracting you in order to allow their buddy (mate) to get closer to you on your other side so they can take your stuff while you're paying attention to the person talking to you. This is especially true if the person appears to be a local.

If the person looks like a tourist and is also wearing a pack like you, they legitimately may be asking for directions. If you believe the question is real, make sure no one is standing close to you, and be aware of anyone moving toward you while you talk to them. Do not start pulling out guidebooks and phones to help them out. Even if no one else is standing nearby, that doesn't mean the person you're talking to isn't going to grab your phone and run as soon as you pull it out.

Most people, even in the poorest areas, have smartphones with Google Maps nowadays. You may get interesting excuses, too, like, "My phone battery died. Do you know where so-and-so is? Can you show me on your phone?"

Don't be tempted by anything like this. If you're outside of your home country, chances are, you don't have a data plan on your phone where you're heading, so just be polite and tell them you don't have data and your phone doesn't work there.

People Claiming They Are Guides

This one is annoying and harder to spot. The scenario here is that you've arrived at a tourist site and immediately someone comes up to you and says something like, "Hello, are you visiting so-and-so today? Let's head over here to get you tickets and then you can enter over here," etc.

The harder-to-spot problem here is that typically, the people who run the tourist site don't even realize or maybe don't care that this is happening outside of the site. And lots of people arrive with tour groups that have prearranged guides, so it's hard to tell a real guide from someone just standing in front.

The reality, though, is that these guides are totally bogus and have nothing to do with the site you're visiting. These are just regular people who hang around and prey on unsuspecting tourists by forcing themselves into your visit and then asking for payment for their "services."

Sometimes these people will insist that you need to be with a guide to get into the site. This is completely false. I think I've been at two, maybe three, places in the world that absolutely required a tour guide, and the ticket counter will make this very clear and assign you a time and place to wait for your guide. Your "required" guide isn't going to bombard you with questions the moment you get near the front entrance.

This guide problem is especially bad in India, and you need to be very confrontational when you say, "I don't need a guide and I know I can get in here without you," in order to get them to back off. They may still try to follow you anyway. Ignore them. They may tell you that you need to buy stuff. Refuse.

People Selling Tours

This tends to occur in major city centers where tourists frequent. Someone will either try to ask you where and how you're going to be traveling, or they will try to tell you about their tour package for a trip. Quite frequently, the people advertising these tours and trips out in public are not legitimate. It may seem like it's smart thinking to advertise tours to tourists who are out and about, but the vast majority of tourists are already going to have bookings like this before they even leave for their trip, which is why this may be a scam targeting people who are new to travel.

What can happen is that you decide to buy a tour from this person, or to see a listing of their tour offerings, and then you head to some office where a number of things can happen. One possibility is that you give them money and the tour doesn't exist and now you're off somewhere else without any way of confronting the tour office. Or you pay for the tour and it's extremely subpar and again you have no recourse. Another possibility is that you get to the office, now out of the public eye, and you get robbed. This is exceptionally rare, though.

I heard one story of a tourist group in China who paid for tickets to a performance show on a river through one of these scam groups, and rather than being in the official bleachers of the show, they were made to sit on the riverbank almost a mile (roughly one and a half kilometers) away and could hardly see anything at all. When they complained, they were threatened with being beat-up and were told to enjoy the show. Don't end up in this situation.

To avoid all of these possibilities, use your hotel or hostel to book tours. Or find a reputable tour company through TripAdvisor. They will know who the legitimate tour companies are and will know which tours give you the best experiences. They may send you to a tour office, but if the hotel is recommending the company, it's likely legitimate.

People Asking Where You're From

This is a gateway to many other scams. It's meant to push on your innate human response to not be rude to someone, but within a couple of minutes, the conversation rapidly turns into offers for tours or trying to sell you something else.

The easiest way to avoid this is just to keep walking or ignore the person talking to you.

Sometimes, if you're in a line (queue) waiting with the person who asks you this, this can be a legitimate inquiry, especially in places that don't get a lot of tourists, but if you're on the move and this happens, just keep walking.

People Asking for Pictures or Asking to Practice English

Both of these are very prominent in China but happen elsewhere, too. The scenario is that you're at a tourist site or in a major city area, and someone walks up to you, starting with something like, "Will you please take my picture?" Then they start talking about how they want to practice English. Or a lot of times, this person will just say, "Hello, I would like to practice my English. Would you be willing to come with me to a coffee/tea shop?" This can be a complete scam, and it especially snares single male travelers when approached by some cute, young female. This can still target couples, women, and groups, too.

What ends up happening is that you go to the shop they talked about and get a menu. You see prices and order something off the menu. Then, when the bill comes, the bill is ten to one hundred times what was listed on the menu. When you start to complain, they show you a menu that has the marked-up prices and swear that's the only menu they have. If you really start to make a scene, you're already off the street and out of the public eye, so they either rob you or beat you up and rob you.

Don't fall into this trap to begin with, and be aware that if you do get trapped that you're in a very dangerous situation if you don't fork over the money. Chances are, there are big men just out of sight waiting for you to start making an issue out of the situation.

Despite being a seasoned traveler, a close friend of mine at home ended up in a similar situation to this once, and when he realized what was going on, he immediately stood up and started walking towards the door while continually throwing bills out of his wallet all over the place as he kept walking. What the staff didn't immediately realize, however, was that he was throwing small, almost worthless, bills from another country everywhere. This was smart. They did quickly catch on to what he was doing, though, and there ended up being a huge confrontation at the doorway as they realized his "payment" wasn't even legal tender there. Things got really nasty and they basically took all his money, but they let him go. That said, they likely let him go because he's incredibly tall, well built, and former military. Someone else might not have been so lucky.

If you're so inclined to try going into a coffee shop or tea house with a local anyway, go to a shop of your choosing, not theirs. And pick something in a crowded area and preferably a known place like Starbucks, McDonald's, or some other major chain.

The Friendly Drinker

This one happens a lot all over the world and can be potentially life-threatening. This happens when you're out drinking, and some locals will start chatting with you. Everything will seem fine, and as the night goes on, it seems you are bonding and having a good time. The next thing you remember is waking up in the street without any of your possessions. What happened? You got drugged.

Someone put something in your drink and you passed out. Since you looked like you drank too much, no one really noticed when you got carried about the bar, and at that point, the person who drugged you can have their way with you. For obvious reasons, this can have especially bad consequences if you're a woman.

How to avoid this? First, always watch your drink. And more specifically, if you drink cocktails, watch your drink being made. If you order beer, ask for it to be opened in front of you. Don't leave your drink unsupervised, and if you do, then don't assume it's going to be left alone while you're gone.

Also, be careful about how much you drink. Another variant of this scam is that you don't get drugged but get very drunk with the locals who then invite you to another bar. Once they have you out and walking (stumbling?) around, they lead you down some alley and proceed to jump and rob you.

Be careful here. Talking to locals is desirable to many travelers, but you can easily be taken advantage of when you're drunk and unaware of your surroundings.

The Dropped Wallet

In this scam, a wallet is dropped in public somewhere. The main catch here is that the person who dropped the wallet is actually part of the scam. Someone else, not the wallet dropper, will try to convince you to pick up the wallet. This person is going to appear to be another tourist trying to do the right thing, but they're also part of the scam. Once you're actually touching the wallet, suddenly the "wallet owner" will reappear and accuse you of stealing their wallet or removing money from the wallet. Suddenly, everyone turns against you and is demanding money from you. If you pull your wallet out, someone grabs it and it's gone.

The biggest thing here is that you're being lured into touching the wallet. Avoid this. If you see someone drop their wallet, and understandably want to do the right thing and help them out, don't touch the wallet, but rather, run after them and let them know they dropped their wallet.

Another variation of this is dropping the wallet in a bus station or train station where you likely have all of your stuff, not just your daypack, and are waiting for your transportation to arrive. You see the wallet drop and run after the person but leave your things behind. Because your bags were on the ground as you ran off, when you come back, your stuff is gone.

Avoid this by never leaving your stuff, ever. If someone does drop their wallet and you're shouting after them, they will likely turn around and respond to you. Someone who doesn't respond to you or turn around when you shout after them is probably a scammer.

The Arm over the Shoulder

The premise here is that you're walking along and a group of drunken guys is singing their way down the street. A lot of soccer (football) teams around the world have chants associated with the team, and that's usually what this group of guys will be reveling in as they go down the street. You're innocently walking along and they seem to joyously want to include you in their celebration, so you end up with an arm over your shoulder and are suddenly in the middle of the group. What you don't realize is that your belongings are being taken right off of your person, and if you resist, you're now in a headlock in the middle of a group that's about to beat you up.

To avoid this, first, don't let the group get anywhere near you to begin with. Being in the middle of a bunch of drunk, rowdy guys on the street is a bad idea regardless of their intention. If you do end up in this arm hold, act fast. Since this is a more aggressive robbery tactic, you need to immediately become violent and get away from them.

No one should be touching you without your permission anywhere in the world. This is not normal behavior to just grab someone in the street. So as soon as you feel someone grabbing you, you need to shove them away and get away from the group as quickly as possible. Literally run.

The Baby Toss

This supposedly used to happen a lot back in the seventies and eighties, but I'm unaware of anyone who has actually experienced this. The idea here is that a group of pickpockets lurks in waiting, and then as soon as you come along, a woman with a baby approaches you. As she gets closer, she proceeds to throw the baby, which is actually a doll, at you, causing you to panic and grab the baby. As you stand there catching the "baby," the other pickpockets run and grab everything they can off of you and run away while you're distracted. Avoid this by being vigilantly aware of people walking toward you, and if they throw something at you, immediately start running forward and past them. I mean, what sane person would throw their real baby at you?

The Jammed ATM

You are incredibly vulnerable at ATMs when you're in unfamiliar areas. One scam is the "jammed" ATM, where you can't get the ATM to work, but someone suddenly shows up to help you out and then proceeds to rob you when the money comes out. A related scam is almost the same thing, except that you are led to another ATM that actually works. What you don't realize is that there was a fake card reader on the previous ATM and someone is already using your card information to withdraw your money while you're walking to the new ATM. The way to avoid this is to always check the ATM for any oddities, and if you have any problems, walk away and use a totally different ATM without assistance.

Another issue is people watching you while you use the ATM, knowing that afterward, you probably have a bunch of money on you which makes you a good robbery target. When you do withdraw money, do it as a separate errand and go back to your accommodation immediately and leave most of the money in your locker or main pack. Be aware of people watching you at the ATM and never reveal your PIN to anyone.

The Freshly Opened Locker

In this ploy, you walk up to lockers at a train station or bus terminal in hopes of storing your stuff for the day. As you're walking up, someone else is removing their stuff from a locker and holds the door open for you to put your own stuff in. They tell you the key didn't work very well, but they'll help you out with it since they already had to figure it out. Already, this should seem odd. If the key doesn't work, then don't use that locker. The main ploy here is that you think the locals are super nice and willing to help.

What's really happening, however, is that the moment they lock the locker, they sneakily hand you a different key. Since most of the lockers around the world charge you for opening/locking the locker (you can hear the coins drop during either stage), you aren't going to test the locker to see if it works since you'll be charged again. After you walk away, they come back with the real key and take your stuff. Avoid this by handling the locker yourself, alone, with no "help."

The Pickpocket Sign

This one is a little different because there may not be someone directly approaching you, but this situation actually makes me laugh because of the irony of the behavioral aspect. What happens here is that police have become aware that pickpockets are hanging out around a certain area or site. So in trying to be vigilant in protecting the public, the police put up signs stating "Beware of Pickpockets." What happens, though, is that most people, upon seeing this sign, immediately go through all their valuables to make sure they haven't already been pickpocketed. What really just happened if you do this, though, is that you've just gone through a list of all the locations of all the valuables on your person for any pickpocket who may be watching you. Now it's really easy for them to pickpocket you successfully because they know where the good stuff is located.

So, by the police putting up the sign, they've actually made it easier for pickpockets to do their work, and so more pickpockets come to these areas. Weird, isn't it? Avoiding this is easy. Don't keep your wallet or any valuables in your back pocket, and don't start going through your stuff when you see these signs. Knowing about this issue, I keep my larger camera on a strap around my neck if I'm using it. It's clearly out in the open, but unless someone plans on ripping it straight off my head, they aren't going to get it. I also don't need to check where it is; I can see it in plain view.

The Resort Checkout Stall Tactic

In this situation, you are staying in a resort or some other type of luxury accommodation. A lot of these places will have combo deals where you can pay money for certain extras or perks, like massages and spa treatments. Usually, they will include a certain amount of credit for these sorts of things as part of the booking. Other times, this will be in the form of a booking promo where "If you book seven days at our resort, you will receive $500 in resort credit to be used anywhere on the resort." Whether or not you have a promo like this, make sure you get receipts for everything you do at the resort, and make sure any promo dollars like this are applied correctly and show up on your receipt.

The scam for this situation then takes place when you are checking out. Typically, people check out just a little before they need to depart. You will go to the lobby and try to settle your bill only to discover the promo hasn't been applied correctly, or there are all sorts of charges you don't recognize, or the charges don't add up quite right. Now, the resort just stalls and says things like, "Oh, well, we calculated everything correctly," or "We can't change anything without a manager looking at it," or "You can't leave until you settle your bill."

They're preying on the fact that you need to leave and they're threatening you as if you're skipping out on your bill. No manager will be around, and now you're being heavily pressured to pay whatever amount they came up with or potentially face the consequences of refusing to pay. You're also further pressured because you don't want to miss your flight, boat, or whatever activity you have planned next. They may even threaten to call the police.

Don't fall into this trap. Settle your bill the day before you need to check out when you aren't under a time pressure or at least request to see your current bill and verify its accuracy. Then, if there are any issues, you can spend as much time as you need making sure things are correct.

MORE BLATANT ISSUES

While there are all sorts of scams that can occur, there are also more blatant issues that are rarely encountered. These are things like muggings, being robbed, and kidnapping. These may require more aggression and a willingness to fight on your part. Taking a self-defense class or martial arts for a few months is a wise idea, not just for traveling but for everyday life. If you ever need to fight for some reason, you're not going to figure out how to do so in the moment. You need to learn beforehand how to fight and have this knowledge and muscle memory on hand when you need it.

There are many self-defense seminars available around the world particularly for women, but if you want to get a serious introduction to something useful for these purposes, I highly recommend finding a Krav Maga studio. If you are unable to find a studio or unsure you want to go this route, Impact Krav Maga in San Diego and Krav Maga Global in Israel both have online programs with a free trial period so you can see these techniques. Check out impactkravmagaonline.com and maxkravmaga.com. Be aware, watching the videos will do nothing for you if you don't practice, practice, practice. Some folks may dispute that Krav Maga is a good introduction to self-defense, but I'm shooting for 80/20 here. Krav Maga will give you a solid foundation to start with if self-defense is new to you.

Now let's talk about some of the blatant issues you will hopefully never experience.

Someone Walking Straight at You

This is a bit more difficult to describe, but you'll know if this is happening to you. Imagine that you're walking down a street and there are few people around. Then you see one of the very few people on this street suddenly made an adjustment in their direction of motion and now they're directly on a collision course with you. It's fairly easy to tell, just by looking at the person, that something isn't right about this situation. Maybe they're coming to rob you, but who knows? Why wait to find out?

If you're in this situation, change your direction and steer away from the person coming at you. If they alter their course to match yours, this is now clearly abnormal from how regular people behave. If they're still coming at you, you have three options: (1) Let them get really close to you, which I don't recommend; (2) Very quickly start moving away from them, running if you have to; or (3) Make it very clear that you're ready to fight, which means getting out in the open and putting hands partially up like you're ready to react to anything.

The second is the preferred option, but if you're stuck with confrontation, most aggressors are going to back off with the third option simply because you're making it clear that whatever is about to happen isn't about to happen easily.

If You Do Get Robbed

I know a lot of people who have been flat-out robbed while traveling. Obviously from some of the scenarios that have been discussed, there's a lot of ways you could be robbed without even realizing it. But the scenarios could start the same and then turn into open robbery. This said, robberies are usually fairly easy to avoid.

If you do get directly robbed, be calm. Chances are, you're going to be at knifepoint, but you may have a gun pointed at you. Remember, people don't want to hurt others normally, and if you're getting robbed, they're trying to take your stuff, not kill you. If they wanted to kill you, they would have done so immediately. So don't give them a reason to hurt you by resisting.

Calmly hand over anything they ask for and they will likely leave on their own. The worst that's going to happen is that you lose your camera, passport, and money. These are all replaceable. And interestingly from listening to my friend's tales of being robbed, most robbers understand that your loss is more the emotional aspect of potentially losing memories of your trip, so if you ask for your memory card out of your camera, they'll probably give it to you because it will calm you down and therefore make you less likely to freak out and they can disappear without having to hurt you.

Almost every story I've heard about robberies could have been avoided, though. A few people have been taking walks on unlit beaches in the middle of the night in MICs and LICs. A few people were walking to their hostel drunk by themselves, through bad neighborhoods, again in the middle of the night. Some people were wearing fancy jewelry and were completely alone. Some people took paths through remote back alleys and walked right into thugs hanging out back there. Almost all of these robberies could have been easily avoided. Most people wouldn't do this stuff at home, so don't do it while you travel.

Robbery at Gunpoint

The major "easy to avoid" exception to the robbery stories that I've heard from travelers has been in the country of Brazil, which has a serious, brazen, daylight-robbery-at-gunpoint problem, mainly in the big cities. From these stories, as a single example, someone was on a famous beach surrounded by thousands of people, and then someone sat next to them with a newspaper, and they look over to see the newspaper is covering a pistol that's pointed at them. There's a good chance these pistols aren't even loaded, but don't take that chance. Remember, people don't want to hurt you unless they have to.

While this is an issue in Brazil, that doesn't mean that you can't be robbed at gunpoint almost anywhere in the world.

My main comment on this, though, is:

Do not attempt to fight someone with a gun.

Why? Gun self-defense techniques are meant to be used when you are *absolutely certain* that you are going to be shot if you do not do something. Anyone robbing you does not want to kill you, so this does not apply. It's also likely that anyone robbing you with a gun is probably not very highly trained in the use of that weapon. If they were, they'd probably have a decent job or something better to do than trying to rob you. Most untrained people holding a gun have a nasty and dangerous tendency to keep their finger on the trigger. Trained people do not do this.

Combine these two things together, and any sudden, quick movement you make toward your robber is going to cause them to tighten up, which means they're going to naturally tighten their fist, and this means their trigger finger is going to squeeze off a bullet in your direction. Instead of fighting and potentially being shot, give the robber what they want and you get to live to see another day.

Kidnapping

Kidnapping is exceptionally rare and is even more exceptionally rare to happen to anyone on a budget trip. Kidnappers are looking for money, and if you don't look like you have a lot of money, it's not worth their time for them to try and kidnap you. The most likely scenario here is you are going to be jumped by a group of people and thrown into a car. If you end up in this situation for some reason, the biggest thing to do is just remain calm. There's really not a lot you can do without seriously jeopardizing your physical safety. Work with your captors and try to make your way to freedom.

Colombia used to be *the* country that everyone thought of with kidnapping, and for a long time, they really did have a very high kidnapping rate compared to the rest of the world, but this was mainly the result of internal fighting with FARC and drug lords. Both of these issues have essentially disappeared nowadays, and Colombia is much safer to visit than in the past.

Being Female

I hate that this is still an issue in the world, but being female unfortunately makes you a target for sexual violence. In parts of the world like India, sexual violence is far more common than it should be, and the culture has not yet stamped out the issues that lead to this kind of violence. Even in many HICs, rape and sexual assault are not uncommon crimes. Planned rape, however, is a rarity while traveling. Forced entry into a hotel room or someone stalking you is rare. There are many people around in hotels and hostels, especially in common areas, so it would be very difficult for an attacker to remain unseen.

Instead, most assaults are going to be crimes of opportunity, and that's where common sense is important. Meaning:

* Don't wander around late at night in areas without a lot of people.

* Don't wander around while completely obliterated by drugs or alcohol.

* Don't hang out by yourself on beaches where few people are around.

* Be very careful to watch where taxis are going and that you're not being driven off to somewhere other than your destination.

* Don't accept the advances of local men unless you are certain you can trust them.

If for some reason something does happen, you are very unlikely to be armed since almost no country will let you enter their borders carrying any kind of weapon. This is where learning self-defense or martial arts comes in handy, and if your attacker is unarmed as well, fight for your life. If your attacker is armed, there may not be much you can do. Either way, if you become a victim, immediately find the police when you are able.

Rape prevention classes are also excellent places to learn the mindset and physical techniques to help avoid this situation ever happening.

ODDS AND ENDS

One thing to be mindful of is that the previous examples are only a few possibilities of the safety and security concerns of travel. Also, safety and security concerns don't stop once you are back in your hotel room.

Always lock up your valuables in your room. Hotel staff and other hostel occupants can easily take anything that's out in the open. Hostels almost universally have lockers, but sometimes they are kind of small. If that's the case, make sure that your bag is always locked with your stuff inside. Most non-scam theft is a matter of opportunity, and while it's easy to cut open a bag to get to its contents, that's still a lot of work, and most criminals are going to go for an easier, quicker target.

Also, never take anything valuable with you traveling. This can include your clothes. I roomed with a guy in Australia who once did his laundry in a hostel and left his folded Calvin Klein boxers on the bed while he went to take a shower, only to come back and find his underwear had been stolen.

Jewelry and electronics are major targets, and while you want to have some sort of camera and probably a tablet while traveling, make sure these are locked up when you walk away.

It's okay to lose your wallet if something happens for whatever reason. Your debit and credit cards are easy to cancel and replace, and your money is just a bit of money. Further, be smart and don't walk around with all of your cards and all of your cash in your wallet. Make dedicated trips to the ATM and then leave your cards and your excess cash in your locker or room. This way, if anything does happen, you are only losing a day's worth of cash and nothing else.

Passports should also be left locked in your bag while you're out. Many countries say that you're supposed to have your passport on you at all times, but this is bogus. The worst that's going to happen if you get detained by the police for some reason is they take you back to your accommodation to get your passport. Passports don't seem like they should be valuable, but the reason they are valuable is because of asylum laws. Say you're trying to claim asylum in the US but can't get there to do so. If you can get a passport with a replaced picture, it gives you the ability to travel to the US and, once there, claim asylum status. The big problem is getting there, though, and that's where the passport comes in. So while the passport is worthless to us beyond traveling, it's a major target to steal for many countries. Worse, people with bad intentions can use passports to smuggle themselves into other countries. Always keep copies of your passport in your bag, in your wallet, and in a third location like your email in case of theft or loss.

Another sort of odd thing to keep in mind are traffic-related issues. There are two main styles of driving in the world: organized and chaotic. Organized driving is probably what most people reading this book experience in their home countries, where people obey stop signs and lights, and people stay in their lanes as they drive. Chaotic driving is something seen in Italy, China, India, and a number of other places. Basically, people don't necessarily follow the traffic rules in the way that you may expect. If you are organized driving in a chaotic driving environment, or vice versa, be aware that you are screwing up their system because you are not driving like everyone else.

The main reason I bring this up, though, is how you're going to cross the street. In most places with chaotic driving, you need to just walk into traffic in order to cross the street. People in cars will not stop for you otherwise, but they will stop to avoid hitting you. This, however, is not true in India, where you will get hit if you don't time your street crossing carefully. Watch what the locals are doing to cross the street and copy them. If you aren't 100 percent certain how chaotic traffic works where you're going, spend some time watching what the locals are doing and replicate it.

ADDITIONAL SAFETY AND SECURITY THOUGHTS

All of these safety and security concerns we talked about may be making you second-guess if you even want to travel at all. But I can't emphasize this enough: most people around the world are just like you. While poverty can cause desperation, most people are not violent and most people respect others. You are unlikely to have any safety and security problems while traveling if you use even the slightest bit of precaution and common sense, just like you would at home. I hope anyone who had some anxiety about safety before reading this is a little more at ease now even though this chapter focuses on all the bad things that can happen.

Even after all my travels, I've never had an issue. There have been a few awkward moments, and the only thing that I've had stolen is an eye mask that I left out on my bunk, and my guess is the other person got confused and thought they had dropped theirs.

In general, you're safe and you're always surrounded by people like you, so you'll be all right wherever you travel as long as you remember to take the same precautions that you'd take at home. The biggest deterrent to any issues is looking confident and being aware of your surroundings. Did someone just walk up behind you? Is that person to your left eyeing your bag? Is the guy at the end of the street sizing you up? Be aware of these things and act like you know what you're doing and you're ready for anything. Simply standing up straight, looking at people directly, looking confident, and being aware of your immediate surroundings are going to deter almost any scammer and thief. Stay in the mindset of not being a victim, and you won't be a victim.

As the saying goes, roughly, "Locks are only there to keep honest people honest." The idea here is that locks don't prevent theft; they deter theft. If someone really wanted to get into something, the lock wouldn't stop them. Deter all theft by staying vigilant.

You may also have noticed that most of the scams were trying to take advantage of someone's normal reaction to "do the right thing." Be aware of this. Don't touch anything that's not yours and don't blindly think that someone is helping you out.

HOW TO HANDLE EMERGENCIES

True emergencies are very rare, but what happens if you really do have an emergency? If you break a leg while cliff jumping or end up in the middle of social unrest or riots somewhere, what do you do? These are serious emergencies and you're going to have to handle them immediately. Emergencies essentially fall into two major categories: medical and non-medical.

MEDICAL EMERGENCIES

If you end up in a medical emergency, your travel insurance is going to be critically important. First, your immediate priority is going to be getting to a hospital and becoming medically stable. What I mean by stable is that you are no longer at risk of dying. If you're bleeding a lot, broke something major, are suffering from extreme dehydration due to food poisoning, or if you have decompression sickness, you need to get somewhere where you will receive adequate treatment and have knowledgeable people taking care of you.

In many of the locations you'll probably travel to, you are only going to have clinics available. This is especially true in MICs and LICs. Most of these clinics will have real doctors, but they won't have adequate facilities to handle significant medical problems. Their purpose is to serve the community around them for things like minor broken bones, sickness, and disease management. Any diagnoses that are more significant will require people to go to a larger medical facility. Clinics are not meant to accommodate significant surgery and/or having people stay for multiple days at a time.

Thus, if something happens, like you break a leg, you're almost certainly going to end up at a clinic first. Use your common sense here. If you know you're having a real medical problem, don't be satisfied with any local response that sounds like, "You'll be fine at our clinic." Go to the clinic, get the immediate treatment they recommend until you are stable, and then as soon as they've done what they can in the short term, ask for a transfer to a bigger facility or a hospital. Likely, this will be in a major city. If you're already in a major city when you have your injury, you'll probably end up at a hospital anyway during the medical emergency.

Before you try to organize getting to a hospital, this is where the medical insurance part of your travel insurance becomes important and you need to call them up on the phone. You're going to want to know what's covered, what isn't covered, and if you need to be transported somewhere else and possibly out of the country to be covered and how that's going to work. Talk to your doctors and see what they're recommending for your treatment and then talk to the insurance people and let them know what's going on. In some cases, taking a plane flight from somewhere remote to a major city could be the best way to go to receive proper treatment. In other cases, maybe you're okay where you are and need to be in the clinic a week, but you'll be fine. There's a lot of scenarios here, but what you don't want is to start getting major treatment at a hospital and then find out afterward that you weren't covered by your insurance there, while the hospital the next street over would have been covered.

Some of you might be asking, "Well, what happens if I'm unconscious?" Well, unfortunately you're no longer in control at that point. You're at the whim of whoever happens to be around you, and hopefully, they make good decisions and get you to proper care. If you wake up somewhere and have a huge bill because you were taken somewhere that your insurance doesn't cover, that's a big bummer, but be grateful that at least you're not dead.

As with everything else regarding safety and security, the best way to avoid these problems is to not end up in this situation to begin with. Evaluate your surroundings and situation and actively think about the risks involved and what might happen if something goes wrong. Don't risk life and limb if your gut is telling you something seems dangerous.

NON-MEDICAL EMERGENCIES

Non-medical emergencies can be a number of different things. You might have gotten your passport stolen, you might be in the middle of a terrorist incident, or you might end up in the middle of a protest, a riot, a fire, an earthquake, or something else.

During a non-medical emergency, the first thing to do is **stay calm.**

I can't emphasize this enough. So many people lose their cool when something unusual happens and it doesn't help the situation at all. Panicking and/or moving too quickly is just going to cause you to do something inappropriate, and then you may end up in a worse situation. Relax, think, and then act.

If you're in a large-scale emergency, like an earthquake or governmental collapse, your first goal is to make yourself safe. "Safe" can look different depending on what's going on. In an earthquake, safe may be standing in the street away from buildings and power lines. In a riot, safe likely means getting away from the riot. In a terrorist incident, this may mean hiding somewhere.

Once safe, you need to keep reevaluating if you're still safe, and you should not consider moving anywhere until you can ensure that you can remain safe while moving. If you're not currently safe, get safe first. Your safety is the single most important thing that comes before anything else you may need to do.

If you've been in a situation involving mass damage or social unrest, you should head to your embassy in the country once you can move safely. This may not be easy if you're on the other side of the country. If you're not close to an embassy, call them and ask what they recommend. If you can't reach them, start working your way toward them.

If what happened to you is extremely localized, like a fire or terrorist incident, you're probably okay talking with local authorities and getting their recommendation on where you should relocate to, who you need to contact, and more.

The main difference between these two situations is the question, "Are the authorities overwhelmed?" If you're in a situation in which the police, firefighters, and paramedics are so overwhelmed with taking care of thousands of calls, you need to get out of the country through your embassy. If you're in a situation in which the police, firefighters, and paramedics can handle the situation, you should talk to them and seek advice.

For any other non-medical emergency, like passport theft or armed robbery, talk to the police department first, and then call whoever is relevant next for your situation. For example, your embassy for a passport theft. If you're not sure what to do next and are not near your accommodation when something like this happens, step into the nearest hotel or hostel you can find. They're used to talking to visitors and will know who to contact and are much more likely to help you than, say, a local shopkeeper who may not speak your language and maybe doesn't even have a phone.

REGISTERING WITH YOUR EMBASSY

Many travel websites really harp on the importance of registering with your embassy in every country that you travel, and I simply don't agree with that advice. If you're in a bad situation, you can find your embassy's information fairly quickly. If you're in a *really* bad situation, your embassy isn't going to be able to help you anyway. Your embassy doesn't track you in a country while you visit, so learn to be self-reliant first and use the embassy as a backup. If the embassy would be able to contact you, you can contact the embassy also. If they wouldn't be able to contact you, you won't be able to contact them either. Please note, I am willing to incur the risk to myself of not registering with my embassy, but you should do what you are comfortable with.

The main program for US citizens for this kind of embassy notification is the Department of State Smart Traveler Enrollment Program or STEP. Their site is easy to find on Google. I enrolled in this when I went to Russia and China because of obvious issues between our countries. I have been shocked at how useless this program has been for those areas since then. I see events happen on the news weeks before I get any kind of STEP notification. In the six years after that trip, I got around ten notifications, the vast majority of which were to avoid Crimea in the Ukraine, which was obvious if you had been watching the news *at all*.

Again, the best way to avoid dealing with these situations is to avoid them in the first place. Something like an earthquake can't be predicted, but don't knowingly watch an angry crowd turn into a riot. Leave the area early. Be smart and avoid problems.

PART 5

AFTER THE TRIP

Coming back from a trip, especially a long trip, can be as difficult as taking the trip in the first place. Plus, it's going to take some time to process your trip and figure out how it really affected you and might have affected your life plans. Let's talk about this a little bit.

REINTEGRATION

If you read the title of this section and haven't traveled much yet, you may be wondering how this is even a topic. But if you have traveled a lot, this chapter heading may have stirred a deep pain in you that made you wince inside a little. Coming back from your trip and reintegrating into your normal life, especially if you've been gone a long time, can be one of the most challenging parts of your trip. You've been out exploring the world and growing as an individual. It can feel like the world that you once knew has turned stale and feels foreign now. Let's explore some of the issues that can come up when you eventually need to return to a normal life.

FEELING ALIENATED

Traveling does interesting things to people, and not all of the experiences are going to make everyone feel warm fuzzies in the long run. For many people, the whole point of traveling is to see what they haven't seen and experience cultures and history with which they may not be completely familiar. That means expanding beyond one's current boundaries. Usually, expanding yourself is a good thing. It means understanding different viewpoints better and seeing that people can be different and that those differences are okay. There are likely a lot of things that most people will discover about themselves that they had no idea were in them, especially about likes and dislikes because they had never been experienced before. The strange part about all this growth comes when you're put back into your preexisting home life, where not everyone around you has had the same life-altering experiences.

To give an example here, imagine coming home from a long LIC trip and hearing people at home complain about the faucet water tasting a little bit funny. Here you are, having been places where the water is contaminated and where most people are so poor they don't have any other choice but to drink that contaminated water, only to come home to incredibly clean, readily available water, and then you hear people moan about a slightly "off" taste in the water. This is going to make you feel very out of place among your friends and peers, especially if you start explaining these feelings to them. You, your friends, and your peers are all experiencing the same things, but you in particular are interpreting a different world than they are. Not everyone is going to have these kinds of feelings after their travels, but the farther you go, the more places and things you see, the more this is likely to happen.

What may feel even more uncomfortable is when you hear people at home talking about groups of people in other parts of the world, and they'll speak with such confidence and surety about people they've never even seen. You, on the other hand, may have been there and seen those people, and you realize the things being said are misrepresented, bigoted, or completely incorrect. Trying to bite your tongue is going to be hard, and you may start seeing some of your friends in a different light than before. Some of them you may not even want to talk to anymore because you didn't previously realize they were bigots, overly judgmental, or racist. Don't worry, though. This experience of feeling out of place is normal. It may not go away, but it's normal.

When people at home start to sound racist or judgmental to you, gently correct them when the opportunity presents itself and feels comfortable or appropriate. All of us are unaware of what we don't know. We may have formed opinions about something but have no idea that those opinions are not factually correct. How else can you discover that you're missing information unless someone else points that out to you? Usually, people are very receptive and are quick to understand how they sounded originally in light of the new information. Every now and then, someone gets a little defensive, but after all, you are trying to tell them that they shouldn't have had the opinion they just expressed, so getting a little defensive is not too surprising. You'll probably find that more often than not, people suddenly get more interested in the truth, then get more interested in how you got your information, and then become interested in traveling themselves. Think of this as a polite way of paying forward the itch to travel while making the world a little more friendly and tolerant in the process.

Your experiences will have made you grow a lot, and of course, the only people who will really understand those changes are people who have also traveled and gone through similar experiences themselves. It's something you'll notice in conversations in the future. You may even pick up on travel topics more than anything else because of how much it has changed you. And travel will be something you and them will be excited to talk about because they know this feeling, too.

Some people may change so much, in ways that others at home don't understand, that it can cause some very negative feelings towards people you knew before traveling. If some of these feelings are bothering you, the biggest thing I can recommend to calm them is to start making friends with people who have traveled. Usually, you'll find these people naturally, but you can always use websites like meetup. com (mainly US-based) to find groups of travelers who meet in your local area.

It's possible that there are hostels around your hometown area, too. You could go down to these and ask if anyone would like to grab a drink and talk about the area since you're a local. It's important not to seem like a scam artist as we just went over. You could also post up a flyer on their announcement board stating that you're a local and just like to help out people coming through and provide your contact information.

Keeping in touch with the friends you made while traveling can also help calm these sorts of feelings somewhat, but traveling and being at home working and living are two very different things. You may find that you drift apart from travel friends fairly quickly once you return home. What do you talk about in your day-to-day that's interesting? It's a lot different when you're experiencing exciting things every single day while traveling.

That said, some people you meet traveling will be happy to see you and talk to you even if you haven't spoken in quite a while. These are some of the most awesome people you will meet in your life, especially since they'll always act like you just saw them yesterday. It's very possible you may be friends with them forever. I can tell you from my own experiences that the world is a surprisingly small place, so you may even run into them again someday. Keeping in touch with these people every now and then just to see how they're doing keeps the connection going.

One thing I've personally struggled with is feeling like I no longer have a home. Other travelers I've met have had families, girlfriends or boyfriends, or a university education waiting for them at home, and this has helped ground them back to where they came from. But I didn't really have any of these things in a central spot during most of my travels, and so after traveling so much, my "home" no longer felt anchored to me. I found so many things I liked in other places but found no single place that has everything I love, and unfortunately that means nowhere on earth feels like it's really home for me anymore. I love lots of places, but none of them are necessarily more awesome than the others for me anymore. If you see that you have these feelings, I suggest forcing yourself to make a decision on what you want to do for the next few years, whether that's moving to another country or staying where you are, and making the most of that time.

CRAVING ALONE TIME

If you've been traveling a lot in hostels, you may find when you come back home that you crave alone time. This shouldn't be too much of a surprise since being in dorms means you've had very little privacy. This feeling may not hit you for a while after you come back, but once your body and mind start to realize that you *can* be alone and that you aren't constantly moving around and doing stuff, this need for alone time may hit you hard.

You may also crave being on a regimented schedule, because travel is usually different day by day. Neither of these should be any worry, and if you're experiencing these sensations upon your return, just be patient; you'll be back to normal in no time. Travel is kind of a special thing compared to at-home living and working, so having some lifestyle cravings after significant time living differently is totally normal.

There are a lot of apps and web pages now that help you practice "mindfulness." Really, these apps are teaching you meditation and stress management techniques, but a huge part of both of those is slowing down, paying attention, and literally "being mindful" of what you're experiencing in the present moment. If you're craving alone time and a regimented schedule, it's likely because you're experiencing sensory overload from always having to prepare for the next unknown moment and not having enough time to process what you've already experienced. Essentially, you've been trying to look at how you've changed, but you've had to always prepare for the future, and then you're not really experiencing the present. Being like this for too long is a really good way to burn out. Trying any of these mindfulness outlets should get you recentered and balanced again pretty quickly, but it may take a few weeks, especially if you've been in that mode for more than a few months.

Headspace and Calm are great companies for this. You may find it really hard to do their exercises at first because your mind is going in a million different directions. Likely, you're still trying to process everything from your trip. Don't worry, this is normal and that's exactly why you need to keep doing the exercises.

BOREDOM

Another common issue people experience is boredom when returning to normal life. When you get to experience the purely self-driven time of doing something you care about, it can be hard to go back to working for the Man, even if you really like your job. Your dwelling may start to seem pointless, and you may start asking yourself, "What am I really doing with my life?" The more you experience passion-driven self-growth while traveling, the more you're going to want to abandon anything that isn't your passion. The thought of making almost no money but living somewhere cheap and doing something fun day to day is going to start really messing with you. Unless you really love what you do at home, you're going to need to have a conversation with yourself, at your own pace, to figure out what life goals are really important in relation to your newly discovered life values. I have no good answers for you here. Only you can be honest with yourself and admit what really matters. Don't wait to have this conversation with yourself if you have these thoughts when you come back, but don't make any snap decisions either.

COPING BY ARCHETYPE

Going back to the archetypes, here are some of the more extreme things you might need to watch out for upon your return home and ways to potentially cope:

- **Gap Year.** Extreme boredom is likely to affect Gap Year travelers. You just had this amazing trip and experiences during your travels and now you're supposed to work till you die? It sounds boring. But remember, even when you're working, you have roughly a third of your day to yourself, you get weekends off, and you have vacation (holiday) time every year. There are plenty of opportunities to keep your feelings of adventure going, but you have to work at it at home more than when you were traveling. Find friends who like trying new things or exploring new areas. You have your life ahead of you to fill with adventures.

• **Hippie.** Alienation and a strong desire to continue nomadic tendencies are likely to affect this type coming home. Luckily for you, there are Hippie types almost everywhere, so you just need to find your local tribe. This will likely help you feel much more at home than otherwise.

• **Retreat.** I think the biggest issue for Retreat types coming back is going to be the immediate reimmersion into the same stressful environment you were trying to get away from. It's like going from a hot tub straight into a cold pool. You were nice and relaxed and then comes a shock to the system. Try to work on the feelings of stress that led to the desire for the retreat. It may mean finding another job role or company to work for. Mindfulness work is going to be key for you folks to maintain a healthy daily lifestyle.

• **Outdoorsman.** With the love of the outdoors, being back in society is going to cause the craving for alone time to feel stronger than before your return. I recommend taking weekend camping trips or living outside of your city to cope with these feelings.

• **Avoider.** This archetype will primarily feel the alienation problem. Being under the nanny state and having to live in the good ol' grind is exactly what you were trying to avoid to begin with. If you must stay at home, try taking non-standard jobs or working in extreme environments like ERs (A&Es). The freedom to use your brain and think through problems may alleviate some of the avoidance feelings.

- **Drifter.** These types primarily feel alienated when they're unable to drift. Honestly, if you can get by doing the drifting lifestyle, I wouldn't recommend stopping unless something stronger is pulling you away from doing so.

- **Explorer.** These types will probably experience some mixture of everything talked about so far. Because this is my type, one of the things I've done is start writing to help others, but doing something that allows you to keep focusing on your adventures is the real key. Maybe this means changing your job or maybe this means moving to another town or city because those things allow you to keep exploring.

- **Out of Comfort Zone.** This archetype usually feels guilt for their "haves" compared to all the "have-nots" they saw during travel. Human beings are pack animals, and simply due to the availability of resources, some packs are going to have more or less than others. As a species, we will never have equal resources. There will always be hierarchies with people who have more and have less. It is terrible that people have to live in poverty, but working to develop technology that aids mankind and teaching skills to underprivileged populations can go a long way to calming the feelings of guilt. Teaching classes online for other countries or taking trips focused around volunteer work are sustainable ways to help those less fortunate even after the trip is done.

- **Pensioner.** Feeling regret for having not traveled sooner or the feeling that most of your life was wasted working and that you're just now starting to live, even though you're entering your twilight years, is common with this archetype. If you feel anything like this, remember, your life isn't over yet and you couldn't have gotten by without working. Use the time you have now and enjoy yourself. Upon returning home, start scheduling your next trip, plan mini-vacations or weekend getaways. Make the most of your time and give yourself that next trip to look forward to. Seeing your friends and family can make a big difference, too.

- **Culturist.** The biggest issue I see here is other people are making you feel like you're crazy because you like another culture so much. This could feel pretty isolating if you don't have like-minded friends. My advice here is, who cares? You know what you like. Keep doing your thing. Not everyone is going to like the same stuff. Maybe join a language club or a local cultural society to hang out with like-minded people or people from your country of interest. If your favorite country is Japan, this should be pretty easy.

- *Eat Pray Love.* Coming back home and feeling like you didn't grow enough is common with these archetypes. These folks may also come to the realization that everything is the same everywhere, and the eat, pray, or love desires weren't fulfilled. If this were me, I would try to remind myself that the internet has made the world really small. You can talk to and find gurus for anything you want, anywhere in the world, and likely communicate with them online. For the love aspect, remember that love is not something you can make happen; you have to grow together with someone organically. Relax and keep meeting people. Love will happen on its own. There's also a good chance you grew more than you realized during your trip, but you need time to process those changes.

- **Foodie.** Can you feel bad after eating a lot of good food? Maybe after gaining a lot of weight. Really, though, I think most foodies will be all right but will likely run into the issues of another archetypal aspect of themselves.

- **Newb.** This archetype will likely feel like a Gap Year or Out of Comfort Zone but may also feel like they screwed up their trip or wasted their time because they weren't prepared. This happens to all of us at some point or another, so don't beat yourself up over it. Learn from your experiences and build on them for the next trip.

HAVE SOMEONE LISTEN

I hope these recommendations make sense, even if you haven't experienced anything I've talked about yet. Traveling is such a wonderful thing. It inspires growth and passion, you meet amazing people, you learn a ton, it's fun as hell, so it's no wonder that you get home and things are just...different. This is an adjustment. It should also be no wonder that what seemed totally fine before you traveled suddenly starts causing all sorts of weird emotions, and now you don't feel like your "normal life" is who you are anymore.

While you're experiencing all of that, it shouldn't surprise you if you're craving your own space and time to process everything. All of this is normal and, in my opinion, totally worth it.

If you are feeling overwhelmed or depressed when you return, it may be a good idea to talk to a therapist. Seeking counseling isn't as taboo as our culture makes it out to be. It's likely you will get something useful out of it and can work through any overly negative feelings that occur with reintegration. You'll probably also figure out your next life steps, too.

PLANNING YOUR NEXT TRIP

You know exactly how you should've packed for a trip right after you get back. You also know exactly how you should have planned the trip and exactly what your itinerary should have been, right when you get back, too. Travel is a learning process. Although I've traveled all over the world, anyplace that's new to me is still a learning process.

Outside of learning by visiting new locations, I continue to refine the things I take with me as I experiment more with packing. Plus, technology changes every year, so that impacts my travels, too. I am also constantly reevaluating places I want to go and things I want to see. You'll find the same thing will happen to you in your travels, both on a broad scale in terms of the countries and cities you visit and on a small scale in terms of what sights you decide to visit and activities you want to experience.

Travel is really a dynamic flow of learning and something that will change you in ways you can't predict. Arguably, travel is a combination of the process of growing as an individual and also the law of diminishing returns, which applies in this case as each new thing you experience changes you less than the similar new thing before it. For example, how many cathedrals can you see before they all start to look the same? Regardless of what type of traveler you are, every experience you have is going to change the future experiences you desire to have.

As with a lot of the feelings that arise after your trip, this changing landscape of your travel desires is totally normal. And it's even possible you may completely switch traveler archetypes as you keep experiencing more things. You may be a Retreat type and become a Culturist, or you may be an Avoider and become a Drifter. This is completely normal. You've traveled, you've learned something new about somewhere else, and in the process, learned more about yourself, and this causes you to change your desires. For you, it could be temples, it could be beaches, it could be islands, museums, paintings, or something else. Your focus will probably shift.

What I recommend for most people is to take a break after your initial trip is complete. If you were on a short trip, you could get by with a shorter break, and if you were on a longer trip, maybe you need a longer break. Nonetheless, it can be good to take a break and not think about traveling for a bit.

Take a break. Reevaluate. Reinterpret. Re-research.

When you start to feel the itch to travel again, look over your list of travel destinations and see what still interests you. Growth doesn't end; it just evolves.

ARE YOU THINKING ABOUT LIVING ABROAD?

Some of you who come home from a trip may start having the desire to live abroad. This happened to me, too, and I followed that desire. I've lived in both Australia and the UK as a result. Let me tell you about my experience living abroad.

As a completely new solo traveler, the first place I went internationally was London. When I got there, I fell in love with the city almost immediately. It has so much history, people from all walks of life, and plenty of different neighborhoods with different vibes. It was almost like a playground. I hadn't been anywhere else internationally except a little village in Germany, and almost immediately, I decided that I wanted to live in London at some point. It took a number of years before I could really act on this. In the meantime, I was explaining this desire to myself by saying, "I want to experience a different way of life, but I want to be somewhere where a language barrier isn't going to get in the way of me experiencing the local dynamic."

When I went traveling next on my first long backpacking trip, I found out Australia has this great live-abroad program for people under the age of thirty-one. Because I was rapidly approaching that age at the time, I decided to live in Australia first. Unfortunately, I was unable to find "meaningful" work in Australia. What I mean by this is that I was thirty at the time and already had a profession and a career, so working in service jobs didn't appeal to me. Because of this, I moved on after a few months of not finding work in my career area. Even still, years later, I regret moving on so quickly and not just taking what was available because my experience there was so amazing and being back at home afterward just hasn't been quite the same. Anything I could have done to prolong my time there would have been desirable.

In the process of moving on, I tried to make my London dream finally come true, almost six years after my initial visit. The work I was looking for was within the video game industry doing computer programming. Yes, that's a niche profession, and it's why I was having such a hard time finding work in Australia. What I ended up finding out was that it's so unbelievably expensive to rent commercial space in London, and video game companies are typically surviving week to week financially, that almost no video game company will go into London for office space. That meant I either needed to live far outside London and commute even farther for work, or I would need to live somewhere else entirely.

In the course of trying to find this UK job once I started moving on from Australia, I began traveling through Southeast Asia. Anytime an interview came up or a recruiter called me, I would just find a place to hang out and do my business call or take my interview tests or whatever. When a job offer did come in, I was literally in the middle of the jungle in Borneo in a place that probably has a population of fewer than 1,000 people. I was also on satellite internet, which is just about as slow as it gets.

I asked if I could start in eight weeks. I was informed that this was unacceptable. They had an immediate need to fill this position and I would lose my job offer if I waited that long.

I asked for four weeks to my start date and was reluctantly given a yes on that timeline. This was a huge rush for me because I was at least a week away from a major airport, and then I still needed to go through all of my stuff in California to pack for living long term in England. Then I also needed to get to England and set up bank accounts, find housing, and figure out how I was going to get to work.

I lived somewhere besides London as a compromise with finding this job. I ended up far north, right on the Scottish border in a city called Newcastle upon Tyne (famous internationally for Newcastle Brown Ale). While this wasn't London, it met the description of what I was looking for in England perfectly.

When I arrived to start working, it was a total mess almost right from the start. In order to get a bank account, I needed a job. In order to start my job, I needed an address. In order to rent a place and therefore get an address, I needed a bank account. Everything depended on everything else.

I went and explained the situation to the property manager I was working with and he just started laughing really hard. After recovering a bit, he goes, "You tried to come here normally? SUCKER! If you had shown up as a refugee, we would have given you a place to live, found you a job, and set your bank account up for you. But doing it the normal way? Good luck figuring that out! HAHAHAHAHA."

Wow. Seriously?

I finally ended up convincing the bank to give me a "provisional account statement," basically an IOU (literally, I owe you) on an account number on the contingency that I was about to have a job, which allowed the place to live, then the work, then the job confirmation letter, which granted the real bank account. This was a nightmare to put into place.

When I showed up in the UK, I had an overweight, max check-in-sized bag, my normal travel pack, and a small pack with my laptop and other electronics. It really wasn't much, although I could go with much less now with what I learned from this experience. The place I rented was furnished and had everything I needed—a bed, couch, dinner table, and a small TV.

On the following Monday, I headed in to start my work.

So there I am, I'm walking in for my first day of work and my manager comes out from the badged area and says, "I just found out we hired someone for this position less than thirty minutes ago. Welcome!" I couldn't believe it. I just whirlwinded my way more than halfway around the planet to be here and my manager didn't even know I was coming?

I asked him, "Did I actually need to start today, or would it have been okay for me to start a month from now?"

My manager responded, "I don't know what they told you, but this position has been open for months. You could have shown up three months from now and it wouldn't really have mattered."

I'll just say, there was a lot of profanity-laced internal dialogue going on after that statement.

To make things even more interesting during this settling-in, I showed up in the UK with a horrific fever. During my first week at work, it got so bad that when the weekend came, I walked over to the hospital and checked myself in for possible malaria.

Being in far Northern England, malaria is not common. Sorry, let me rephrase that. In far Northern England, malaria doesn't exist. So when I checked myself into the hospital, they were skeptical of my malaria claims to say the least. They asked me why I thought I had malaria and I answered, "Well, I was deep in the jungle two weeks ago and now I have a horrific fever and feel like death. This is kind of what they warn you to look for, right?" Well, there wasn't much arguing with that logic and they checked me in.

The UK has national medical care which is great, but being a foreigner, I wasn't sure how this was going to work. Luckily for me, as I found out, you only need to be working in the UK in order to get into their medical care system for free. One of the triage nurses turned and asked me, "Why did you say you were here in the UK?" I responded "work" and was immediately taken back and given care, even though I didn't even have a medical ID number. It turned out I had some really, really nasty strain of influenza, but I did not have malaria.

After this first really rough couple of weeks in the UK, everything finally settled down and I got into more of a rhythm with working, cooking, and hanging out with people. I was also trying to date. What was really interesting to me when I got into this phase of living was that things didn't really feel different than they did in the US. This sounds weird to say even now, but let's break down one of my days to see what I'm doing.

First, I'd wake up and have some breakfast. Then I go to work and work roughly eight hours on typical workday stuff. There was an adjustment period to the work culture during which I became known as the "blunt American" pretty quickly (different work cultures between countries). But that calmed down as I adjusted to their work culture. Then I would go home, work out, eat dinner, screw around on my computer, and watch TV. On the weekends, I'd go out, sometimes to house parties, sometimes to bars, but even this felt familiar.

After a few weeks, it started to really dawn on me that nothing I was doing in the UK was really different than being at home in the US.

The main difference was the social interaction, and in my opinion, the British were very warm in that almost anyone was up for a pint. Things felt much less cliquey than in the US, and it's been my experience that non-Americans are always curious if the shows about American high school are actually accurate in the way they portray how the jocks, nerds, band geeks, and other groups don't hang out with each other, and I always have to inform them that it's mostly true. So being in a place where everyone got along more or less was great.

Beyond this more socially lubricated culture, my food, my clothing, my drinks, my hair products, public transportation, going to the mall, fast food...nearly almost everything was the same as being in California.

I had to think about this quite a bit, and having seen many other places traveling already, if you're living anywhere in HICs, and arguably a lot of places in MICs now, too, you're going to have the same amenities that you would have pretty much anywhere else. All of your activities are likely to be really similar as well. A lot of this stems from globalization.

So why go somewhere new to live?

Well, the only reason can be for that social and cultural difference.

But that's what really surprised me as it turned out. If you're living and working somewhere, the social and cultural experience is really only about 10 percent of your experience.

When you're just traveling, and not living and working somewhere, you're seeking adventures and the main cultural spots, so a huge proportion of your time is experiencing unique cultural differences. But when you're planted somewhere and working day to day, the cultural experience part of your day to day drops to a considerably smaller percentage. There are still ways around this, but not if you're taking the career-driven approach that I took in the UK.

So what to make of all of this? Ask yourself these questions:

- If you're thinking about moving somewhere abroad, ask yourself why.

- Is it to experience something new?

- Is it to learn about another culture? And if so, how much different is that culture from your own?

- Is it to experience adventure?

Many people are trying to get away from the boredom at home and do something different. However, trying to integrate into another system is hard. Potentially really hard. Trying to square away bank accounts and healthcare numbers and the like took a lot of time and effort, and all of it was about as interesting as sitting in a bank and talking to someone about interest rates and account types. I would imagine this is not the definition of adventure for most people.

Honestly, I think a huge part of what made Australia so fun and the UK so familiar was a change of scenery in that I wasn't doing my normal career in Australia. I was working in my usual profession in the UK, so not much changed from at home. This brings up the questions: "What is driving your desire to live somewhere else? Is it boredom with the day-to-day at home? Do you need a break from your career? What's driving this urge?"

An interesting thing I should mention here was that my limited belongings made a huge impact on my life while I was in the UK and Australia. Because I basically owned the bare minimum to get by, I had almost nothing to clean. I had no clutter in my place, and I didn't have to worry about saving up to buy more stuff. All of these things left me completely free to go out and spend my money with my friends and also freed up all my time to do the things I cared about. You might try this experiment at home before you commit to moving abroad.

Should you move abroad if you're thinking about it? There are no directly clear answers here. You're going to have to figure out what you want out of living abroad and if that's actually right for you. If you're really excited about it, do it. You won't regret it. Just try to avoid using moving abroad as an excuse to get out of a boring day-to-day situation at home, because you're likely to find that most things are pretty similar everywhere. At that point, it's really your own lifestyle that you're trying to change, and not your surrounding environment.

If you do decide to move abroad, the process is almost certain to be difficult because the procedures within countries aren't clearly linked together in one easy-to-follow format nor are they explained anywhere as a checklist. The closest I could find for the UK, whose process I already know now, was the "How to Migrate to the UK" page on WikiHow.com. That WikiHow page, however, is missing an incredible amount of relevant information, so it's really just a starting point at best.

I can almost guarantee that a similar situation is going to be the case no matter where you want to move. Websites like expat.com may put you into contact with others who can answer specific questions, but you're still going to have to figure out the key components.

In general, if you move somewhere, you will need these things and probably in roughly this order:

1. Figure out your work visa process. This will likely go in one of two directions. Either you find work at a company and they sponsor you for a work visa, or you will apply for your own work visa and then start looking for a job. The first way is cheaper because the company will probably pay for your visa, but if you can't find work immediately, you will have to go the second route. Be aware

visa applications can take months to put together and process and typically have an expiration date a few years out. When you get the visa, the timer on this expiration may start ticking immediately. Finding the government website on how to apply for the visas is a fairly straight-forward Google search. In some countries, you can hire a representative who will help you with the visa process, but these services are usually very expensive.

2. Find work. Most developed countries will likely have job listing equivalents of things like LinkedIn and Gumtree, and you should be able to find those online pretty easily.

3. Find somewhere to live. Be aware, a job may be required to move into a place if you are brand new in a country. Again, country-specific websites like Craigslist or Gumtree will help you find these places. I would call a property manager, landlord, or realty company before you leave and ask what the requirements are for foreigners to get a place to live.

4. Set up a bank account. I would call a bank ahead of leaving and ask what the requirements are for setting up a bank account.

5. Set up a tax ID. This may or may not be done through your work.

6. If there is national health insurance, set up a national health insurance ID. Again, this may or may not be done through your work.

There may or may not be extra steps you need to take before or after your arrival. Also know that permanent residence or becoming a citizen in your new country is a possible option, so look for information on those possibilities as well.

THE REMOTE CAREER REVOLUTION

During COVID-19, many people all around the world started remotely working from home. Hopefully, that trend will continue into the future. Already in the early days of COVID-19, many employers had already stated that remote work would remain a permanent option for their employees. If you're someone with remote working options, what this allows you is the ability to work in another country while staying there on a tourist visa. Typically, these last for ninety days. This may allow you to have the live-abroad experience without having to jump through all of the hoops of actually getting a work visa. The main downside to this approach is that you can't rent a place to stay under a tourist visa. Long-term Airbnbs, VRBOs, or other similar vacation rentals are likely going to be your best option here. It's something to think about.

CONCLUSION

YOU'VE GOT THIS

Well, we're at the end here. I hope after reading everything in this book you now feel confident that you can take any kind of trip that you've been thinking about. It's really not that bad. Think about your trip, plan your trip, get your stuff together, take your trip, and then come home. Obviously, there are a lot of things that you need to work through to make a trip happen, but nothing is so strange or unnatural that it should prevent anyone from going out and traveling around the world.

Because my intent was to leave you with all the key components of traveling, I've had to talk about some scary situations that could happen, but I can't stress enough that these events are rare, and I've never met a single person who has been worse off after their trip.

In fact, the reality is quite the opposite. Everyone I know who travels, regardless of their style of traveling and what they're looking to get out of travel, loves traveling. And the more you travel, the more you want to travel even further and farther than you did before. Having adventures makes you want to have even more adventures.

For first-time travelers, I hope that most people will read through this book first and then skim it while going through the steps and getting their trip together. If that's you right now, I want you to know that after having read through this book, you really do know all of the major parts of traveling now. While you may run across situations that I didn't cover in these pages, you now know enough to work through them. Don't be nervous or scared about your trip. You're now an expert who just needs to go out and get some experience.

If you're a seasoned traveler and picked this book up, I hope you found at least one new thing in these pages. Travel is a large subject area. It's essentially a subject where you have to relearn how to live on a day-to-day basis, and we as humans do a lot of really varied stuff daily, so this is naturally a huge topic. My views are not the only views out there, but I've been surprised how niche most traveling tips are, so using my background in science and engineering, I wanted to break down the subject of travel into principles rather than specifics. If you have a wildly differing opinion than me on something I've presented, let me know. I'd be curious to hear it. Contact me at andrewwatson.com or through social media. Just like you, I can only be the sum of the experiences that I've been exposed to, so I'm curious if there's something out there that I don't know about yet.

For everyone in general: get out there, get traveling, and go adventuring! The more we all travel and the more we all see the world, the more we understand each other despite our different cultural backgrounds, and this unites us together around the world. I love the feeling I get when I find out that someone I'm just meeting has spent time traveling the world. Immediately, we are able to bond on a deeper level and know that we're going to have a lot to talk about.

If you see me somewhere out there on the road, don't be afraid to say hi! In the meantime, check out my blog at andrewwatson.com for gear reviews, tips, tricks, and deeper dives into some of the material covered in this book.

Have fun, good luck, and stay focused on your dreams. Stay safe, and have a blast out there!

APPENDIX

COMMON UNIT CONVERSIONS

There are a few common and easy-to-use rough unit conversions you should know. The following will help you navigate, purchase necessary items, and more.

Big Distances:

- 1 mile = 1.6 kilometers (km)

- 1 km = 0.6 miles

These numbers for distance aren't completely easy to work with, but if you need to know km and know something is 5 miles, add half and another 10 percent of the original number. So:

- 5 + 2.5 + 0.5 = 8 km

Similarly, to go from km to miles, take half and add 10 percent again. So to get miles from 8 km:

- 8/2 = 4 and then 4 + 0.8 = 4.8, so round to 5 miles

It's not exact, but it will get you close enough.

Small Distances:

- 1 yard (yd) is roughly equal to, but slightly shorter than, 1 meter (m) over shorter distances.

- 1 yd = 3 feet (ft)

This is helpful especially for scuba diving. If your depth gauge is only in m, then 30 m is going to be approximately 30 yd, which would be 90 ft. Now, 30 m is actually closer to 99 ft, so you can see the error here, but this should be close enough to help you out quite a bit. Remembering 30 m as 100 ft will work well.

Weight:

- 1 kilogram (kg) = 2.2 pounds (lbs)

- 1 lb = 0.45 kg

To do the conversion, double it and add 10 percent of the resulting number, or half it and *subtract* 10 percent of the resulting number. So for 5 kg:

- 5 x 2 = 10, then plus 10 percent of the 10 is 10 + 1 = 11 lbs

Or the other way:

- 11/2 = 5.5, then minus 10 percent of the 5.5 is 5.5 – 0.55 = 4.95 and round to 5

Volume:

It's not uncommon in many parts of the world to see things like salads, food, and liquid measured in grams (g), but guess what? This is super easy. It's actually the definition of the milliliter (mL) that 1 mL is 1 cubic centimeter. And 1 cubic centimeter of water is 1 g.

So because 1 liter (L) is 1000 mL, 1 L of water is also 1000 g or 1 kg.

Because this is based on water, heavy solid material like granite or steel isn't going to weigh the same (it's closer to 3 g per mL), but for food, which is mostly water anyway, it's close, so 500 g of soup is going to be roughly 500 mL of soup.

Other conversions for volume include:

- 2 cups (c.) = 1 pint (pt)

- 1 pt is also roughly equal to 500 mL

- 1 pt is also 16 ounces (oz), or 1 lb

Therefore, 500 g of soup is roughly 1 pt of soup, and a 250 g steak is about an 8 oz steak.

Temperature:

Pretty much the entire world uses Celsius except for the US and a few island nations. The real conversion equation is:

- $32 + 9/5 * C = F$

But that's a little unwieldy. So to roughly quick convert between them, instead use:

- $C * 2 + 30 \approx F$

Dates:

Dates almost everywhere in the world are in DD/MM/YY format instead of the American MM/DD/YY format. If you aren't 100 percent sure which format you're looking at, be sure to ask.

Time:

It should seem odd that time shows up in the unit conversions, but many countries say "half one" or "half two" to describe a time of day. Something to be aware of is that different languages treat this phrase differently. In some places, "half one" is 12:30, and in others, it's 1:30. Be careful to ask for clarification if someone throws you a "half" time value or you're risking missing buses, tours, trains, etc.

Also, for those in the US, most of the world relies on "military time," meaning a 24-hour clock. To adjust for p.m. hours, just add 12. So 5:00 p.m. becomes 17:00.

For one last oddity with time, a few countries flip 12:00 a.m. and 12:00 p.m. In the US and much of Europe, 12:00 a.m. or 00:00 is the sundown 12 on the clock. In a few places, this is 12:00 p.m., but 12:01 a.m. and 00:01 are still the starts of the a.m. cycle.

If you have time said like any of this to you and you aren't completely certain you know the intended time, ask.

Building Floors:

There are two different systems to count building floors. Some countries start with floor one being the ground floor. Other countries start with the floor above the ground floor as floor one. Be aware of this and make sure you check the signage on the floors to determine where you are.

RESOURCES

These are listed in roughly the order they appear in the book.

Determine Your Traveler Archetype

Foodie Show: *Chef's Table* on Netflix

Rough Budget Calculations to Keep in Mind

How-to-Travel-Cheap Book: *How to Travel the World on 50 Dollars a Day* by Matt Kepnes

Destinations by Archetype

Foodie Website: The Fork—thefork.com

Foodie Website: Yelp—yelp.com

Foodie App: Google Maps and search for restaurants

Day-to-Day Time Management and Logistics

Travel Things-to-Do Research: Trip Advisor—tripadvisor.com

When to Skip a Destination

Country Safety Research: *CIA Factbook*—cia.gov/library/publications/the-world-factbook/

Getting around during Your Trip

Flight Booking: Matrix ITA—matrix.itasoftware.com and then use BookWithMatrix.com

Flight Booking: Google Flights—google.com/flights

To Go in Groups or Alone

Group-Splitting Money App and Website: Splitwise—splitwise.com

Sample Itineraries

Free Calendar-Making Tool: WinCalendar—wincalendar.com

Trip Timing and Budget Tweaks

Country Weather Research: World Climate & Temperature—climatemps.com

Draft Your Itinerary

Financial Advice: *Mr. Money Mustache—Early Retirement through Badassity*—mrmoneymustache.com

Minimalism Book: *The Life-Changing Magic of Tidying Up: The Japanese Art of Decluttering and Organizing* by Marie Kondo

Vaccinations

World Vaccination Recommendations: Traveler's Health Centers for Disease Control and Prevention (CDC)–cdc.gov/travel

Physical Fitness

GORUCK–goruck.com

Visas

Visa Research and Help Obtaining Visas: VisaHQ–visahq.com

Set Up Your Bank Accounts Properly

Travel Bank Account Research: Nerd Wallet–nerdwallet.com

Recommended Banks for Travel Accounts: Schwab Banking–schwab.com

Recommended Banks for Travel Credit Cards: Bank of America–bankofamerica.com

Booking Your Trip

Hostel Booking Website: Hostel World–hostelworld.com

Hotel Booking Website: Kayak–kayak.com

Hotel Booking Website: Booking.com–booking.com

Compare Travel Insurance Plans: TravelInsurance.com–travelinsurance.com

Couch surfing–couchsurfing.com

Airbnb–airbnb.com

VRBO–vrbo.com

What to Pack

Minimal Wardrobes: Project 333 or look up "Capsule Wardrobes"–bemorewithless.com/project-333/

Good Bottles for Toiletries: Nalgene, check Amazon

Good Shaving Cream Substitute: King of Shaves–shave.com

Good Collapsible Camp Cup: Sea to Summit X Cup, check Amazon

App for Text-to-Speech PDF Reading: @Voice

Right before You Leave

Home Theft Deterrent: FakeTV, check Amazon

Language Issues

Language Translation: Google Translate

Scuba Diving Safety

Diving Insurance: DAN insurance–diversalertnetwork.org/insurance/

Knowing Is Half the Battle

Medical Training: American Red Cross–redcross.org

Safety and Security

Online Self-Defense Training: Impact Krav Maga Online—impact-kravmagaonline.com

Krav Maga Global Online Training—maxkravmaga.com

Traveler Safety Registration for Embassies: Department of State Smart Traveler Enrollment Program or STEP—step.state.gov/step/

After the Trip

Meet Other Travelers: Meetup—meetup.com

Meditation and Mindfulness Practice: Headspace—headspace.com

Meditation and Mindfulness Practice: Calm—calm.com

SPECIAL THANKS

I would like to thank a bunch of people for helping me out during the mammoth task of writing this book. First and foremost, thank you to my partner, Kimbrie Gobbi, for being a continual sounding board and reading this book in its various drafts, multiple times. That was a lot of work that she wasn't getting paid for and she never once hesitated to reread something.

I would also like to give a huge thank you to Kelly Lydick for her editorial expertise and knowledge of the publishing industry. Without her guidance and editing, as a first-time author, I'm not sure this project would have ever seen completion. I can't explain how much I appreciated your editorial comments, which were both funny and thoughtful, and how you kept me going during the never-ending editing process. Now that this is finally coming out, I'm embarrassed at what I originally sent you, but such are the woes of a first-time author. Thank you so much for sticking with me and straightening me out!

Thank you also to Kyle McEachern and Sharon Hunt for providing much-needed general feedback on drafts in the middle of this project.

Thank you to Gerard Baker, Annette Bombosch, Lauren Farmer, Jakob Kierkegaard, Julian Luca, Emily D. McCarthy, and Tiffany Widdowson for reading this book and providing me a blurb. All of your comments and feedback uncovered some things that I needed to fix in here that I would have been embarrassed to have published. I can't thank all of you enough.

I also want to say thank you to Tucker Max (yes, that Tucker Max) for giving me some free mentoring on how to go about writing this book and explaining how to find editors as a first-time author. I was initially bummed out that your book publishing process (at Book In A Box at that time, which is now Scribe) was not right for this book, meaning you declined to take me on, but you explained how I could move forward when you were at no obligation to do so. Without your initial advice in the early days of my writing, I would not have found Kelly or known where to start on the formal process of writing a book.

Beyond that, thank you to everyone at Scribe publishing. Thank you, Rikki Jump, for continually following up with me during the pandemic because I was definitely about to lose sight of this book during that time. Major huge thank you to Katie Orr for guiding me through the publishing process and getting everything squared away. Thank you to John van der Woude and team for turning my ridiculous placeholder images into useful and professional-looking illustrations. Thank you to Michael Nagin for the awesome cover art. Huge thank you to Skyler White for helping me choose a title. Looking back now, it's almost funny. I was seriously so nervous about picking a title that I wanted to vomit, and you got me through that. Thank you again! Thank you, Erin Michelle Sky, for your amazing cover text work and marketing insight. Thank you, Braxton Benes, for all the wonderful grammatical feedback during the numerous back-and-forth iterations in the final editing stages. The interaction was fun, and I learned quite a bit as I both laughed and cursed while sparring with the Chicago Manual of Style. I'm sure by the time this is published, I'm going to be missing folks from the Scribe team, but I want you to know I appreciate your work and a big thank you to you as well. All of you have been the best.

I also want to thank Neil Strauss (yes, that Neil Strauss) who randomly happened to be going on the exact personal journey that I was going on at the same time for his book *Emergency*. We had crossed paths many times during the late 2000s, and when I asked you about writing advice during your *Emergency* book tour in 2009, you were very encouraging and honest with me about the publishing industry and writing process. Your words about selecting a book topic helped me narrow in on this book a few years later. I always had a book in me. I just wasn't sure how to get it out, and you laid out the terrain and explained the destination to me so that I could start my own journey. Much to my luck, just as I was starting the publishing process for this, you put on a one-time "Creativity & Storytelling Masterclass" and that completely changed my thinking and approach to writing. I only wish that I had the opportunity to be a part of that earlier in the process of this book. In my life, you've been like the big brother I don't have who has similar interests, gets into something and messes everything up, and then passes your knowledge onto me so I can mess it up in my own unique way. Truly and seriously, I wouldn't be who I am today if it weren't for you, Neil. You're actually why I even thought about writing to begin with. Your writings and classes have helped me be a better person and live my life more fully, so maybe my writings and eventual classes can help others do the same, too.

Thank you to Michele Desrochers, Kimbrie Gobbi, Manda-Lou Kitson, Danielle Mandich, Jennifer Scharf, and Erika Vorrasi for teaching me all about feminine hygiene. Even with my medical background, I would not have guessed that the subject area was as complicated as it is and that there's so little consensus there.

Thank you to Paul A. Escajadillo and Alden Kirkman for your marketing help and for trying to get me to think like a marketer. I just can't make myself think that way still, but you both taught me a lot and I appreciate both of you taking the time to help me.

There are also many more people who were around in some way or another during the process of writing this, and thank you to all of you for your support and encouragement. There were times I wasn't sure this book was ever going to get done, and all of you motivated me to keep going. Thank you, truly.

ABOUT THE AUTHOR

Andre Watson is a self-funded world traveler who has been to roughly sixty countries across all seven continents. He started writing and blogging in order to help others experience their own adventures. He has lived in the United States, Germany, Australia, and the United Kingdom. Andre received two bachelor's degrees, in physics and computer science, from the University of San Diego (USD) and a master's degree in computer science for computer graphics from the University of California at San Diego (UCSD). He has worked as a software engineer on defensive missile systems for the US Navy and now works in the video games industry as a programmer. His game credits include *Watch Dogs*, *Planetside 2*, *Free Realms*, *Just Dance 2014*, *Cookie Jam*, and *HGTV: MyDesign*. He is an endurance athlete (GORUCK and Spartan), an EMT, a photographer, an artist, and has significant training in survival, combat, and exercise physiology. He lives with his girlfriend and co-parents three very cuddly cats. He can be found online at andrewatson.com.

CONSULTATION

If you've gone through this book and really want to plan a trip but just don't have the time or genuinely have no idea where to start, I am available to help you. I'll work with you one-on-one and we'll go through this whole book's process from beginning to end. I'll make sure you are completely squared away for your trip and that everything is tailored to your desires. If this describes you, contact me through andrewatson.com.

Made in United States
Troutdale, OR
05/06/2024